Promise Them Anything

Promise Them

Anything

THE INSIDE STORY
OF THE MADISON AVENUE
POWER STRUGGLE

Edward Buxton

STEIN AND DAY/*Publishers*/New York

First published in 1972
Copyright © 1972 by Edward Buxton
Library of Congress Catalog Card No. 72-187100
All rights reserved
Published simultaneously in Canada by Saunders of Toronto Ltd.
Designed by Bernard Schleifer
Printed in the United States of America
Stein and Day/*Publishers*/7 East 48 Street, New York, N.Y. 10017
ISBN 0-8128-1453-3

Contents

Preface

THE TAXI CAB noses through the crowded New York City traffic. Mary Wells, blonde and brilliant young president of her own ad agency, is riding with her executive vice-president, Fred Lemont and another passenger. They are on their way to a client, but Mary presumably has other things on her mind. Her agency will be going public in a few weeks.

"You worked at the Bates agency. Who took out the big money over there?" Mary asks Fred.

Fred, the first of three executive vice-presidents Mary will have in three years, answers thoughtfully. "Well, I know that Rosser Reeves was supposed to have walked out with over two million dollars."

"Oh, I know that!" replies Mary impatiently. "But who made the *real* money?"

A marketing executive arrives at the Ogilvy & Mather offices for a meeting on a new product. The agency and client people are assembled in the conference room awaiting David Ogilvy, chairman, Hall of Fame copywriter, Order of the British Empire, owner of a twelfth-century French château, the man whose Rolls-Royce awaits to take him to his town house each evening. There he is now, tossing his head as he joins the group. The General Foods executive extends his hand and says, "Hello, Dave."

The salutation causes a perceptible shudder through the half-dozen agency men present. The General Foods man may not have noticed. Later, however, as this executive is leading the meeting, telling the agency what will be expected of it in introducing his new product, he politely directs some of his remarks to Ogilvy at the far end of the table. Each time he does this, he mentions him by his first name. "As you see, Dave." "Now, Dave, we will want—" The Ogilvy & Mather executives wince. Eyes dart back and forth. Papers shuffle.

The meeting over, the General Foods man, now obviously aware that something was amiss during his talk, asks one of his close friends at the agency, "Something seemed to be wrong. Did I say anything out of line?"

"Oh, really it is nothing. Don't worry, for goodness sakes," the agency friend explained. "It's just that—er—*He*—is never addressed as 'Dave.' It's *always* 'David.'"

Ed Vellenti, a copywriter, has just resigned from Kenyon & Eckhardt. He is packing his portfolio as the senior vice-president enters and makes one more last plea: "Ed, please, I just can't figure out why you haven't been happy here with us?"

Ed continues with his packing. Over his shoulder, he replies: "When you hire a Napoleon, don't put him on K.P."

When twenty-nine-year-old Jerry Della Femina was hired by the hard-rock Ted Bates advertising agency at $65,000 a year plus expenses, he reported in wearing a green suit, a dark tan shirt, and a bright lemon-colored tie and carrying a gold typewriter.

George Lois, flamboyant head of Lois Holland Callaway ("When you've got it, flaunt it" was one of his better-known campaigns) opens a client meeting. His words are: "You better believe this. What we've got here is a ball-breaker of an idea. It's so goddamn exciting that every one of you in this room is going to wet your pants."

The superstars of Doyle Dane Bernbach included many highly strung art directors. Helmut Krone, now of the Case and Krone agency, was considered one of the most volatile. His outbursts, especially those directed toward the young traffic men who came to his office checking up on jobs, were notorious. One day, one young traffic man had enough. During his noon hour, he visited a butcher shop and purchased two pounds of raw meat. On his return, before a startled audience, he tossed the slabs of raw meat, piece by piece, into Helmut's "den."

"What good is happiness if it doesn't bring you money?"— slogan of the Golden Ulcers, an elite admen's luncheon club.

1

Why Is There So Much Bad Advertising?

WHAT is bad advertising?

It is any advertising that doesn't give the normal reader or viewer a fair and reasonable chance to understand the message. Is that asking too much? Wouldn't you think that any big, important corporation that makes a good product, gets a decent price for it, earns reasonable profits, and has a good name to protect would be willing to concede this much to its audience of potential customers?

It is not too much to ask, yet many big companies get caught in lies, misrepresentations, misleading claims, spurious demonstrations, half-truths, false testimonials, and contrived picturizations. This includes big and prestigious companies. American Home, Bristol-Myers, Campbell Soup, Coca-Cola, Colgate-Palmolive, Carter-Wallace, Firestone Tire, Lever Brothers, Mattel, Pfizer, Philip Morris, Sterling Drug, and J. B. Williams are just a handful out of hundreds of large corporations that have been called to account for advertising action that, if not actually illegal, has been sufficiently questionable to be cited by the Federal Trade Commission (FTC) or the Food and Drug Administration (FDA).

The reasons why companies take these risks will be discussed later, but first, here is a closer look at the main types of malpractice. Basically, they fall into several general categories.

One questionable practice is the spurious demonstration. When Colgate-Palmolive, for example, shows Madge, the manicurist, soaking customers' hands in Palmolive dishwashing liquid, they are hoping TV viewers will be impressed by the mildness of the product It is pretty convincing, but it is a sham. The dishwashing liquid in the commercial is cold. It does not begin its cleaning action until it is mixed with hot water. When this happens, the hands in hot water are certainly not getting a beauty treatment. An ad for Vel dishwashing liquid used a similar trick when it dipped roses in the liquid. Roses react differently from human skin. Or take these other examples of questionable demonstrations. Easy-Off window cleaner showed two windows: one cleaned with Easy-Off, one with a competitive brand. The Easy-Off window was "demonstrably" cleaner than the other. Why? Because the other window simply hadn't been wiped as vigorously, says the FTC citation. Or Chevron gasoline in a commercial shot on the West Coast showed exhaust from two cars collected in large plastic balloons. The one from the car using Chevron collected clear, almost white exhaust. The one from the car using a competitive brand was inky black. The trick? The motor of the competitive car was "unusually dirty," said the examiners. The FTC was also unhappy about the sign hung on an impressive building in the background. It read: Research Center. The building was a city hall.

Another common ploy used by advertisers is the identical ingredient that is made to sound like something special. Shell Oil for years bragged about the Platformate ingredient in its gasoline. In order to prove how much more mileage cars would get with this gas, they ran the long series of commercials showing cars breaking through paper barriers. Shell, the winner by nearly a mile—every time. No wonder, since according to the FTC, the other cars were using a gasoline not commonly available to motorists. All major gasolines contain the same special ingredient used by Shell. Recently, Wonder Bread was called by the FTC in this same type of advertising. The charge was that their "enriched" bread was not much different from all breads available in the marketplace. The enrichment was a government requirement. Another example: For years Anacin has talked about an "ingredient doctors recommend most." The hope perhaps is that people will think it is a doctor's prescription. The "ingredient" is simple aspirin. Which, of course, doctors do recommend.

Another group of misrepresentations is visual. Campbell Soup caused a tempest recently when the FTC charged that it put colorless glass marbles at the bottoms of bowls of soup shown on television. This was done to force the chunky stuff up to the surface. Libby foods has often shown its canned fruit cocktail in open display in ads. The types of fruit were correctly represented, but several years ago the photographer, in preparing the ad, used nicely cut pieces of fresh fruit. The product in the can was not at all similar. After heat treatment, the fruit was drab and faded in color. This conduct, which has not recurred in recent years, was never cited by any of the Federal regulatory agencies. Many of these visual tricks are said to be necessary because of the heat and light requirements of TV film studies. Hence, shaving cream has been substituted for whipped cream; molasses has been added to coffee to give it body; glasses have been sprayed with water to simulate coolness.

False authority is another popular abuse. A white coat may be worn by the pitchman in the hopes the viewer will think he is a real doctor. Or when this was prohibited, they dressed the man in a business suit and placed him behind a desklike table, with a shelf of heavy textbooks in the background. Most readers and viewers are alert to this kind of put-on by now, as they are to the celebrity testimonials. Who really believes that the star actually is so carried away with the product that he would stand up and make a pitch for it, except for money—which, by the way, is very good: $25,000 originally, plus residuals (additional payments for each time the commercial is aired). This has often added up to over $100,000 for a single commercial.

Health and nutrition claims are constantly under the gun from the Federal Trade Commission. The common ones are those that promise questionable dietary advantages. Such as Profile bread for weight watchers; the FTC charged that it is merely sliced thinner. Or Hi-C orange drink; the FTC said in its complaint that its claim that it was better than orange juice could not be justified. And many of the claims for margarines that promised too much in the way of the healthfulness of polyunsaturated oils. The cosmetics people for years were allowed to use any ingredient so long as it was not harmful. The FDA didn't question whether it worked or not. This resulted in many misleading claims that went unchallenged. Cosmetic companies for years talked about "hormone" ingredients, which actually did little more than sit on the skin. Many of the moisturizers and wrinkle remedies have also been almost useless. Many health claims are very subtle. Ads for Salem and Marlboro cigarettes, for example, with the dramatic outdoorsy look, are in fact selling an implied health benefit, according to research. But no complaints have been issued against the advertisers.

An annoying category of malpractices is the whole area of warranties, guarantees, and "bait" prices. Many of the big tire, automotive, and appliance companies have fudged these assurances in small type and legal disclaimers. Recent legislation has brought most of these practices under control, but there are still some abuses. The price lures that are used to get you into the store and then sell you something at a higher price are more frequently tricks used by local advertisers. These, too, are being more rigidly policed of late.

Recently, there was a rage of contests, sweepstakes, and games that were certainly misleading. The typical ploy was to offer a fantastic number of prizes worth a million dollars or so. In actual practice, there were nowhere near the promised number of prizes awarded. The FTC charged that Procter & Gamble, for example, offered 50,026 prizes worth some $92,000 but gave out only 559 prizes worth $559. Other big companies involved were Coca-Cola, *Reader's Digest,* the McDonalds hamburger chain, and most of the major oil companies. Fortunately, these misleading contests are apparently on the decline.

The last category of falsity in advertising, which is also a subtle one, is what is known as *corporate-image* advertising. Many major companies often run ads that claim far too much in the area of supposed contributions they are making to society (environmental control, ecology, conservation, and so forth). Too often they overdramatize or overcredit themselves for actions that merely whitewash their larger guilts.

There are many other petty, paltry, and sneaky devices advertisers have used and still use. For example, the claim "starts to work instantly," which can mean no more than that the pill begins to dissolve. Relief may be a long while off. Or "stop germs." In this case, "stop" may mean "arrest," not "kill." Or when something is certified by the U.S. Testing Laboratory; this only means that a private company in New Jersey that uses this name had tested the product. Or "steaks and chops of lean red meat," a claim made by Ken-L Ration pet foods for years; the FTC charged that they failed to say that the beautiful meats shown in the ad came from horses. Or when a glass company showed how clear its car windows were in comparison with squiggly competitive glass; they filmed empty air, according to the FTC complaint. The car window in the commercial, the FTC charged, was all the way down.

There are others, too. Next time you watch TV, you can play the game called "Look for the hook." For example, a commercial for a spray starch shows two T-shirts side by side. Both have just come from the drier and are badly wrinkled. The demonstrator then sprays his product on one of the shirts and says, "See how it begins to work instantly!" The starch isn't working; the fluid is. If you sprayed *plain water* on the shirt, the wrinkles would begin to flatten out. Or this one: when Bufferin shows its glass men on TV to demonstrate how fast the product goes to the head "while the other brand is still in the stomach." The exaggeration here? The time-span difference in relief is a matter of seconds it takes to get to the bloodstream. Actual relief is still 6 to 10 minutes away. Neither of these examples, however, has resulted in a complaint from any Federal agency.

Another area that bears careful watching is the dramatic put-on, that is, the commercial that makes a big joke out of the product. If you watch carefully, you'll see that the line between playful exaggeration and reality can get pretty fine. Procter & Gamble, for example, recently stopped using a commercial that showed Bounty paper towels noisily sucking up liquid like a vacuum cleaner. People were taking the demonstration literally.

Does it seem hard to believe that giant corporations such as those mentioned in the examples given would confuse and mislead millions of potential customers, often deliberately? Perhaps it is hard to accept, but in order to do so, you must understand how they got into the bad habits to begin with. There has always been some misleading and deceptive advertising, particularly in the years before government regulations took over. Directly following World War II, however, when companies began getting highly competitive, advertising took on a much more aggressive tone of voice and put a keener edge on its selling claims and propositions. It was a period advertising people call the *hard-sell era*. It coincided with a period when companies began making a lot of what the trade calls *parity* products. These are products with literally no visible or significant difference in quality, performance, or price. In nearly every product category—soaps, instant coffee, margarine, soft drinks, cereals, cosmetics and toiletries, drugs, and many other packaged-goods products—there appeared four or five major brands that were almost identical. All could be good, worthwhile products made by reputable firms. The drug and food products generally were approved by the government for purity and safety. But the nub of the problem was parity. Too many products, too much alike.

So you see the situation. Four or five giant companies, each selling its own brand of basically the same product. So how do you outsell your competitors? How do you make your product sound different, better, or worth more than your competitors'? Advertisers, with the help of their advertising agencies, did it by various, often devious, means. One of the most common is what the trade calls establishing a *preemptive claim.* That is, saying or demonstrating something that apparently can be said *only* about *your* brand, and no other. And this is where the tricky part comes in. This is the hacksaw in the cake, the way out. You are starting off with an almost identical product, and you have got to make it sound like it is something special, very special and exclusive. For example, suppose Dash detergent can do nothing more or less than the other major detergents. It is a parity product. Here is an example of how the Procter & Gamble people and their advertising agency managed some years ago to convey an impression of superiority. They announced proudly in ads and commercials: "Only Dash gives you whiter, cleaner, Dash washes." Sounds exclusive, doesn't it? But look closely. What kind of washes? "Dash washes." Of course only Dash can give you that because there is only one product named Dash. And the same advertisement backs this up with another preemptive claim: "No other product can match it." Obviously not, and for the same reason. There is only *one* Dash. In order to "match" it, any other product would have to come in a Dash box.

This kind of flimflam has been called various names inside the business. One especially appropriate term is the *weasel*. It is that indeed. A slippery, elusive animal. They are also sometimes called *disclaimers*. That is, you first claim something big and bold, and then down below, as obscurely as possible, you *disclaim* it. You don't have to be a literary genius to write preemptive claim, hard-sell advertising. It may help to have a little larceny in your soul, however. One woman copywriter was so clever at putting together convoluted English that sounded great but said next to nothing that she became famous in the business as "Weaseler's Mother." It is reported that some of her handiwork could actually make grown account executives burst into tears when they finally discovered the "hooker," the one tiny word, deftly inserted into the headline, that made the great extravagant promise possible.

Had the hard-sell era of advertising confined itself to relatively few products and companies and their ad agencies, the damage might have been less. But advertising, always an imitative business, saw the influence of these big firms and big agencies setting the precedents for all advertisers big and small. It was the thing to do. It was smart. It was shrewd. It was good old basic competition. And the legacy of hard-sell advertising became expensive. It served to erect massive barriers of disbelief among millions of youngsters then growing up. It tarred all advertisers, good and bad, with the same brush because the result was that fewer people believed in advertising. As one adman ruefully admitted, his ten-year-old came to him with a magazine ad one day and asked, "Daddy, is this true or is it an ad?"

Perhaps the most famous of the hard-sell wizards was Rosser Reeves of Ted Bates & Company. Some of his classics included the hammers in the head, the glass stomachs, the breaking chain, and other irritants. At one point, the noncreative, unbeautiful reputation of Bates became a hazard. Reeves, according to contemporaries in the shop, tried to change his image. After his book *Realities in Advertising*—a textbook of hard sell that stamped him as a "hard-rock Pete"—appeared, he sought the advice of his creative assistant Jerry Gury, a man of good taste, to help change his image. Gury taught Reeves how to become more artistic. He took him to art galleries, the theater, and also taught him how to "create" art masterpieces. One consisted of a technique known as "ice tray art." Reeves was instructed to freeze various colors of paint into cubes in the tray. They were then dumped onto a canvas and allowed to melt and mix. When dry, the concoction was framed beautifully. Hard-sell Reeves proudly displayed them on his walls.

One of the best descriptions of this era of advertising, which fortunately is fading fast, was the expression used frequently by the noncommissioned British officer in an Eric Ambler book: "Bullshit baffles brains." This was literally true. A great many people have been "bullshitted by advertising claims," and some still are. A product called Vivarine, made by J. B. Williams, was only recently advertised to women as a way to save their marriages. The claim: The product would make the wife more exciting to the husband when he comes home from work. The real story was this: The product is made of simple caffeine and dextrose. Not unlike coffee and sugar. This claim was promptly challenged by the FTC—as will more and more claims that are based upon thin-air promises. Moreover, the parity products will be much more difficult to bring on the market in the future. Companies that used to steal the formulations of drug products and come out with similar products in a matter of weeks will find that the FDA prohibits them from doing so. The FDA will insist upon a clear and definite superiority over the existing brand. This is fair not only to consumers but to companies as well. Previously, a firm could spend several years and many millions of dollars launching a new product, only to see it copied at little cost by a competitor. "Me-too" products may soon be a thing of the past.

In order to appreciate the problem of weaseling that manufacturers are faced with, consider the United States government, with its cigarette warning. For years, they have tried to find a way to make an absolute and declarative statement about the hazards of smoking. They tried first: "Warning: Cigarette Smoking May Be Dangerous to Your Health." The antismoking forces considered this too weak. Yet, like the advertisers, the government cannot be guilty of making an absolute statement that it cannot substantiate. At the present time, it cannot state unequivocally that smoking actually does cause cancer and heart trouble. The government resorts to a weasel when it says, "Warning: The Surgeon General Has Determined That Cigarette Smoking Is Dangerous to Your Health." The hedge is the surgeon general. "He" has determined. He is thus expressing an opinion. It is not a fact. Hence, the weasel is necessary, or the government would be caught in a lie.

There is still a heavy residual of the old-time hard-sell philosophy in the business. Too many people were trained to believe that truth could not stand alone in advertising. It needed a twist, a grabber, an attention getter, a visual come-on. Hell, that was what advertising was all about. If you had to stretch a little, okay. It was permissible under the ground rules of poetic license, trade puffery, dramatizations. The result: All the marbles were picked up by the men who were best at twisting and stretching. And these men are still around, not creating ads, but directing them. And on the client side, the older opposite numbers are still demanding this kind of advertising.

Ad makers of this old school still approach advertising from the wrong premise. As soon as they face the typewriter or drawing board, they begin making up ads. They start thinking up ideas, concepts; in short, they start thinking up fiction. This is the direct opposite of legitimate journalism or communications, which starts off with the premises "let's tell the news," and "let's convey the facts."

Another reason for so much bad and unbelievable advertising is that few ad makers know, or most are never taught, how to convey believability in messages. They simply don't understand the anatomy of truth as it applies to a projectable, communicable message. To be fair, this isn't easy. You may have all the facts and research to tell you that Brand X is a better floor cleaner, but putting this in a message that other people will believe is a very difficult thing. You have to know first, for example, what people

9

already believe about floor cleaners, what they are prepared to believe, what they are capable of believing. This is the homework that seldom gets done. This is why absolutely truthful messages come across as false and incredible to the viewer or reader

Too much emphasis on entertainment developed bad ad-making habits. Television spawned this problem. The medium was an entertainment vehicle, so admen thought they had to entertain audiences before they could sell to them. Right, up to a point. But too few admen were skilled entertainers. They simply copied vaudeville, nightclub routines, visual jokes, and sight gags. And most of them copied badly. Others used, and still use, old-fashioned pitchman techniques. The stand-up presenter who is as out of character and out of context with modern living as P. T. Barnum. Still others borrowed from foreign movies, off Broadway, Hollywood; sometimes they succeeded, but often as not, the message got mangled in the techniques. The era gave a lot of art directors and still photographers a chance to experiment, but it hurt credibility.

All the blame, however, cannot be put on the old-timers. Some of the young ad creators have brought with them new bad habits that, in turn, make for either ineffective or confusing and superficial ads. Young people are very uptight about being contemporary. They place great importance on doing things that are fashionable, whether these are the latest European film techniques, art graphics from Pop artists, or new avant-garde poster techniques. Whatever, they force these fads into their messages. Maybe it works; maybe it doesn't. More likely, it is pleasing only the creative man and perhaps his sophisticated friends.

Advertising language is another serious drawback to believability. Over the years, admen have come to believe that the language of persuasion has to be clever, a lingo, a cant, a zingy kind of patter, or it won't get attention. So ad makers write ad language. "All the flavor, all the time," "springtime fresh," and so forth. They are right; it catches the audience's attention—and immediately tells them: "This is fake, phony. It's advertisingese." Still another mistake: ad makers have been told that the new creative philosophy includes a don't-take-yourself-so-seriously attitude. This means admission of fault, playing up minor product faults, and the like. A little of this goes a long way, and in unskilled hands it's a bomb.

Believability begins with the messenger. If the viewer doesn't buy him, he won't buy the product. If he comes on silly, loud-mouthed, or pompous, the message has no chance to be believed. Too many inappropriate testimonials are used today, and they erode credibility.

Believability needs a frame of reference. Audiences have to see something immediately in the message that relates to their own area of experience. "That actually happened to me." "I know someone just like that." "That's *me* they are talking about." Too few ad makers know enough about the life-styles of their audiences to hit them with this shock of recognition.

All the above limitations to believability should not imply that honest advertising is dull, unimaginative, or uncreative. Headlines, illustrations, and TV commercials can be compelling, exciting, and provocative for the simple reason that truth can be more exciting than fiction. Moreover, there is truth in humor, truth in storytelling, truth in put-ons and playful exaggeration, and truth even in slice-of-life dramatizations. But in all these forms, the truth can be lost or booted away if the ad maker doesn't know how to convey it believably.

It is too bad this skill is so rare. It makes for so much bad and unbelievable advertising done by people who, for the most part, really want to be believed.

Some creative men really do try. Take George DeCoo. When he was a copywriter for Ogilvy & Mather, George was given an assignment to make a radio commercial to be broadcast in farm states for a Shell insecticide called Aldrin, which was used primarily to kill corn grubs. George, a streets-of-New York boy, knew nothing about corn grubs, but he got a great idea for a commercial. He wanted to tape the sound of grubs actually eating the roots of the cornstalks. A new needle microphone pushed into the ground could pick up the noise, he maintained. It was midwinter, which made the two most important ingredients of the commercial —growing corn and corn grubs—difficult to obtain. George persisted. He started growing corn in the offices at Ogilvy & Mather. Under hothouse conditions, on the Fifth Avenue window ledges, he got a few stalks out of the soil.

Getting the grubs was a different matter. He discovered that at this time of year, the only available grubs were in the laboratory of the Oklahoma State Agricultural Station. Moreover, there was an additional complication. He learned that there are laws against transporting grubs across state lines. George pushed on. He found a loophole. The grubs could be brought to New York City provided a state inspector came with them, armed with a spray gun. This was arranged. Grubs and inspector were flown to New York and arrived in the Ogilvy offices for the encounter with the cornstalks, now a foot or so tall. A tense crowd gathered around as the grubs were slipped into the earth beneath the stalks, along with the needle microphone. Wires were attached to a tape player so that all could hear. The room was hushed. A minute, two minutes, five minutes went by. Nothing happened. Patience. Then "a noise like a goddamn popcorn factory" came out of the tape machine. It roared away while the crowd applauded. The commercial that was eventually made and run on the air won a prize, the copywriter's Gold Key Award, for George DeCoo.

The modern, dedicated, and usually younger adman does not have the bad habits of the earlier generation of admen. Most of them are basically honest, basically interested in selling products by fair and legitimate means. So they are just as annoyed as the FTC or consumerists about weasel-worded, fake, unbelievable advertising. They are also annoyed about other things in advertising, especially unprofessionalisms such as poorly conceived ads; hackneyed, badly executed ads; imitative, me-too ads; and ads that permit the gimmicks to get in the way of the message. The good adman today tries hard to be a competent professional. He likes his business. He believes advertising can play a useful and indispensable role in marketing. He wants to be proud of his work.

In spite of himself, however, he may still turn out some advertising that is less than perfect, unsatisfactory, unrewarding. Why? Here are some of the chronic and persistent problems.

First, good, outstanding advertising—is a very difficult thing to create. It may look easy, but behind the simple page advertisement or the thirty-second TV commercial are an enormous amount of work, a tremendous amount of specialized skills to be orchestrated, and a complicated network of approvals and okays.

Imagine, hypothetically, a copywriter who is asked to write an ad for a major airline. The group head tells the copywriter: "The client wants something fresh, different, exciting, gutsy, and *hard selling*—you know, put more bottoms in those seats." He adds as an afterthought, "Don't forget the new CAB regulations, the new IATA fare rates and restrictions, and remember the FTC is very rough these days. Got to document every goddamn comma. And we don't want any trouble with the NAB [network code], they are very touchy about strong competitive claims right now."

The young writer goes out with his assignment. "Fresh, different, hard selling?" he muses. And all those restrictions. He knows he can't possibly understand the fine print and the legal interpretations of them all. Sitting in his cubicle office, the copywriter faces his task. Before he starts being "fresh" and "different," he has to know what is old and overused. This means he will have to read and study all airline advertising, current and past, to see what has gone on before. If he has been on the account long, he has done this homework anyway. He will then have to check the latest research on the motivations and reasons why people travel, why they chose one airline over another, what gripes they have. He will then check recent test scores of ads and commercials for his airline and other airlines to see which kind of appeals and techniques are stopping readers and attracting viewers. He might as well try to outguess the researchers now, before he goes to all the work of making a commercial or an ad.

Also, if he is going to be "fresh" and "different," he is aware that the supervisors will expect him to come up with new, contemporary ideas and graphics. This means he should, as he usually does, refresh himself on the latest "in" creative styles and designs. Last year it was Art Deco; the year before, psychedelic art. He might look at some of the exhibits in the art department or the new work of photographers and artists. He should, if he has time, visit the Museum of Modern Art or browse in Greenwich Village. If he is going to get in on the TV commercial part of the job, he will also want to check up on the latest reel of airline commercials,

13

perhaps catch any good new movie playing in town, and spend a little time at home watching new commercials.

"Got a world-beater idea yet?" his group head asks a couple of days later. "We'll be looking over some rough and scuffy ideas later this week.'

This warns the copywriter that time is running out. Also that he is competing with other creative men for the best ideas to be picked at the meeting. This reminds him of previous meetings, meetings in which ideas he submitted were "shot down in flames," as they say. He tries to reconstruct the previous objections.

"Too complicated. Client is cost-conscious," said the associate creative director.

"Not stylish enough. No flair," said the senior art director.

"Got to be more ballsy than that," said the copy supervisor.

"The marketing people won't like that economy approach," said an account man.

"Too competitive," said the top creative director. "We don't want Washington on our backs."

"It's been done before," said an executive TV producer. "American Airlines tried it in 1965."

"The audience segment we are interested in will respond negatively," said the research executive.

"Too cute," said the account supervisor. "Trying to win an award?"

"Trying to say too much. Keep it simple. More like a poster," said the associate creative director, art.

"Where the hell is the USP [Unique Selling Proposition], the *real* difference?" asked the group head, copy.

"They'll never buy it," said the senior vice-president of creative services.

"Good try," said the junior account executive. "Better luck next time."

This is the real situation the creative person faces. The young copywriter is faced with an echelon of critics ahead of him. On the copy side: a copy group head, a copy supervisor, an associate creative director, a creative director. On the art side: an art director; an executive art director; an associate creative director, art; a creative director, art. Also there are TV producers and directors, copy research people, market research people, and the entire account staff (the men who must like the ad or they "can't sell it"). Higher up, of course, within the agency are management supervisors, executive vice-presidents, and the president.

All these before the ad or commercial idea even gets to the client. At the client, there is the whole other echelon. Ad director, marketing director, group vice-president, and so forth.

So you think it is easy to write an ad?

The system is identical in all big ad agencies, such as J. Walter Thompson, BBDO, Young & Rubicam, McCann-Erickson, N. W. Ayer, and Leo Burnett. Despite the fact that the young copywriter's job looks impossible, he has in fact many things going for him. The research he needs is usually available simply by phoning for it. He is working in a stimulating creative environment among other bright young creative people. This keeps him on his mettle. He learns his trade from all those critics who supervise his work. He comes to realize why the idea has to have a unique difference, why the graphics must be outstanding to get attention, why the account and marketing men insist upon directing the message to the right audience, why the TV director asks for a concept that has not been visualized before so that his ad won't be confused with competitors'.

A big agency like J. Walter Thompson offers the young copywriter a host of services he can use. Seminars conducted by department heads, guest lecturers in the auditorium, reviews of competitive commercials, after-hours refresher courses, a social hour in the dining room after work where he can meet and trade ideas with associates, a house organ to tell him what the rest of the company is doing, and a complete library service. He can even take a course in public speaking right in the office.

Yet it is still hard. And it is the same anywhere in the business. At an agency like Ted Bates, there is a selling philosophy that has to be understood. Here the approach to ad making is different: more basic, less entertaining, more hard sell. At Doyle Dane Bernbach, there are other high creative criteria to be met. Here the account people have little to say about the creative product, but the older, senior creative men can be very demanding, often clannish and superior. At Ogilvy & Mather, the strong influence of

15

David Ogilvy still dominates. And David wrote his own book on how to make ads. The young writer had better follow it. At Wells, Rich, Greene, there is another philosophy, another point of view. Ads here have to be more dramatic, yet product-oriented. At Norman, Craig & Kummel, there is an approach called *empathy*, described by them as, "If you see a person who is seasick, and you feel sorry for him, that is sympathy. If you see the same seasick person and feel sick yourself, that is empathy." Get that into an ad. Or at Leo Burnett, there is something vaguely known as the "earthy, common-touch" advertising that must be learned. At Carl Ally, it is a bold, straight approach. At Lois Holland Callaway, advertising with a flair, dramatic emotion, and often famous-people testimonials. At BBDO, ads all have to contain the "three basics"—the product, the problem, the unique solution—and "break the boredom barrier." At Grey Advertising, it would be wise to remember that President Ed Meyer got his start in the business in Bloomingdale's basement. He and his associates are retail-oriented.

The copywriter trying to push his way through this thicket of approval has, in theory, the backup support of his creative supervisors. They are expected to help fight his battle. In many agencies, this support is fainthearted or nonexistent. In others, it is excellent. Curt Berrien, a management consultant, tells about a copywriter at William Esty who once had a campaign for a beer account totally rejected by the account supervisor. On his way back to his office, he ran into the creative director, who asked what he had in his hands. "Three weeks of wasted time, a beer campaign that the account man won't buy," the copywriter replied.

"The hell he won't," said the creative director, grabbing a phone. When connection was made with the account executive, the creative director lashed out, "What's this about rejecting Jim's beer campaign. Who the hell are you to judge creative work? As a matter of fact, that campaign is not only great, it's the greatest beer campaign I ever saw! If you can't sell it to your client, goddamnit, I'll take it over myself!"

The account man caved in quickly. Then the creative director turned to the copywriter and said, "Let me see that stuff, is it any good?"

There are many handicaps to turning out good creative work. One of these is laziness. A fantastic number of creative people are goof-offs. Especially in the big factory agencies. Take any sizable creative department of say thirty to forty people, and maybe 50 percent of them are busy at any time. They can look busy. In fact, many are very imaginative in this respect. A copywriter, for example, can make a clatter of noise on his typewriter writing letters, messing around with a plot for a short story or novel, writing poems, or revising his résumé. An art director can cover his drawing board with meaningless scribbles, and nobody would dare question what assignment it is. Or he can be interviewing models, which sometimes seems to take up 90 percent of his day. Or a TV director or producer can sit in his darkened office and screen film footage against a blank wall for hours. They could be Donald Duck cartoons for all anybody knows. Directors and producers also have unlimited license to be out of the office. One didn't occupy his office in person for 2½ months. He didn't even visit it on paydays when he came by to pick up his check. Another took a two-week European vacation and was never missed. It was assumed he was on location somewhere.

Creative people goof off in many other ways. They spend afternoons in museums, movies, sitting in a cool bar on a hot day, or taking the afternoon off with a date at the Central Park Zoo. If anybody asks, they are "researching" material. Dave Scott, a supervisor at Ted Bates and other shops, likes motorcycling. He might take a day or two without notice any time the weather is nice. Still, when he is on the job, he is a top performer—and tough. They call him "Dread" Scott. Another copywriter took a one-hour nap every day between 2:00 and 3:00 P.M. on the john in the agency's men's room. Others actually sleep in their chairs, facing the window, of course. Creative people are expected to spend time meditating. One top copywriter couldn't stand meetings and regularly popped off to sleep if the meeting lasted more than twenty minutes. Another, who did his sleeping at home and always came in after ten o'clock, had an arrangement with his secretary to turn the light on in his office, put a cup of coffee on his desk, a piece of paper in his typewriter, and a lighted cigarette in an ash tray.

It would be unfair to leave the impression that all creative

17

people are lazy. Creative work is never a nine-to-five kind of thing. It's not something turned on like a faucet or, as an account executive once said at a meeting, "If you are going to have an idea, have it now." So it is true; a creative man might properly spend many hours apparently idle and immobile while thinking up concepts. It is no joke that many of the best ideas come to the creative man at crazy times: while shaving in the morning, while driving a car, or lying in bed. The ad problem is supposedly sitting in the back of the creative man's head, waiting for some catalyst to spark a solution. It may come from a fragment of a conversation overheard on a subway; it may spring from a breakfast-table squabble with children; it may come the hard way, from hours of listening to recorded tapes of consumers talking about the product. For example, a woman copywriter faced with a problem of how to advertise a can of mixed fruit was staring at a clock when she got her idea: "Make a clock with a different fruit for every hour." It made a pretty magazine picture, and the client decided to make actual wall clocks of the same design. As a premium offer, it sold 40,000 clocks. And many times a big idea leaps full-blown out of a heated argument between a couple of keyed-up creative people. "That's *it* for Christ's sake! Write it down quick!"

An eye patch used in Hathaway shirt advertising gave David Ogilvy, of Ogilvy & Mather, his first big claim to creativity. As David described to a friend, "Fame in America hangs on a very slender thread. I was shaving one morning when I decided to see what I would look like wearing an eye patch. I improvised and came up with the idea for my Hathaway shirt campaign." Bill Bernbach, of the Doyle Dane Bernbach agency, says that many of his best ideas have come from long, searching talks with the heads of companies. He recalls one visit to an upstate New York brewery. The beer, Utica Club, was not selling. The two men sat long into the evening discussing the problems. Bernbach was seeking an idea, a concept, a reason why people might buy the beer. The president of the brewery was more concerned with keeping the brewery going.

"It is getting harder every year," the old president said.

"Why is that?" Bernbach asked. "Too much competition?"

"Partly, but I guess the real reason is—I don't have to make beer as good as I do. I'm too fussy, too old-fashioned. I don't use substitutes."

That was all Bernbach needed to know. His first headline was: "We don't have to make beer as good as this." It turned the company around.

The laziness that hurts advertising is the shortcut, easy-way-out approach to ad making, when writers and art directors simply shove a bunch of elements together and call it an ad or a commercial. A little of this, a little of that, a big picture of the product, something to please the account executive, something to flatter the client, then render it all up slick and professional. The result is no more an ad than a manikin is a human being. Many ad agencies operate like this. They beg, borrow, and steal the ingredients of an ad. They beg the proposition from the client. "Give us something to say." They borrow techniques from ads and commercials used by successful competitors. Norman, Craig & Kummel invents a successful White Tornado in the kitchen for Ajax, and directly Ogilvy & Mather comes out with doves in the kitchen for Lever. Compton Advertising and Procter & Gamble, trying to catch the same excitement, rush in with a clothes washer ten feet tall. Advertising is full of imitators. Next comes word-for-word plagiarism; this is the step beyond copying. Here the lazy ad agencies and creative people literally trace the layout of an ad right off the page. A copywriter once did this for the Spanish tourist bureau, tracing an Ogilvy & Mather ad for Puerto Rico right down to the last detail. David Ogilvy was so mad he dashed off a letter to the agency accusing them of "deplorable plagerism." The copywriter, in answering David, was brief: "If you are going to criticize someone for *plagiarism,* you ought at least know how to spell the word." This must have stung, for David is one of the most literate writers in the business.

The unrelieved sameness of so much advertising is not always the fault of creative people. Clients often insist upon creating ads that answer competition. This means doing the exact same thing as the competition is doing. Too many ad agencies give in to these requests even though they know that usually the result is sheer confusion in the minds of consumers. This is why all Detroit car advertising looks the same, why so many cigarette brands are indistinguishable, why it is so hard to find differences between the major soap products. Not only are the products made of the same ingredients but so is the advertising. If Procter & Gamble uses slice-of-life vignettes (two housewives talking), so does Colgate-Palmolive, and Lever Brothers. If Buick shows a picture of their car standing in a field with a pretty girl leaning on the right rear fender, so do ten other Detroit manufacturers. It is absurd, but like so many other axioms in advertising, "That's the way it's done." These are the rules of the lazy creative people or of clients who feel safe only when they are copying the competition. "If they are doing it, it must be right."

Here are a couple of illustrations of how far client domination of advertising can go. American Can once had an ad manager who was so determined to write the ads himself that he used to chase over to Compton Advertising almost every day with a new idea. He usually headed straight for the copy supervisor's office with a "Hey, how about this?" The obliging supervisor would hand him a pad of paper and let him sketch the idea. Most of them never got through the mill, but the ad manager kept trying. One morning he arrived in the agency office before the supervisor. Too impatient to wait, he seated himself at the typewriter and started banging away. A few moments later a woman from the accounting department stopped by the office, said good morning, and handed the man an envelope. It was payday. She assumed he was the copywriter who belonged in the office.

Another eager ad writer was the P.R. manager at General Dynamics. He was such a frustrated writer that for four years, and through two ad agencies, he had to write every single ad himself. The ad agencies, D'Arcy and later Ogilvy & Mather, both had to resign the account. The stuff the P.R. man was writing looked like technical articles in aerospace journals. A third story of too much client involvement concerns the product manager of a major food company. He desperately wanted to write the ads but knew that his management would never allow him to do so. So the product manager would send his ideas over to the agency, demanding that they be shaped up into layout form exactly as he directed. Then a week or so later, the product manager and his superiors would have a visit from the agency. The work done by the product manager via the agency would be presented. The product manager would say, "Hey, now you guys are coming up with some good stuff, let's buy this."

Clients' hypersensitivity to criticism results in much spoiling of ads. If one commuting friend doesn't speak highly of his current advertising, the client may kill the campaign or possibly fire the agency. The same thing happens with his golfing partner, a member of his luncheon club, his father-in-law, his wife, or possibly his teen-age children. If a single word of criticism arises, it is taken as gospel. Never mind the thousands of people in the consumer research program who liked it. "My wife has got to like it, too!" shouted one head of a big company. "She's a woman, and has damn good taste, too!" Another very sensitive source of criticism is any member of a board of directors. One such criticism ruined a big agency presentation. The agency was about to unveil a complete fall campaign for a large bank. Ads, commercials, posters— a complete package. Just before the presentation began, the director of advertising said, "We had a call this morning from one of our directors. He brought up a good point. He said that we should never use the color red in our advertising. Red is cheap, not right for a bank." He paused. "We agree with him. Now go ahead with your presentation." How could the agency go ahead? They had dozens of full-color illustrations, commercials, posters, and so forth. No red?

Bad or certainly dull advertising is often caused by lawyers. In their grim determination to spell out the letter of the law, they often castrate ads. An oil company lawyer once changed a headline from "More Power" to "tends to promote beneficial engine performance under certain conditions." And this was supposed to go on an outdoor poster. Others are great on disclaimers. They will let you say something as long as you use a bold asterisk followed by 150 words of explanatory copy. Lawyers make up most of the bureaucracy in Washington. That's why advertising people have so much trouble clearing ads with the various departments there.

In summary, much of the bad advertising today is caused by the following factors: First, the sloppy habits gained during the unbridled laissez-faire days of the hard-sell era of advertising. Next, the sheer difficulty of getting good creativity up through the thickets of approval on both the ad agencies' and the clients' sides. Third, client interference, which often results in dull, conservative advertising or advertising that tries to copy competition slavishly. Fourth, creative laziness. That is, taking the easy way out in making ads by imitating other people's advertising or putting together ads without care and imagination. Fifth, interference from other sources (legal departments, code authorities, and Washington), however meritorious, nonetheless handicaps the creator of bright, interesting, and informative advertising.

Is it any wonder then that $50,000-a-year creative people have chucked the business? Like Tom Johnstone, who is now building houses in the Caribbean; Judd Irish, who is running an investment service; Gene McMaster, who is operating a ski resort in Vermont; Tom Meyer, who is selling lobsters by mail from Maine; Ed Hannibal, who is writing novels; Walter Wier, who is living in Paris; or Jack McCarthy, who is serving as a correspondent for Irish and English newspapers. There has to be an easier way to make a living.

2

How Advertising Got That Way

THE LEGACY of bad advertising presupposes a business with shabby beginnings. Has it always been a kind of con game? A fast-buck, opportunistic operation? Was the bad seed planted way back when men like Albert Lasker accumulated more than $50 million; when Atherton Hobler, a founder of Benton & Bowles, reportedly earned $700,000 in the depression year of 1932; when Bruce Barton was a multimillionaire and a member of Congress?

In order to understand the present state of advertising, it might help to review briefly the growing-up years of advertising. Back in the days when the advertising business was strictly a business of advertising agents, the enterprising agent would buy a block of newspaper or magazine pages from the publisher at a 15 percent discount. He alone assumed the responsibility of selling these pages to potential advertisers. If he sold them, fine, he got his money back plus the 15 percent override that was his profit. He was a risk taker, a gambler. And sometimes he lost. When this happened, it was often too late to inform the publisher that the space was unsold. The empty page usually ran with a last-minute design or more often with the standby words "Compliments of a friend." The "friend" was the luckless agent who was stuck with the page. In the days of the early ad agents—men like N. W. Ayer of Philadelphia, George Batten of New York, J. Walter Thompson of Chicago and New York, and his partners Mr. Lord and Mr. Thomas—took these chances all the time. The only way to prevent it was to hire more aggressive salesmen or—and this was a breakthrough at the time—to make the space more attractive to potential advertisers by helping them write the ads. The early agents, riding the day coaches between cities, scribbled headlines and copy on the backs of envelopes. They told the health sanitoriums of H. K. Kellogg in Battle Creek, Michigan, how to tell their story to millions of magazine readers. They helped phrase the messages for the early Hoover carpet sweeper, the brewers of Milwaukee, the soap people in Cincinnati, the meat-packers of Chicago, the watchmakers of New England. They literally taught their clients how to advertise, thought up their slogans, designed their trademarks.

As time went on, competition grew. In the early part of the century, newspapers and magazines grew in size and number. Billboards and painted signs entered the area of commission sales. Agents traversed the farm lands of the Midwest paying farmers for permission to paint ads for Clabber Girl, Gold Dust Twins, and Bull Durham on their barns or to paint the entire barn free for the privilege of using the roadside exposure for their ad. As competition intensified, the agents became more innovative and resourceful. An agent named Albert Lasker hired an itinerant copywriter, reputed to be the best in America, for $50,000 a year, an unheard-of salary in the early days of the century. Others devised gimmicks to help promote sale of their space. The coupon was invented. The money-back guarantee was a sensational advance. Imagine, a manufacturer so convinced of his product that he would give a full refund if the user was not entirely satisfied. Incredible. The agents also invented the door-to-door sampling, some of the first mail-order catalogs, return postcards, and other ingenious merchandising tricks that fascinated the hardheaded, production-minded company owners of the day. They let the admen assure them that pictures of their faces and of their plants would sell goods. This was doubtful, but it sold advertising space.

It was an advertising man who told the Postum Company of Battle Creek to put its cereals in boxes. It was another advertising man's idea that put William Wrigley, Jr., in the chewing-gum business. Originally, he was selling baking powder and giving chewing gum away as a bonus The gum proved more popular than

24

the baking powder. (Proof that some things never change: Only recently, in 1970, Dr Pepper, trying to introduce its drink in Puerto Rico, offered a blowup plastic pillow as a premium for a carton of the drink. The pillow proved more attractive than the Dr Pepper. So the offer was reversed. Buy the pillow, get Dr Pepper free.) But more on the services of the original ad agents. Other ad agents began advising manufacturers on how to make their products easier to sell and, hence, more needful of advertising. They helped the manufacturers design attractive packages, told them how to hire salesmen, and finally actually advised them on what they should make, where to sell it, and what price to put on it.

By the 1920s, when Baron Collier was hiring F. Scott Fitzgerald to write slogans for the considerable number of billboards he controlled as an agent, the ad agency business had added quite a number of services. Many of them were not structured yet as departments or specialties, but the agent more and more became the marketing advisor of his client. Ted McManus, who had written the classic "The Penalty of Leadership" ad for Cadillac, and other talented automotive admen were advising Detroit on what style of cars to make. Others were telling food manufacturers to put vitamins in their products, to package them in wax paper, to use live steam to sterilize the Schlitz beer bottles, to sell raisins in handy boxes, to put trademarks on oranges, to make their products more convenient to housewives. These were valued and profit-producing services for manufacturers. Today it seems incredible how much power the old-time ad agency had with its clients. They almost ran the companies, often took over shares of stock in exchange for ads, and made millions. Most manufacturers in those days still believed that if they made a good product, it would find its own market. Admen, however, wouldn't let them believe this. They continued all through the first half of the century to cajole, needle, and harass, if necessary, their advertising prospects to be more marketing-oriented. The selfish objective was of course to increase the use of advertising. It worked, too. Manufacturers did look to the advertising agencies for these ideas; they did increase their spending on advertising; and often as a direct result, the consumers got better, more convenient products.

Into the thirties and forties, ad agencies were offering more and more services. There were also many more agencies, lured no doubt by the fabulous financial successes of some of the advertising giants of the era. Raymond Rubicam, Bruce Barton, Sterling Getchell, Albert Lasker, William Benton, Phil Lennen, Stanley Resor—all millionaires, some many times over. So, with more agencies competing, the race to outservice was on. The heaviest investments went for top writers, especially when it became obvious that a first-class writer could overwhelm a big client. A young man named Bill Esty, up from Philadelphia on a visit to Lever Brothers, reportedly earned a check for $130,000 in one day. Next came top artists. Norman Rockwell, the *Saturday Evening Post* cover artist, was touted by ad agencies. Well-known novelists and poets were offered. Then came the first Hollywood and famous-person testimonials. All were competitive services of ad agencies.

Something else happened during the period between the thirties and the early sixties. It was broadcast advertising. The new sound waves began to overtake the print media in glamor and, eventually, in profitability. The days of the great radio shows were a special bonanza to ad agencies. Now they could buy programs in huge network proportions, hundreds of stations at the same time, and all using the same sixty-second commercial. The agencies, seeing the enormous potential, literally took over broadcasting. They made and produced the shows themselves. A Chicago agency, Blackett Sample & Hummert, almost cornered the soap-opera market. At one time, they had seven shows a day wrapped up. Others became specialists in the big musical programs —hundred-piece symphonies, brass bands, opera, and jazz. The race to outservice competitors in broadcast expertise was furious. Young & Rubicam, J. Walter Thompson, Benton & Bowles, Dancer-Fitzgerald-Sample (which succeeded Blackett Sample & Hummert), Lennen & Mitchell, and later Ted Bates and William Esty dominated the broadcast era. Their coffers filled rapidly. So rapidly, it became truly embarrassing. The Internal Revenue Service warned Ted Bates to "do something" with those enormous reserves of capital or else declare it profit. Large amounts were used to finance Bates' successful overseas expansion.

This largeness of income obviously spurred agencies to offer more services. After all, they were collecting enormous fees (15 percent of $1 million for writing a few hundred words of radio copy); hence they felt honor-bound to offer their clients part of this loot. So now they began to spend it on new services and presumably useful contributions to the clients' selling operations. Research became an expedient way to spend large sums of money. Still new and mysterious, it had an enormous financial appetite. Viennese doctors appeared in the research departments, field staffs of hundreds of women combed the country, filling out questionnaires by the tens of thousands. Then other services were invented. Shiny and elaborate test kitchens manned by home economists with master's degrees sprung up. Audition rooms, casting departments, photo labs, packaging and design studios. Actual medical labs (complete with hamsters) were installed for agencies handling drug products. The conference rooms grew into indoor arenas. A wide assortment of intellectual specialists arrived, including anthropologists, sociologists, behavioral scientists, mathematicians, statisticians, type designers, fashion stylists, speech and drama directors, song writers, lyricists, librarians, and resident psychiatrists. With the advent of television came a new army of people. Producers, directors, stage designers, film editors, grips, prop men, script girls, animators, cinematographers, Broadway gag writers, and elevatorloads of charlatans, many of them refugees from musty corners of industry.

All this cost money. But for a long while, the cash flow was no problem. An annual $10-million budget for one cigarette brand brought the agency a net commission of $1.5 million. For this, the creative requirements might not exceed five or six commercials for the whole year. At $50,000 apiece, how much is left? Hence the offer of all these other services, which had now become known as *peripheral*. This they certainly were when you consider that the agencies of the previous generation managed quite nicely with a few good writers and artists. Some of the clients had absolutely no need for gag writers, a big test kitchen, the sociologist, or the behavioral scientist. He was selling a pack of gum or a bottle of beer. How complicated can you get? However—and here was the hitch—he was being charged for them anyway under the 15 percent commission system. The agencies, as a general practice, spread expenses proportionately among all their clients. Take it or leave it.

27

Many a client, after being paraded through the sumptuous surroundings of his ad agency, asked himself, "Who needs all this horseshit?"

For example, here is a story that happened not so long ago; it would be unlikely today. An ad manager of Coca-Cola arrived at McCann-Erickson, his ad agency, on a wet, stormy day. At the time McCann had a ground-floor reception room that announced visitors before they went upstairs. The ad manager was announced and proceeded up the elevator. He was met by Norm Herwood, a young man who worked on the account.

"Hi," said Herwood. "Glad to see you. But—er—what the hell are you carrying your shoes for?"

"Young man, if my wet shoes dirty up the plush carpets of this place, you can be sure that Coca-Cola, as your biggest client, will have to pay the cleaning bill."

The walls began cracking earlier than many admen realized. It wasn't the recent recession, as many ad agency people believe, that caused advertisers to look around for an agency with fewer but more relevant services. This trend had actually started during the lush prosperity era of the soaring sixties. American Tobacco, for example, comparing costs against results back in 1962 sat down with its ad agencies (BBDO, SSC and B, and others) and said with unmixed candor: "From now on, boys, we split." The offer: a guaranteed *reasonable* profit for the agencies after all necessary and requested services were performed; beyond that, the company demanded a refund of the balance of the unused portion of the 15 percent commission. Anticipated savings were estimated at from $2 to $3 million per year. It should have shaken the business to the roots. And it did cause some clamor. But it had to be accepted. In truth, many big advertisers, especially heavy broadcast spenders, had been getting rebates for years. Now, however, it was out in the open; clients were getting fed up with paying for unwanted, unnecessary services. Actually, "paying for" is an inexact phrase. The commissions don't belong to the client. They supposedly belong to the agency. What the clients, in effect, were asking for was a better use of the commissions. "We don't want to see it pissed away on a lot of frivolous services and window dressing. Use it instead to make better ads, or split it with us."

The overexpanded services began to fall out of the agencies like overripe fruit. BBDO folded up its children's marketing group. Kenyon & Eckhardt sent its doctor of behavioral sciences packing. Foote, Cone & Belding closed down its mock supermarket and turned the space into a storeroom. J. Walter Thompson cleaned out gag writers, stage designers, test kitchens, and an elaborate showpiece called the TV workshop, which was being used mostly for home movies. Coordinated Communications Inc. called in the experts to find out why its multimillion-dollar computer was not working properly and were told that everything would be fine if they spent another million on new-generation advances. CCI told the experts to stuff it. The Interpublic Group of Companies, Inc., got out the biggest broom of all. They wiped out eight companies and some four hundred executives, including a crowd of such unorthodox experts as interior decorators, food scientists, social workers, State Department specialists, international banking experts, five Army generals, and a dozen $40,000 generalists who never knew why they were hired in the first place. They also shuttered all the "creative islands" located in penthouses and other exotic and isolated places. And more. They dumped several company planes, including the luxurious flying living room assigned to Marion Harper (called "Harper's Ferry"), a ranch and riding academy, a Swiss financial firm whose nature and functions were vague, two of its Centers for New Product Research, including an expensive eye camera to measure pupil dilation of eyeballs when exposed to ads. They also dumped their chairman, Marion Harper, who must certainly have earned the long-distance record for expanding agency services. At its zenith, his conglomerate was indisputably the fullest of the full-service agencies.

In some cases, the brooms swept too clean, the axes pruned too close to the roots. The ad agencies still desirous of calling themselves "full-service" (anything you need, we got it) were reducing their services so sharply that whole departments were wiped out, leaving perhaps a department director nakedly exposed on his own. He became the figurehead for a service that was no longer there. The profit squeeze that began to hit the ad agencies demanded many of these cuts. It simply became unprofitable to house a six-man public relations arm just to wing out a press release on a new copywriter once a month. It was impractical to keep up a sales promotion department when all they produced was a few brochures now and then. Young & Rubicam took a hard look at its research department and decided that it could reduce the staff from 178 to 9 without feeling any pain. Lennen & Newell decided it was cheaper to put all its TV production in one outside TV firm, thereby whacking off a dozen insider pay-rollers. Media departments, never a well-paid operation, and one that top management itself rarely visited, were now subjected to cutbacks to the bone. Funny bones, as it turned out, because the reductions in quality of media service soon became an acutely sensitive subject in client-agency relationships. This, more than anything else, gave impetus to the development of outside media-buying services.

Here's an example of how this kind of service evolved. One cold winter night in 1967, a visitor dropped in at a trade paper office. It was after press time, so there was a chance to visit. The young man, Dick Gershon, was then a media director at a major agency, Benton & Bowles. Gershon, a modest, intelligent man, had spent many years at his agency learning the media end of the business. Benton & Bowles was considered one of the top media agencies in the city. It had trained many of the best men in the industry. Since he was at the top of the department, Dick was himself a qualified expert on media problems of all sizes and shapes. This was the conversation, as the trade paper editor recalled it:

"I have an idea," Dick began, "that there are a lot of small ad agencies who really don't know how to buy good time or space for their clients. They are faking it. Doing the best they can. But they are handicapped by low salaries, short staffs, unappreciative management."

"So?" the editor asked.

"Well," he replied, knowing that what he was going to say would be a radical suggestion, "I think I might go in business, sort of as a media department for people who don't do it very well for themselves."

"But," the editor said, "this is what ad agencies are in business to do. This is their first and major responsibility. If they don't buy space, they aren't advertising agents."

"True, but if they don't buy it well enough, they may not be in business at all."

"How would you get paid?"

"Simple, a percentage of what I can save them. With my experience in bargaining and negotiating for big clients at Benton & Bowles, I can get better prices on buys. Besides, I see a time when the agencies who will be my clients won't need anything but a planner on staff. I'll handle all the rest, at a savings to them. And they'll get better media service all around."

"An agency with no media department at all?" the editor asked incredulously.

"Right," said Dick Gershon.

And he was right. Today, four years later, a dozen or more ad agencies have turned over the entire media function to people like Dick Gershon. Using these services didn't threaten the existence of the agencies. It merely permitted them to offer their clients a better media service, coordinatd by the agency but executed by the outside media expert. It was a significant milestone. This kind of a service, together with the other new outside specialists who were particularly expert in bartering for and negotiating prices for spot TV time, became a permanent fixture on the scene. But not without some vicious criticism from some of the large ad agencies, who saw their mainstay operation dangerously threatened. Hurried meetings and panel sessions were set up to debate the issue. In a session at the Waldorf, six top media directors of major agencies blasted the trend. They predicted it would be dead in six months, a year at the most. "Typical of those experiments clients like to try out." Herb Manaloveg, of BBDO, a dean in the media fraternity, said, "They ought to be horsewhipped!" A year later, Herb was president of one of the largest of these new firms. Three of the others on that same panel—Sam Vitt, of Ted Bates; Paul Roth, of Kenyon & Eckhardt; and Bernie Kanner, of Benton & Bowles—had left their agency media roles within the next eighteen months.

The appearance of the media services was especially opportune for another important development: the birth of the *creative-only* agency. The media services made it possible for almost any team of young, ambitious professionals to start an ad agency without a large structure of account executives, media departments, and other functions. A new agency could, in theory anyway, be launched from a hotel suite, a loft, or an apartment. This opened the door to a whole generation of frustrated, thirty-five- to forty-five-year-old creative men who had always longed to start an agency but could not kitty up the needed capital to go out on their own. Now they could —with a few months' expenses for an office, some furniture, a girl Friday, and reasonable luck—make a go of it. Dozens upon dozens tried it. During the years between 1965 and 1971, more new agencies were formed than in any period in the history of advertising. Not only in New York but in Chicago, San Francisco, Miami, Houston, and Philadelphia, where a new precedent was started. A fledgling agency there was frankly composed entirely of unemployed creative men, a kind of blind-leading-the-blind enterprise. Many of these slapped-together agencies failed within two months. Others, within six months. Those that stayed alive a year or more generally squeaked through.

The major problems of these new agencies were lack of adequate capital, the wrong chemistry among the partners, a shortage of salesmanship (most good creative men are poor stand-up salesmen), and the long lag in waiting for the first account to come in. In order to avoid long-term commitments in leases, investment in furniture, and other overhead, many of the new creative-only agencies and independent services began business in hotels. The Gotham, a marble lump of elegance on Fifth Avenue (also once known as a haven for high-priced call girls) was the site of the first office of Mary Wells, Dick Rich, and Herb Greene. A half-dozen others followed them at the same address. Several others, including Gene Case and Helmut Krone and June Colbert, started business in suites at the Plaza Hotel. Case and Krone served room-service coffee at $1.50 a cup to impress visitors. They also used the ornate fireplace as a file cabinet. Some took over girl friends' apartments or sublet space in employment agents' offices. One, Warren Muller Dolobowsky, got a buy on some empty floors in a brownstone in the Turtle Bay area of midtown on the East Side. This was dandy, except that the only telephone was in the bathroom, the kitchen was used as the president's office, and the empty bedrooms rattled with mice.

How serious is the trend toward outside services? Let this story tell: It was easy to see fear on faces in a crowd. The people may have smiled, talked glibly, greeted each other with hearty handclasps, even told jokes. But it was there, the tightness at the corner of the mouth, the furtive eye movements, the gulp of coffee or cocktail. This was in the spring of 1971 in the ballroom and foyers of the Plaza Hotel in New York City. It was at an all-day seminar held by the Association of National Advertisers (ANA). The genesis of the fear: A business was coming apart at the seams. Obviously and unmistakably, the ad agency business, as it had operated for more than half a century, was under the gun, in deep trouble, maybe dying. The theme of the seminar, which was attended by the top executives of both major advertising agencies and major corporations, was "The New Needs of Advertisers." Not shocking in black and white, but terribly so when the "new needs" revealed at this seminar clearly appeared to be services no longer sought or expected from advertising agencies. They were, in effect, being given their walking papers by the all-powerful Association of National Advertisers, which represents the major clients of the major ad agencies.

"This is nothing new for Christ's sake," waxed one ad agency president during a morning coffee break between sessions. "We've seen this before. Outside services, moonlighters, free-lancers, so now they call them independent services, what's the difference? It doesn't mean the business is going down the fucking drain."

"How about at your agency? Any of your clients using these services?" an executive asked.

"Absolutely not," the president replied with force.

"Not even media services?" (Media services buy time and space. Ironically, the basic original function of ad agencies.)

"Especially not media services! I'd tell them to go straight to hell if they did."

He moved away from the group quickly then. Before he left, there was moisture on the temples of his handsomely tanned face. He had just told a barefaced lie. His agency at the very moment was deep into this problem. At least three of his major accounts had been and were using outside media services, outside creative services, and outside sales promotion services. All functions a full-

33

service agency such as his ought to be providing for its clients. Obviously, his agency was not the only one. The whole top-ranking tier of big, full-service shops had seen at least some of their clients experimenting, trying out, testing the new outside services. Now, as they milled around the coffee-and-croissant buffet under the crystal chandeliers of the lush foyer, they did their best to hide their fears. Many of them, when asked direct questions on the subject, avoided answers or, as agency president John did, told outright lies. What else could they do? Can a surgeon admit he doesn't perform surgery? Can a lawyer confess that he doesn't write his own briefs for clients? Can an adman say he doesn't make ads, doesn't place ads for his clients? If he admits this, then what the hell *does* he do for his commissions?

William Claggett, a top marketing executive for Ralston Purina and one of the leaders of this seminar, put the fat in the fire at the very first meeting of the day. He revealed the results of a survey the ANA had recently made among a hundred or so of their members. He presented the results in a dramatic fashion. The figures in large type on the slide projection spoke for themselves: 76 percent of the companies surveyed had *switched* some services away from advertising agencies either to internal house agencies or to outside independent services—76 percent! If asked previously, most of the agency men in the ballroom would have guessed perhaps 10 percent, maybe on the outside 15 percent. But three quarters of the major companies in America in this survey had turned away from ad agencies for services ad agencies traditionally offered. It was a staggering fact. But then to add to the drama, Claggett had had dozens of the key company executives in the survey reveal their reasons on tapes. Because the matter was so serious, and because the top executives did not wish to reveal their identities, the voices on the taped broadcast to the assemblage were those of professional actors.

The disembodied opinions rang through the vaulted ballroom: "Our agency has not been responsive to changing times." "We find it easier to work with smaller groups." "The time factor was important to us, we couldn't wait months for jobs that can be done in days or weeks." "Too many echelons of executives at the

34

agency." "The independent services we use seem to have more spark and enthusiasm. Get down to work faster." On they went, nearly all on the same theme of failure. A few, to be sure, said they still preferred to work through their regular ad agency systems. "Until we run into trouble, then we might change." The effect on the audience was visible and audible. The squirming in the chairs, the whispers, the nervous coughs, the shuffling of papers in laps, the shoulder shrugging. It was a black morning for ad agencies. Perhaps the death knell for the full-service agency.

This bad news should not have come as a surprise. There had been ample warnings. No one could deny that some thirty to forty creative workshops had been set up in New York City, Chicago, and elsewhere in the past eighteen months. These agency men knew this, of course, but they assumed the brash young kids were starving to death. The agency men had belittled them at every chance they got. They derisively labeled them "frivolous, smart-ass boutiques." They implied they were superficial, perhaps even immoral: "creative teams living together." Like "toadstools," they will be gone after the shower dries out. They knew, too, about the new media services. First there was one, a flamboyant character, a rough talker, who reputedly had made a quick million. "A shady character, foulmouthed," they said. Then there were several more media services. Then ten more, twenty, and at this point, thirty-eight independent media services. Still the Greek chorus chanted, "They'll be gone in a year. A passing fad." The same ad agency executives had also heard of other independents who were chipping away at their business. The new-product workshops, the new direct-marketing firms, sales promotion firms, broadcast TV production firms, merchandising specialists, all doing work that agencies traditionally performed for their clients. This, too, got the same back-of-the-hand, "insignificant pip-squeak operators" comments from the elder citizens.

As this historic day at the Plaza wore on, ad agency forces put their own men on the platform in rebuttal, not defense. "Piece-mealism," scoffed the spokesman the august American Association of Advertising Agencies (4As) had selected to present a white paper on the subject. "They [the independents] are inefficient,

35

inexperienced, unreliable." As if to demonstrate the great powers of the old-line big agency, this spokesman, John Monsarrat, formerly a senior executive at J. Walter Thompson, said, "A full-service agency has in-depth personnel strength. Why, if the client needs or calls for it, we can fly three men to a midwestern city over a weekend to check a particular sales situation." Advertisers in the audience might have said to themselves, "Who needs an army of high-priced executives chasing around the country? What we need is a couple of smart creative brains to get out some good ads for us."

Another defender of the status quo took the stand. Archie Foster, president of prestigious Ted Bates & Company, himself the author of the "Move up to Kool" cigarette campaign, and also the current chairman of the 4As. His brief for the full-service ad agency was in essence, "If you can't be smart, be big." Or, as he put it in his address, "When clients sit down with us for a one-hour meeting, we have already had a thousand hours of meetings beforehand." Again, advertisers in the audience might have said, "That's just it, can't you see it! We don't want a thousand hours of committees, we just want a couple of bright young people who we can sit down with face to face and get the ads done." He also added that an ad agency relationship with its client should be like that of husband and wife. Like the wife who tells her husband "you are working too hard, drinking too much, spending too much." The executives in the audience glanced at each other knowingly. Archie was saying, "Agencies should be hand holders, intimate custodians, bosom buddies." Advertisers at the meeting might have thought, "Bullshit, we've had it with the pandering, socializing, arm-around-the-shoulder nonsense. We want to see more attention paid to making good ads. Spare us the good-time-Charlie crap."

Toward the end of the day, there were signs that maybe the earthshaking message was getting through. Vic Bloede, president of Benton & Bowles, an old-line, blue-chip shop, was heard to say, "Hell, if we can't beat them, we'll join them. We as an agency will offer separate services on the same basis as the independents if that's what they want." This sounded like heresy. This isn't the way the Establishment wants things to trend. They will defend their full services until the last. They feel that if they don't, the ad agency business as they have known it will disintegrate, fall into a fragmented industry of small, specialized experts, and spell the end of an era—a fat, profitable era—for the major ad agencies.

3

The New Men Take Over

BEN COLAROSSI, a young man in his early twenties, with curly chestnut hair and a quick-flashing Latin smile, got off the Lexington Avenue subway at an uptown station on a summer day in the late 1950s. Ben, ordinarily a cocky, outgoing person, was nervous and uneasy as he climbed the stairway to the street. He was on his way to the Ruppert brewery to apply for a job in the advertising business. At this moment, young Colorassi had no idea that he was about to become a small but significant part of a profound change that was to take place in the business of advertising. When he reached the street level, Ben's chances looked dismal. It was pouring rain. He had six blocks to walk to the brewery, far enough to completely drench his carefully pressed suit and soak the package he carried under his arm, his portfolio of art samples. "I've always been a lucky bastard," Ben said later. The advertising manager, along with several other brewery executives, happened to be passing through the reception room just as Ben arrived. The group stopped and looked at Ben, "Like I was some kind of an insult—then they laughed."

"What can we do for you, kid?" the ad manager asked.

"Gimme a job. I'm an artist's director. Or could be—will be someday."

The entire group studied sopping-wet Ben for another few moments, then laughed some more. The portfolio of art samples was a lumpy mass under his arms; his shoes squished with water.

Then Ben remembered. He fumbled in his trousers pockets and came up with a dog-eared business card. "It's from Tony, you know, down in my neighborhood. He's your distributor. I do Tony lots of favors in the taverns. He thinks I draw good. He sent me." The "neighborhood" Ben was referring to was the Lower West Side of Manhattan, Hell's Kitchen.

Ben didn't get a job at the Ruppert brewery. Instead, the executives sent him to their advertising agency, the old Biow Company in Rockefeller Center. In a few short years, Ben was on his way up. From his first job in the art department bullpen, he moved up rapidly to a full-fledged art director; to a TV commercial director, flying back and forth to Hollywood; to creative director in charge of a large department of writers and artists; and finally, in less than ten years, to head his own ad agency, Creamer-Colorassi, with offices on the fortieth floor of a midtown skyscraper, far above Hell's Kitchen.

Another young man, also in his twenties, also a subway rider, but this time from Brooklyn, was Dick Rich. Dick had the name and address of an advertising agency he had heard about that actually hired people on the basis of talent alone. Never mind the right connections, the proper college, the big interview stuff. "If you can produce," he had heard, "you're in." The agency was Doyle Dane Bernbach. They hired Dick as a junior writer. His salary could not have been more than $100 a week at that time (early in 1960). Dick produced for Doyle Dane Bernbach and for several other ad agencies in rapid succession. Among his best ads and commercials was one for Benson & Hedges that told about the "disadvantages" of the new extra-length cigarette. Like many of his ideas, this one hit a jackpot. At one point in this meteoric rise, Dick was standing uncomfortably in a crowd of people in the ballroom of the New York Hilton. He was to receive several awards that evening. "Jesus Christ!" Dick said, tugging at the collar of his tuxedo shirt, "I've never worn one of these mother fuckers before."

Dick doesn't even work in advertising any more, except as a consultant now and then for major corporations. He retired in 1969 with over $2 million, his share of the pie when Wells, Rich, Greene, the advertising agency of which he was a founding partner, went public. Mostly now Dick dabbles in the stock market from his renovated brownstone town house in the swank Upper East Side section of Manhattan.

Neither of these young men would have thought of themselves as revolutionaries when they first broke into advertising. They had no way of knowing that Ben, the Italian art director, and Dick, the Jewish writer, were to personify the character and the catalyst of the upheaval in advertising generally known as the *creative revolution.* Ben, for example, was only one of dozens of other Italian art directors, with names like Paccione, Brugnatelli, Scali, La Rosa, Travisano, Cappiello, Ammirati, Auditore, Cammaradella, Ragoti, and Palazzo, who all became part of the new wave of creative people who shook up the business in the 1960s. Nor did Dick Rich, at the time he got his first job, identify himself with another ethnic wave, the Jewish writers who brought in names like Koenig, Levenson, Papert, Reider, Hampel, Tolmach, Solow, Meadows, Tannenbaum, Isadore, and Rosenfeld. The Jewish cadre that entered the business is generally credited with changing the language of advertising. A change toward a fresher, warmer, friendlier, and more powerful voice. Together, these two new forces were (along with other newcomers) responsible for the vast and sweeping improvements the business was to experience.

It was indeed a revolution. Perhaps it was not noticeable in any sudden fashion to the general advertising audience. But it certainly was noted and recognized within the business. Almost overnight, there was a sudden new respect for creativity, for the big idea, for breakthrough, standout advertising. First there were the early Volkswagen ads, then Polaroid, Alka-Seltzer, Braniff, Xerox, Benson & Hedges, and many others. It was different advertising. It broke all the rules. It got attention and got itself talked about. At first the staid old agencies along Madison Avenue scoffed at this trend. "Superficial nonsense, done by brash young kids. Wise guys with no background, no training." It will go away, they thought. But it didn't. Instead, it gained momentum, for by now it became embarrassingly and increasingly evident that this wild, fresh stuff was getting results. Volkswagens were indeed selling. So were Polaroid cameras. Braniff airlines, with its multicolored planes, was carrying more passengers than competitors.

Benson & Hedges 100's were acclaimed the fastest-growing cigarette on the market. Something important was happening. It was not all glamor and mystique. These new-wave kids had something that was suddenly highly marketable: genuine imagination, a freshness and boldness that could not be denied.

The reaction up and down Madison Avenue, after the first attempts by the senior citizens on the speechmaking circuit to belittle and disparage the new kind of advertising, was a sudden switching of gears. "Well, hell," they told their clients, "anybody can do that kind of crap, if that's what you want." So they tried—and found it was far from simple. In fact, it wasn't anything that could be copied or adapted, as an agency president discovered one day when he presented an ad to a major client. The ad had been literally traced line for line, comma for comma, from a well-known Doyle Dane Bernbach ad. The client simply shook his head and noted, "Not the same thing. Something's missing." When the old-line agencies found they couldn't "borrow" the techniques, they finally decided that they would have to hire their own resident Jewish writers and Italian art directors. The race was on. The salaries of these new-wave creative people began to skyrocket. Young men in their twenties, who had been earning less than $10,000 a year, were suddenly getting offers for $20,000, $30,000, $40,000. A team composed of a Jewish writer and an Italian art director was packaged by enterprising placement agencies and sold for price tags of $75,000 to $100,000. McCann-Erickson snapped up a whole creative department from one of the hot new shops for a price reported to be nearly half a million dollars. Some of these youngsters were hiring financial advisors to negotiate their deals. The few agencies that had some of these much-sought-after talents on their staffs were forced to give quantum raises every few months to fend off the raiders. Some could not be held. They changed jobs as often as three times a year, leaping from one golden pinnacle to the next. The largest and stuffiest ad agency in the world hired Ron Rosenfeld at a salary often mentioned as $100,000 per year. Besides, they gave him carte blanche to hire all the assistants he wanted, design any kind of working quarters they wanted, and as an added fill-in, they could all wear any hair styles or clothes they wished. An enormous concession for this hundred-year-old, blue-chip company. Ron, by the way, had never attended college, wrote his first ads for a Chinese restaurant in his hometown of Baltimore, had nothing of the high-pressure-salesman mannerisms about him. He was, however, fresh from the creative coup of "soft whiskey" for Calverts, which saved the brand while earning millions for Seagram.

The most disquieting and unsettling reaction to this new development in creativity, at least to the conservative, old-line agencies, was the welcome it seemed to be getting from clients. Especially among the major multimillion-dollar spenders in the packaged-goods fields. Procter & Gamble, Miles Laboratories, Philip Morris, Gillette, as well as some of the major airline and liquor accounts. The very companies who for years were considered the implacable advocates of rigid, formula advertising. These were the ones who were blamed time and again for dull, irritating advertising. It had been the standard rejoinder in ad agencies when something new and fresh was presented to agency review boards: "We like it, we think it's great, but we can't show it to the client. You know these guys, they'd never approve it." Now these important big advertisers were switching their accounts, or parts of them, to these bright new creative people. During the sixties, Doyle Dane Bernbach, the agency with the brightest creative reputation, jumped its billings from less than $50 million to more than $250 million.

How did it come about? Why did the advertising agency Establishment become so vulnerable to such a radical, abrupt change-over? In order to understand this, a brief glance backward at the business is required. During its first seventy years, roughly between 1885 and 1955, the advertising business was growing up. There were many tumultuous years, but by the late thirties, it had become a mature, quite-respectable business. Concentrated largely in New York City, where nearly 70 percent of all national advertising originated, it soon began to attract personable young graduates from the Ivy League colleges, notably those with no particular professional interest in mind and no special talents. It was the same group that during the previous generation had drifted naturally toward Wall Street. It became a stylish profession, about which Franklin D. Roosevelt once said, "If I hadn't gone into politics, I think I would have liked advertising." It was also the business that attracted Chester Bowles and William Benton, both Yale graduates. They both retired as millionaires to go on to other careers: Bowles became ambassador to India; Benton, senator from Connecticut.

It would be unfair to say that the advertising agency business was snobbish or exclusive. Yet it was indeed often run as a sort of private fiefdom for well-to-do sons of good Eastern families. It could hardly be said to welcome eager, ambitious, hungry young men. In fact, it was the kind of gentlemen's profession that once caused the old blue-chip N. W. Ayer agency to write a memorandum to its executives politely chastising "quite a few of them" for failing to pick up their salary checks on paydays. "Some offenders are six months behind," the memorandum stated. A wag answered this memo by writing, "Nobody can live on Ayer anyway." And this was also true. The entrance salaries were so small that few but those with independent incomes could afford the first few years. There were actually no-pay apprenticeships in operation in some of the larger agencies during lean recession years.

Part of the attraction of advertising was its reputation—a combination of glamor, imaginative people, a certain libertine life-style —and quick fortunes. Some of this was partly true, but most of it had been inflated by novelists, moviemakers, and short-story writers. During the 1945–1960 era, it was in fact a fairly conservative business. The big, well-established ad agencies were playing it safe, holding on to their stable, profitable positions. Thanks to a munificent commission system, nearly all were profitable operations. It wasn't difficult. The result was that during this period, the top management level of ad agencies was peopled by relaxed, sensible, and unimaginative businessmen, men who sincerely believed they were serving their clients with what their clients wanted. "Let's be realistic, we all want to eat," was a typical catchphrase during these years that, in effect, simply said, "Don't make waves."

At about this time, a significant development took place.

Marion Harper and two young copywriters about his own age, which was then about twenty-five, looked out of place in the gin mill on South Wabash Street, a block away from McCann-Erickson's Chicago office on Michigan Avenue. The conversation, over ten-cent beers, took place after work. Marion had arrived by train from New York a few days before on a secret mission for H. K. McCann, his boss and mentor. He had spent this time ploughing through all the creative output of the Chicago office. He would ask for a batch of Pillsbury, Maytag, Standard of Indiana ads, then retreat into an empty office to study them for hours. The local office staff was not especially happy about this mysterious investigation of their work. Still, the young man had orders from New York.

The two copywriters were simply curious. One was Bob Smock, a hot young writer up from an Indiana radio station and at the time writing one of the top quiz shows on the networks.

"Tell me, Marion," Bob asked, "what's with the big probe into my radio commercials?" Earlier in the day, Marion had asked for a six-month supply of Bob's commercials.

"It's the coming thing, the wave of the future," Marion replied.

"What thing, for Christ's sake?"

"The advertising business is changing, no more seat of the pants. It's all going to be scientific. Proof, evidence, exact measurements."

Bob Smock and the other young copywriter looked at each other and took a swallow of beer. Then Bob asked: "Sorry, Marion, I don't get it. How's all this going to happen?"

Harper, standing there in the garish, blinking lights of the little bar, looked like a man who had the great secret of the ages about his person. His eyes shone, his head nodded, jiggling his tight, curly black hair. The word came out softly, conspiratorially. "Research," he said.

Marion was always ahead of his time. Always right, always wise, always premature. Research did become the God Almighty of advertising, but not for another decade. By that time, Marion was president of McCann-Erickson, and the new research he had predicted was behind him. He was now setting the stage for the Interpublic Group of Companies, a far wider, more visionary scheme than any advertising research program.

Coupled with this conservative and safe attitude on the part of management during these years was the hope to pin all advertising down to an exact science. On this, both clients and ad agencies agreed. "We've got to be more accountable." "We've got to be more knowledgeable about how people respond to advertising." "It's time we stopped guessing about what is good advertising and what isn't." Sensible aims. Typical business-like thinking. So the era of research was born. Ad agencies began to invest heavily in research departments. Every facet of advertising that could be tested was measured with slide rules and the new computers. There were pretests, posttests, eye-camera studies, palm-perspiration analyses of emotional response to ads, recall tests, message-retention tests, readership studies, motivational studies, audience-profile studies, demographics, psychographics, focus-group studies, and on and on.

All this new emphasis on research, although costly to ad agencies, made one thing much simpler. It was no longer difficult to sell a client on a new campaign. Where previously the agency people had to put on elaborate presentations to convince a client that their new approach was right, now a few turnover charts highlighting research results did the selling job. There was nothing to argue about. There it was; the figures didn't lie. Yes, there were some frauds and fakes. Oftentimes the actual field research was not done. Other times, it was done only among secretaries and office workers. Many times, the high guru research director's credentials were suspect. One doctor got his degree in ophthalmology. Many field supervisors simply wrote out the answers to most of their questionnaires themselves. In fact, a study showed that some 40 percent of all national surveys were faked. Still, the enthusiastic belief in research dominated the decade or so before 1960.

In this environment, who needed creative people? All that was required of the ad makers was a facility to implement the research. You didn't need a vocabulary; you just strung together words that were known to test high, such as "new," "mothers," "easy," "you," "your," "free," "hurry," "limited time only," and "use this handy coupon." Demonstrations were great according to research, so whole staffs were installed to work on before-and-after gimmicks or other "laboratory" tests to prove the superiority of one brand over the other. Art direction was even simpler. Research told precisely what kind of pictures invariably rated high: dogs, babies, family scenes, sentiment, modest cheesecake, outdoor scenes, sailboats, freckle-faced kids, and so forth. The range was limited, but never mind, how could you go wrong? Certain type styles were more "readable" than others, so here again, art direction was simplified. Copywriting became bead stringing. Using the short list of high-tested words, it was merely a matter of putting them together in order, plus following a few other simple research findings such as: it is best to mention the brand name seven times in each one-minute commercial; restate the user benefit three times in each message; raise the sound level of commercials above the program level; and keep the package on screen at least 28 percent of the time. No sweat, boss.

Obviously, this kind of creative straitjacket began to take its toll among writers and artists in the ad business. The good ones began to drift off into other fields. Or if they stayed on, they tried to sublimate their creative urges by doing creative work on their own. At one point, some thirty novels were being clandestinely written by creative people at J. Walter Thompson. Art directors were becoming Sunday painters or getting involved with underground moviemaking. The creative supervisors were carrying home briefcases full of research reports instead of copy to review. It wasn't long before there was a hierarchy of creative supervisors composed of executive art directors who couldn't draw, creative directors who couldn't write, who were managed on top by company officers who were concerned only about finances and client relations.

It might have been the recession of 1959–1961 that marked the turning point. Or it could have been the realization by many major manufacturers that many of the new products they were introducing were bombing, failing miserably in the marketplace, despite the fact that all their expensive research had told them to go, go, go. In any event, the disenchantment set in. The Edsel automobile, researched as nothing had ever been researched before, laid a historic egg. In other instances, those studies were found to be manipulated rather than merely unreliable, and the FTC was moved to lash out against "spurious, misleading research studies." It was not only advertising research that was subject to abuse. Many of the high rated quiz shows were found to be rigged. One client found that he was being asked to pay for a research report that he had already bought from a previous firm. And ads began to look so much alike that one client found that every time he ran one of his $50,000 commercials, 35 percent of the people who saw it went out and bought his competitor's product.

In any event, at the time Ben Colarossi and Dick Rich entered the business, an era was ending. Bill Bernbach, one of the leading exponents of creative emphasis, told an impressive audience of national advertisers at the Plaza Hotel one day early in the sixties, "If we had gone by the research we would never have run with the Avis campaign, 'We're Number Two.' The figures all said it would never work." By this time, Avis was already the most successful and talked-about campaign of the period. A saltier comment came from George Lois, then partner in the hot young Papert, Koenig, Lois, which was at that time picking up accounts so fast they could hardly absorb them. Lois said, "Fuck research, that only tells what you had for breakfast. Let's make some ads with balls!"

So the time was ripe, but who was going to fill the void? The big Establishment ad agencies considered themselves resourceful enough and deep enough in talent to meet the challenge. Didn't they have writers who had worked on the college magazine at Princeton? Didn't they have art directors with degrees from the Yale School of Fine Arts? Weren't the executives themselves men of culture and education? Of course they were creative! But then they would look around at some of the new "upstart graffiti writers" and see the ads for Volkswagen apparently appealing with clattering success to snobbish intellectuals. Yet they were written and designed by kids in blue jeans and jackets, who had either no education or a few night school courses in a subway college. Or they would be forced to laugh with everyone at the imaginative ads for Talon zippers or London Fog raincoats. Who made these things? Shep Kurnit at Delehanty Kurnit & Geller? "Why hell, he's nobody but a Brooklyn guy who used to run an art studio." Or Dick Gilbert's shop doing the London Fog ads? "Christ, Dick was just a radio time salesman a few years ago!"

The reaction got bitter and sometimes frantic. Dignified old BBDO thought it had an answer for a while. It had been experimenting with something called *brainstorming*. You put a bunch of people together in a room, and let them all shout ideas and random thoughts. Then somebody would blow a whistle, and you'd collect the gibberish into patterns. Then more shouting, more collecting, classifying, and whatnot. It was supposed to develop "latent" creative powers. It did produce a certain amount of publicity for a while, but the most imaginative campaign idea BBDO had during this period was the Tareyton ads with the black-eyed people saying, "I'd rather fight than switch." Other big agencies tried ways to get more creativity out of otherwise-uncreative people. They invited editors to their offices to give them lectures. They hung up exhibits of paintings and photography in their corridors, hoping no doubt that some of this creativity would brush off. They held pep-talk meetings, urging creative people to "pull out all the stops," "don't worry, we'll show your stuff to the clients." Nice old Cunningham & Walsh conducted tours of Greenwich Village, taking their creative people to see the Electric Circus and other "educational" sights. A number of the big, conservative agencies actually passed the word along that they would have no objections if some of the younger creative people wanted to wear beads or jeans, or let their hair and beards grow. They wanted clients to see that they, too, had some hippies on staff.

None of these efforts produced very much in the way of original thinking. Some copying and adaptations of currently fashionable creative campaigns, but almost nothing in the way of fresh, breakthrough advertising. And the reason was clear. It was a talent shortage. A people problem. The big agencies simply didn't have the right kind of creative people on staff. Long years of recruiting "our kind" had resulted in echelons of dry, sterile, and unimaginative minds. But it was something else, too. There was an enormous social and cultural gap as well. The well-educated, carefully selected creative people in the big shops were not snobs exactly, but they were light years apart in life-style experience from the new breed of creative people. Most of them came from, and lived in, comfortable surroundings. Westchester, Westport, the North Shore of Chicago, Grosse Pointe, Michigan. They were out of touch, or never had been in touch, with ordinary working people: the blue-collar households, the middle-income housewives, and the burgeoning new generation of rock-music-swinging youngsters. Of course, they had their research, which purportedly told them what these people were like; what they were interested in, and so forth; but it was a poor substitute for reality. It was a case of misunderstanding that often bordered on contempt. The people who had been creating the ads didn't know how to talk to the people who were supposed to be reading them.

In truth, these advertising executives were so out of touch that many stories cropped up about their trying to put nickels in subway turnstiles, getting lost in Greenwich Village, referring to guitars as banjos, mistaking the *Yellow Submarine* for a war movie, and naming Wayne King or Guy Lombardo as their favorite band-leader. The gap was especially wide in the language of advertising. Since they had no direct knowledge of how ordinary people talked, what expressions and words they used, these advertising people developed their own advertisingese. A fake, false, make-believe jargon that passed for dialogue between the actors in TV commercials, in the headlines in ads, or in the words of singing radio announcements. It accounted for much of the dull, dreary, irritating advertising of the 1945–1960 period, for much that was inane and ridiculous. Some of it revealed actual and unmistakable contempt, a patronizing, down-their-noses regard for the soap opera–horse opera millions who watched TV or read newspapers and magazines. The "boob tube," the "idiot box," although passed off as jokes, were truly the way these people felt about their audiences.

Looking back, it now appears that the main thrust of the new wave of creativity came mostly from one area: the Seventh Avenue–Macy's–Gimbels arena of advertising. This was where retailing was king. Advertising here was different from the big, national advertising campaigns done on Madison Avenue. Here advertising was created and produced for one purpose only: immediate sales action. Madison Avenue had its four-color magazine ads, its corporate-identity campaigns, its image-building investments. Over here, results in the cash registers were the only thing that counted. Creative people here took the service elevators to the department store top floors, where they worked in cubicles or in loud, messy open areas, grinding out ads by the yard. They worked long hours, fought hard for their ideas, were under the gun all the time. Bernice Fitzgibbon, longtime ad manager of Gimbels and previously at Macy's, where she authored the famous line "It's smart to be thrifty," called this *item advertising.* You made up an ad for a particular item, ran it the next morning, and if by noon the item hadn't sold out, "Somebody's ass would be in a sling!"

It was only natural that this kind of strong, sales-pulling advertising would carry over from the department stores to a small group of advertising agencies in the nearby area. These were of an altogether-different stripe from the posh Madison Avenue companies. One, for example, was Grey Advertising. Its founders— Arthur Fatt, Herb Strauss, and Larry Valenstein—decided that the name "Grey" sounded better than their own names on the door. They chose it from the color of their office walls. Another agency took a similar step and called itself "Daniel & Charles," after the first names of Danny Karsh and Charlie Goldschmidt. These agencies recruited their creative people from the neighborhood department stores. They hired people like Bill Bernbach, Ben Alcott, Paula Green, Ed Meyer, Bernie Kahn, Manning Rubin, and other hard-working, retail-oriented people. Naturally, their experience in advertising designed for direct, fast sales action was helpful. But they had an additional advantage. They were close to the public, close to the fast-changing moods of the big audiences, close to the new trends in fashion, style, theater, and entertainment. They had the common touch so necessary for communicating with large groups of people. They had to be sharp about things like new words and expressions, new apparel styles, new concepts in home furnishings, new fads, and new products. They were hip, savvy, contemporary. They had to be; it was their life-style. They were Sammy Glicks, running hard and fast for success.

It was said later, with some truth, that Madison Avenue was hit on the blind side when this new, fresh, action-oriented advertising charged in on them from Seventh Avenue and Broadway. The old, established ad agencies certainly were not prepared for this kind of an assault They were, of course, aware that those retail outfits did their own kind of advertising and that some of them had their own kind of ad agencies. But to them, it was nickel-and-dime business. No science, no research, no review boards, no campus recruiters, no training programs, no stature. So when it hit them, as it did when these very people from the wrong side of Fifth Avenue began to make themselves heard, they were ill equipped to understand it, much less to combat it.

Here is a closer look at some of the individuals who arrived in the vanguard of this new kind of advertising.

William Bernbach is a good person to start with. There have been many men over the years who have established great creative reputations for themselves. Some, like Leo Burnett, David Ogilvy, George Gribbon, and Rosser Reeves, were contemporaries of Bernbach. But none were in the same class with him. He literally invented a new kind of advertising. A friendlier, warmer, more personal point of view. He came from the heart of the retail arena. He worked with Grey Advertising on ads for shirts, watches, liquor, fashion, and soft goods. He knew how to get the direct, fast sales action typical of this school of advertising. But he added some extra touches of his own. He believed, for example, that people might appreciate something a little more than just value and bargain prices. They would respond to an appeal to pride and personal satisfaction, would buy products with intrinsic beauty, quality, and high fashion. He tried this with one of his first accounts when he set up his own advertising agency. This was Orbach's, a noisy bargain-center kind of retailer on Fourteenth Street. His now-classic ads delivered a clear and unmistakable message: "high fashion at low prices." Orbach's became so successful that they moved to much-larger quarters uptown.

Bernbach brought another dimension to advertising: an absolutely frank honesty. An early anecdote best illustrates how this evolved in Bernbach's advertising. One of his first accounts was a Brooklyn bakery called Levy's. Bill was from Brooklyn, still lived there, and knew the bread Levy baked was a good product. He had been called in now because sales were down.

Sitting in the small office of the bakery on his first visit to Levy, Bill asked, "Why isn't your bread selling? Have you cut the quality, changed anything?"

"No," the baker said. "Same bread. Best we can make. People just don't like it anymore, I guess."

Bernbach then asked, "You make a lot of different kinds of

bread—which one do you think is the very best one? The one that people should hear about?"

"The Jewish rye," was the immediate reply. "It's beautiful."

"That's funny," Bernbach said. "You never mention Jewish rye in your advertising. Never once. Why?"

The head of the company shrugged, "Well, you know,—it's Jewish. Maybe some people might think—they are anti-Semitic—or something."

Bernbach thought for a minute. Then said, "It's your best bread —sell it. With a name like Levy—people are going to know you're Jewish." And Bill proceeded to tell him how the advertising should be handled. The results were the now famous poster ads, "You don't have to be Jewish to love Levy's rye bread," featuring blacks, Italians, Chinese, Indians, etc. Bill Bernbach understood ordinary people. And how to talk to them.

Bernbach's contributions also include his fantastically successful training environment, which produced at least a dozen ad agency presidents and hundreds of creative stars throughout the industry.

Another typical revolutionary of the period is Julian Koenig, a graduate of Bill Bernbach's agency, but an individualist in his own right. Koenig began in the same Seventh Avenue environment as many of the other new-wave creative people. A superb writer, he spent quite a number of years trying to convince some of the Madison Avenue agencies where he worked to break out of their molds and do something fresh and different. He was totally un-successful until he went to work with Bernbach and wrote some of the first historic ads for Volkswagen. A typical ad simply head-lined "Lemon," which then went on to show why it was unlikely that an owner of a Volkswagen would own a car that was a lemon because each one was inspected 382 times. Throughout his work on Volkswagen, and on many other accounts at DDB, Koenig de-veloped a refreshing new approach to advertising. Stated simply it said, "Don't take yourself too seriously, be human, admit a fault once in a while." This was heresy to advertising fundamentalists, whose credo was always to make the advertisers look big, powerful, pompous, perfect. Now Julian seemed to say through his ads, "Give a little, tell the truth, how much can it hurt?" It apparently didn't hurt a bit; in fact, for Volkswagen, Avis, and many other "honest" advertisers that Koenig worked on, sales went up astonishingly. Julian later went on to start his own agency, win the coveted Copywriters Hall of Fame award, and make some other marks. More about him later.

Carl Ally is another typical adman who belongs smack in the middle of the creative revolution in advertising. Carl—a sensitive, thoughtful person in spite of his tough-talking, scrappy personality —was a fighter pilot in World War II and in Korea. He began his advertising career in Detroit, working as a copywriter for Campbell-Ewald, the agency that handled mostly General Motors assignments. Later he moved with this same firm to New York, and still later, he joined the fast-rising Papert, Koenig, Lois firm. Carl's main forte was an approach that said, "Let's cut out all the bullshit and tell the story in plain, simple English." When he left PKL to set up his own agency, he had surrounded himself with a cadre of like-thinking and very bright creative people, including Jim Durfee, Amil Gargano, and a group of young enthusiasts. Almost immediately, they began turning out an "Ally kind" of advertising. It was completely individual. Soundly conceived, carefully put together, and (as Carl had always maintained) "no bullshit." When asked once to describe this philosophy in more specific terms, Carl replied, "It's like I'm selling my used car to a friend. A real friend. I don't want to screw him—after all, I might be seeing him again. So what do I tell him? The truth, the good and the bad, the whole story. Why should I con him?" This, too, was a new dimension in advertising. A unique approach. Advertisers and their ad agencies simply didn't think this way previously. They had forgotten that they, too, might be seeing their prospects and customers again in the future. Ally later went on to do remarkable campaigns for Volvo, Hertz, Northeast Airlines, IBM, and other giants. His advertising and his own personal philosophy reflect a strong sense of business responsibility to society.

George Lois—a tall, rangy, semipro basketball player and the ultimate Greek—would hardly be comfortable in the hushed, conservative environment of the large, famous-name ad agencies. He is, however, very comfortable in the penthouse offices of Lois

Holland Callaway, overlooking Fifth Avenue. This complete antithesis of the old-line adman is the perfect example of the new breed. Loud, laughing, an arm-waving salesman, George is also a very talented art director. He has designed more than a hundred covers for *Esquire* magazine in his spare time. George Lois brings a different facet to the new advertising: a flamboyancy, a flair, and a go-for-broke attitude to ideas and concepts. More than anything else, he wants his advertising to be seen, talked about, cause a controversy, but, "For Christ's sake, don't ignore me!" This has led to some wildly bizarre advertising for such staid old clients as Edwards & Hanley, the Wall Street brokerage firm. Their TV campaign, you may remember, featured testimonials by people like Joe Louis, the ex-heavyweight champ, saying, "Edwards & Hanley, where were you when I needed you?" Or another for Maypo cereal with Mickey Mantle, tears streaming down his face, crying, "I want my Maypo!" He also used Margaret Mead, Andy Warhol, and other famous personalities in unexpected, delightful, and successful campaigns. He even used a chimpanzee to do a commercial for Xerox photocopiers. Lois brought a devil-may-care approach to advertising that shook up a lot of people and rang up a lot of sales. His contribution to the revolution was, as he might put it, "We made the lazy bastards get off their fat asses." The business needed some of this prodding.

Mary Wells Lawrence—chic, glamorous, blonde superstar—is a brilliant product of advertising's creative revolution. She came to New York City from Ohio, where she had written copy for a Columbus department store. Her real working experience, however, began from the same base as many of these other new pacesetters: Macy's, Doyle Dane Bernbach, and later, Jack Tinker & Partners, a creative, experimental operation that was started by Interpublic. Mary is a dynamic, ambitious, tremendously success-oriented person. Wherever she worked, she brought her own exciting charm, coupled with a shrewd, sharp knowledge of salesmanship. Her advertising philosophy was clearly an extension of her own personality. She likes glitter, beauty, drama. She wants to be loved; she wants to be admired; she wants to stand out. All these personal traits emerged in her advertising. It stood out boldly, dramatically for Braniff International airlines when she dressed the hostesses in Pucci outfits and teamed up with her art director Phil Parker to shock the airline world by painting every Braniff plane a strikingly different and brilliant color (baby blue, canary yellow, blushing pink, and so forth). On the Alka-Seltzer account, she was credited with some of the earliest and greatest commercial episodes, including "Whatever shape your stomach is in, Alka-Seltzer will make it feel better," which was filmed with a hilarious series of stomachs of everyone from bikini girls to pneumatic drill operators. Later, when she started her own agency with Dick Rich and Stu Greene, she utilized this philosophy even more for Love cosmetics, Benson & Hedges, American Motors, and TWA. Mary also added a new importance to an old, but often neglected, advertising technique: capitalizing on the owner and employees of a company. A hundred years ago, advertising used the picture of the founder in ads, but Mary updated this. She made a national figure out of Roy Chapin, president of American Motors. She made TWA employees the stars of the TWA commercials, showing them as they worked hard to win a million-dollar-bonus contest. She did somewhat the same thing with Royal Crown dealers around the country. This contribution was particularly timely. It helped counteract the growing attitude on the part of all Americans, especially the young, that companies were all huge, impersonal, money machines. Mary also helped propel the creative revolution by the sheer force of the fantastic publicity she generated toward herself and thus toward the exciting new advertising as well. More about Mary Wells Lawrence later.

The five personalities described above are by no means the only revolutionaries who brought about the great change in advertising during the sixties. Taken together, however, they typify the movement, the momentum, the radical turnaround in the business. All, as you notice, had a solid retail experience, usually with department stores. All were from middle-class, average backgrounds. All were rebels, rule breakers, antitraditionalists. All, too, were warm, human, outgoing, and essentially friendly people who respected audiences and understood their feelings with an intimacy born of firsthand knowledge. All had a tight, unquenchable core of vanity and ham inside. A priceless quality in the top creative person and the successful adman.

What actually happened to the surface of advertising as this new trend took over? Did all the excitement take place only in the ads and commercials produced by these new heroes? No, there was an outward, visible explosion as well. The business came to life again. For creative people all over—in New York, Chicago, San Francisco, Philadelphia, and other major cities—it was as if gold had been discovered. Suddenly, there was something worth working hard for. Something that promised quick, practical rewards. Creative people and creative departments were, almost overnight, in brilliant focus. And the eager young kids took advantage of everything they could seize. Looking the part, playing the role, or, to borrow one of George Lois's headlines, "If you've got it, flaunt it!" became the order of the day. Any night of the week, you could hear excited, loud-talking young creative people, jammed into the bars and restaurants near the ad agencies, bragging, boasting, trying out new ideas on each other. Michael's Pub, Ratazzi, Charlie Brown's, Manny Wolf's (near Papert, Koenig, Lois), Costello's, Charley O's, and dozens of others in midtown New York. In Chicago, it was the bars at the Wrigley, Prudential, Palmolive, buildings and Rush Street bistros. They compared salary offers; they debated heatedly over which were the hot shops and which agencies were those you shouldn't be caught dead in. They placed bets on their individual heroes. Who was going to start his own agency first? Who was going to knock off a great new account single-handedly? Who was going to be the first to go public?

Along about this time, and very much a part of what was happening, two new terms came into prominence and promised new jackpots of money. One was the *creative team*. It had been discovered that Doyle Dane Bernbach, Daniel & Charles, Delehanty & Kurnit, and a few highly creative agencies owed some of their success to the remarkable results produced by a top writer and top art director working closely together, actually sharing the same office, spending their entire days and evenings bouncing ideas back and forth, and coming up with some of the most sensational of the new stuff. So now there was a rush among creative people to find the right partner, the perfect counterpoint to their special talents. Some of the brightest were boy-girl teams, and word had it that they really worked together, all day and all night. And some of it was true; the in-town "mousetrap" apartments began to flourish. The ideal team obviously was the by-now-acknowledged magic combination of the Jewish writer and the Italian art director. As far as individual talents are concerned, this may have been correct. As compatible personalities, the two volatile ethnic strains didn't always produce harmony. There were stories of drawing boards being hurled across rooms, typewriters used as missiles, and battles with T squares. Management also found, somewhat later, that nothing much happened at all. Many of the fabulous twosomes simply spent whole days corking off or phoning the placement agencies looking for better offers.

The decorum of ad agencies certainly began to take on a different look. Women copywriters began wearing pants, plunging necklines, and peekaboo blouses. Men began sprouting beards and handlebar moustachios and wearing buckskin jackets and jeans to the offices. Many an agency executive was heard to remark, "Who in Christ's name was that in the elevator. Does *he* work for us?" The smell of pot began drifting down the corridors. The office hours became looser. Many of the creative people preferred to work only at night, staying in the offices often until dawn. Some slept on the vice-presidents' couches, took showers in the presidents' private bathrooms, turned the conference rooms into movie-making labs. Management tried gracefully to look the other way. "What the hell," they thought, "we've got to go along with this or be accused of being a 'square' agency." They stretched pretty far on occasions. One agency president paid for a trip to Europe so that a model, pregnant by one of his top art directors, could get a quiet abortion. Others tossed in sports cars as fringe benefits. Some issued special stock so that the ambitious young people could get the "piece of the action" they were now demanding. Offices took on new embellishments. Creative people no longer had to abide by the stuffy office-manager rules of neat, tidy cubicles. They could hang anything they wanted on their walls. So up came the nudes, antiwar posters, psychedelic art, neon signs, barber poles, wooden Indians, spittoons, and other expressions of personality. Management did its best to keep clients away from their creative departments, although they wanted to be sure they got a glimpse now and then of a hippie boy or girl in the hallways. It set the right tone.

Clients were enchanted. For years they had been sitting through long, boring meetings conducted by gray-suited elder statesmen, with their inevitable flip charts and graphs. Now they were entertained by zany creative types who literally danced and sang their way through proposed commercials. These charged-up, loud-voiced rebels shouted their ideas, pounded the mahogany conference tables, and laughed loudest at their own commercials. It was fun. It was what the advertising business was supposed to be. It worked. Many an idea that once would have never even reached the conference room now got a full hearing. And best of all, who cared whether the research director was present or not.

The gray eminences from the mill towns of Pennsylvania and Ohio were now sitting face to face with sexy, sweet-smelling young creative girls who were pouring on all the charm they could muster along with their sparkling new ideas. The young men were equally entertaining as they spouted their ideas laced with outrageous cusswords, many of them refreshingly new to the serious-minded clients. No wonder the word got back to management, "We want more of these creative meetings. It makes much more sense to talk to the actual creators themselves, person to person. This way we cut out all the crap." There was a noticeable loosening up of client language during these creative upheavals. They began to ask with a straight face for "more balls, less bullshit" in their advertising. The creativity bit was contagious.

The growth of the team system necessitated some physical changes in ad agencies. The quiet routine of agency operations was soon disturbed by crews of interior designers, carpenters, and other construction people knocking down walls, tearing out partitions, restructuring whole floors. The aim was to erase the now-outdated symbols of separation between copy and art. For fifty years, copywriters had dominated the front offices. These were the college graduates, the thinkers, the idea generators. Art directors, in the back of the office, were the mere implementers of the copywriters' ideas and words. All this was changed. They were now on equal footing. The new creativity, the "now" advertising was mainly a new visual look. This was the TV era; the film and art directors moved to the limelight. "Concepts" became the magic word. It meant words and pictures working together. No longer did the words precede the layout and design. Now teams gave blushing birth to the concept in full partnership. This meant, of course, that they would have to be together, if not in the same new, larger office, at least in intermingled, side-by-side offices. All this accomplished several things. It stepped up the noise level in creative departments as the shouts and disagreements rang through the new office layouts. It made for many cozy arrangements for the boy-girl teams. It generated a lot of light, but not so much fire. As sage old Leo Burnett once put it, "After all the talking and meetings, somebody has to go off by his lonely self and write the ad."

Despite its faults, the team concept worked efficiently for some ad agencies. At Daniel & Charles, Jack Tinker & Partners, Delehanty Kurnit Geller, deGarmo, Doyle Dane Bernbach, Grey Advertising, McCann-Erickson, and Papert, Koenig, Lois, teams produced outstanding work. They also accomplished something else that did not please management. After working successfully together for a year or two, the teams discovered that they were ready to go into business for themselves. During the 1965–1968 period, team after team set up their own shops: Chappel Fiore Endelman; David, Oksner & Mitchneck; Calderhead, Jackson; Kurtz Kambanis Symon; Spade & Archer; Scali, McCabe, Sloves; Case and Krone; and Rosenfeld, Sirowitz. After it became apparent that two creative men alone had little chance for success, many of these shops wisely included a marketing man to team up with the creative pair.

The other hopeful experiment tried at this time was something called the *creative island*. The promise here was based upon dubious belief that somehow creativity would germinate and blossom better if the environment was right. "Freedom," "permissiveness," "looseness," "group-think," and other magic keys were supposed to release pent-up imaginations, let out inhibited ideas, spring loose talents people didn't even know they possessed. It was an exciting theory. Everyone rushed to try it out. First you needed a very bright cluster of handpicked creative types. The way-out, blue-sky dreamers. The wild-eyed, bushy-haired types. The youngest, most undisciplined writers and artists. And maybe a moderator type, but no ham-fisted, wagon-boss supervisor. The monolithic old Ted Bates agency surprised everyone with one of the first creative islands, which they called the "Blue Birds." This was to differentiate them from the straights, who were called the "Men from Iron City."

Other agencies raced to introduce their own islands. J. Walter Thompson picked easygoing, good guy Sid Olsen, a former *Life* editorial writer and a fine ad writer as well, to head their island, which they called "Group Seven." They built a special suite within the dreary and semilit confines of the old Graybar Building and decorated every piece of furniture—couches, chairs, walls, and so forth—with polka dots! Coffee and refreshments were on hand at all hours. Permissiveness and freedom were practically rampant while it lasted, which wasn't very long. McCann-Erickson, eager to follow the fashion, discovered that they didn't have any really creative people to populate the island, much as they wanted one. Judy Wald, the enterprising placement agent, solved this. She sold them a whole package; six writers and artists were delivered en masse, tightly wrapped in long-term contracts. Many others tried, with varying results, mostly bad. The cold realization finally emerged: "We're pissing away a lot of money on these freaks, and what are they producing? Zilch! They sit around all day drinking Cokes and rapping among themselves. Besides, all the regular working stiffs are getting damn well frosted."

The islands rapidly disappeared. But the notion of the "right creative climate" persisted. Agency management simply could not figure out how they could get the creative juices flowing. Something had to be done because this amazing creative revolution was indeed getting a lot of fanfare and publicity. Clients talked about nothing else. It must have finally occurred to agency management, in the big shops anyway, that perhaps they had been hiring the wrong types for a long period of time. That what they needed was a little fresh seeding here and there to be accomplished by bringing in a few of these name personalities. This they did, and again with middling-to-miserable results. The new superstar was never welcome. He was sandbagged and mousetrapped on all sides. When he did produce something fresh and different, he discovered that the account executives didn't really plan to sell the blue-sky stuff to the clients. They certainly would not recommend it. They only wanted to prove to clients that they were capable as an agency of cranking it out. This is the straw-man ploy. The preparation of ads and campaigns are shown, only to be shot down dramatically before the "real thing" is presented. Ron Rosenfeld, the $100,000-a-year man, took this kind of treatment at J. Walter Thompson for just about a year before quitting. Jerry Della Femina and his group sweated out about fourteen months of this at Ted Bates before they trooped out to start their own shop.

As the creative revolution marched ahead, the management men on top began to get deeply concerned. Some $300 million in big billings had been switched out of the big Establishment agencies to smaller creative shops in the mid-1960s. "What else can we do?" was the lament. There was one more move, and they tried it. After much soul-searching, they decided that the trouble with the creative climate was at the top. Management itself didn't have the right attitude. It looked down on creative people. Treated them as second-class admen. Didn't sympathize, understand, care enough. "Well, goddammit, if that's how they feel, we'll make the president of the whole agency a creative man. That ought to satisfy them!" And again, the monkey-see, monkey-do pattern took over. All over town there was a sudden rash of new creative presidents. Steve Frankfurt, thirty-eight years old, a Jewish art director and big award winner, was made president of Young & Rubicam. Vic Bloede, creative director, went to the top at Benton & Bowles. Chet Posey, a onetime creative director, moved from vice-chairman of McCann to president of Jack Tinker. Art director Bill McCaffry became president of deGarmo. Larry Dunst, only twenty-eight years old, an *enfant terrible*, became president of Daniel & Charles. Bill Free became president of Marschalk; John O'Toole, president of Foote, Cone & Belding; Milt Gossett, president of Compton; Bill Betz at Esty; Paccione at Leber Katz; Hanno Fuchs at Richard K. Manoff; Stan Tannenbaum at Kenyon & Eckhardt; Bill Wall at Rockwell, Quinn & Wall; Paul Foley at McCann-Erickson; and many others down the line.

Was this the answer? For a while it seemed to work. Creative men in theory had a voice to top management. One of "their guys" was up there. Also, it was believed that it took the pressure off clients who were harassing many agencies about their lagging creative images. "Look," they could say now, "creativity is our most important product, we've even made a creative man president!" Not all clients were impressed. Upon a closer look, they could see that the chief executive office, the real "button," was somebody else. Ed Bond at Young & Rubicam. Charlie Goldschmidt at Daniel & Charles. Impressive young Milt Gossett had an ironfisted chairman and vice-chairman up ahead of him at Compton. The new presidents were, for the most part, mere figureheads. Also, it turned out that many were considered inept at supervision and often arrogant with clients. Where are they today? Of those listed above, the following are missing: Frankfurt, McCaffry, Fuchs, Paccione, Posey, Wall, Free; all have gone on to other jobs.

The life-span of the creative revolution lasted roughly the full decade from 1960 to 1970. It is not completely over, for many of the valuable, constructive changes endure. The creative aspect of advertising has become more important, more respected. Creative men's salaries are higher. Their piece of the action is larger. And the revolution did indeed sweep away a great deal of bad and corrupt advertising. It brought a fresher, warmer, more honest approach. It also paved the way for the successful establishment of a score or more bright, innovative ad agencies founded by some of the more successful and talented creative men of the decade. These are the men to watch in the business.

4

How Ad Agencies Grow

Two CREATIVE SUPERSTARS are on the phone.

"You can talk, huh? . . . How about the broad on the switchboard? . . . She's okay . . . Beautiful . . . Now listen, here's the thing, we meet this guy tonight. Six o'clock. He's all checked out. A hundred percent. So we sit down, nice and loose and have a couple of beers . . . What? . . . Sure, *tonight*, that's what I'm say-ing. Jees-us H, man, already you are dragging your ass? Huh? . . . Nobody's going to *see* us for Christ's sake. We're meeting him at Hurley's gin mill. It's strictly a hard-hat joint. At Sixth and Forty-ninth Street. You got it? . . . Okay, now stay with me. This guy is a first-class white-shoe type. M.B.A., BBDO, Westport, you know, like he played lacrosse and that shit. Take my word, he's first-class. And, don't forget, we need a character like this just as much as he needs us. Maybe more. Besides, he claims to have this big account knocked up. Positive. And I mean one million five or six. That's just for paying the rent. He's also got a couple of other cute ones sitting in the freezer. See what I mean? So we meet him. Have a couple of beers, nice and loose. What can it hurt? Yeah, yeah, no, don't bring any samples or crap like that. He knows all about us. Awards, titles, salaries. He knows. He's done some checking, too. So tonight, it's just the chemistry thing. We get acquainted. A couple of beers, a couple of laughs, you know, look each other over. No sweat, no push, like I'm saying, stay loose, don't fuck it up. By the way, you still wearing that ratty sweater? . . . Huh? No, no, don't change. It's okay. I just asked . . . Yeah, fine. Fine. See you. Six o'clock. Hurley's. It's a hard-hat joint."

An ad agency is born. In the style of the 1970s

The origin of the "white-shoe" label is obscure. It stands for the front man in the ad agency, the one who does the talking. He has the right accent, straight teeth, wears a J. Press suit and tie, exudes the right background. The term may have come from the days when white bucks were in style at Yale and Princeton.

Well, maybe it is not all that easy. Maybe more like these same two creative superstars have sat down over a couple of beers with about ten different white-shoe types before they finally shook hands. It's that chemistry thing. It has to be right. By this time, there are enough horror stories in the executive suites of newly formed agencies to put the aspiring partners on their guard. Palazzo Davis & Vellenti changed the names on their shingle twice in the first year and then folded somewhat ingloriously into a third agency. One man showed up on two different shingles, in two years, and both agencies failed. Mary Wells Lawrence, of Wells, Rich, Greene, appeared to have chemistry problems with men when she started her shop. Dick Rich left early in the association. Fred Lemont, her executive vice-president, tried hard to make it work but eventually left also. A smooth bank type, Herb Fisher, from Detroit, took over the pivotal spot for another year; but he returned to banking. The man there now, a genial Irishman, Dick O'Reilly, has lasted longer. Bill Free and his wife Marcella, two creative stars, were partners when Bill left Marschalk, where he was president, to set up his own shop. Spade & Archer, a promising young shop (named after the partners' favorite mystery-book characters), split up three ways after a bumpy couple of years. The youngest of the trio of partners, Al Sklar, was stranded in the Milan, Italy, office. (What they were doing with an office there, when they had almost no billings in New York headquarters, was a Spade & Archer mystery.) Other partnerships have gone through equally tumultuous times. One group, hoping to save their marriage, all agreed to see a psychiatrist and go by his recommendations. That didn't work either. Another team would never enter the same room unless it was to meet a client or their lawyer. Advertising people in general are apt to be temperamental. Advertising agency partners can be very temperamental.

The difficult problem right now, as ad agencies are forming up for the seventies, is the troika structure. It has come to be standard practice that an ad agency cannot be successful unless it has three key men: The account-marketing type (white shoes), a creative guy, copy, and a creative guy, art. The two creative men are almost always friends and buddies. They probably have worked together or are working together when they launch the new venture. The third man may or may not come from the same agency, and as indicated before, he is quite likely to be a stranger introduced to them. Here are two examples of why it is necessary to have all three men. A year or so ago, a young agency, Case and Krone Inc. —Gene Case, copy; Helmut Krone, art—started their own shop. Both were superstars with more than a hundred awards each to their credit. They came from great shops (Jack Tinker and Doyle Dane Bernbach). Their sleek penthouse offices overlooking the Plaza Hotel were sumptuous ($60,000 per year rent). It looked like they would make out like Gangbusters. But they didn't. The beautiful suite of offices was dreadfully quiet for months. Then they got the message. They went out and got their third man, Pat McGrath, from Benton & Bowles. In less than a year, the shop zoomed up to nearly $15 million in billings. Since then, however, Krone has left.

A second case is almost identical, except that they supposedly did have a third man to start with. The partners were Ron Rosenfeld, Len Sirowitz, and Marion Harper. The first two were superstars out of Doyle Dane Bernbach (Ron had had a brief stopover at J. Walter Thompson). Marion Harper was the empire builder himself, the former president of the global advertising agency network, the Interpublic Group of Companies. Marion at this time was on his own, starting several ventures. One of them was to be this bright new ad agency. It was launched with much élan and elegance at a breakfast press conference at the Regency Hotel. Then they set up business in the posh Dorset Hotel. Len and Ron operated out of the sitting room; Marion, supposedly out of a connecting bedroom. However, there is some doubt whether Marion Harper ever spent much time there. Ron and Len (like Gene and

Helmut) limped along with one small account, Swissair. Finally, they dropped Marion, who had not brought in expected accounts, and picked up Tom Lawson, a bright (Harvard M.B.A.) account man, the youngest vice-president Ogilvy & Mather had ever had. Again, the success formula proved itself. They, too, were up to $15 million in less than a year. Big, blue-chip accounts, too, like Hartford Life, Lanvin, Charles of the Ritz, and Carter-Wallace.

So the troika arrangement is the way to go, but the three men must be able to get along. They all need each other. They must work together closely. But they are different types. The account-marketing man is a businessman, a disciplinarian, a planner, and a strategist. The creative men are, more than likely, jumpy, genius types, high-strung and high-keyed. Agency partners, especially young ones, seem to have more extracurricular problems than other business partners such as lawyers, CPAs, and the like. They are likely to be hung up with divorces, girl trouble, private financial troubles, or other idiosyncrasies. One, for example, was a drag-race nut and neglected his business. Another wanted to work only afternoons so that he could play golf mornings. Still another was more interested in shooting a feature film while the partners ran the struggling new shop. A fourth got so tied up in social issues that he was lost to the business.

The story of how Mary Wells Lawrence left Jack Tinker & Partners to set up her now-outstanding ad agency has been widely discussed. According to some former associates, Jack Tinker had just had a heart attack. It was clear he couldn't run the agency, at least for a long while. Marion Harper, head of the Interpublic Group of Companies, so the report goes, rushed to the Tinker offices, which were then in the penthouse of the Dorset Hotel. There were, at the time, six partners. Two of them were clearly the most likely successors to the ailing Jack Tinker. One was the brilliant and gorgeous copywriter, Mary Wells; the other was Myron MacDonald, a senior adman who was account supervisor on the $20-million Alka-Seltzer account. Marion had to make a decision fast.

He chose Mary.

Mary was, of course, delighted. As associates reported, she wanted the position badly.

Myron MacDonald reacted. Reports say he stormed over to Marion's office the next day and threw down his ultimatum. "I won't work for that girl!" The implication whether voiced or not was that he would quit—and as account supervisor on Alka-Seltzer the account conceivably might move with him. It was apparently too big a risk for Harper to take. He went back to Mary. Behind closed doors—there were no eye-witnesses—Mary resigned. One executive on hand said "She whirled out of the office, hair flying, eyes flashing."

At the time she had no accounts to start her agency but it was well known that she and Harding Lawrence, president of Braniff and later to be her husband, were very good friends. The Braniff account did become the first account the new Wells, Rich, Greene agency announced a few weeks later. As it turned out the implied threat of MacDonald—the possibility of losing the Alka-Seltzer account—had little strength. MacDonald soon was replaced in favor at Miles—the makers of Alka-Seltzer—by Bill Weilbacher, another partner. MacDonald later moved on to LaRoche McCaffry & McCall where he was just in time to be a large stockholder when that agency went public. He did well for himself. Although he was with this shop less than a year he reportedly gained nearly a half million in stock value plus a five year contract for $75,000. He now lives in Arizona where he is said to be writing a book on his Interpublic experiences.

In the history of ad agencies, many accounts have been "stolen." A classic case—the names cannot be mentioned because it may still be in the courts—occurred in a midwestern shop where the owner had permitted the junior partner to service the major accounts from a New York office, supposedly for convenience. The junior partner very carefully and one by one convinced the clients that the "old man" was getting too old. He signed them up singularly to go with him. When he owned the bulk of the agency's business, he presented the ultimatum to the president in the home office. The witnesses say the owner was so shocked that he dropped to the floor with a heart attack that left him partially paralyzed. The remaining takeover was simple. The owner could no longer manage.

Of course, the new agency must have accounts soon, or the

limited capital they start with evaporates. Years ago, agency executives used to walk out with an account. A classic court case, the
Duane Jones affair, ended this. Mr. Jones, while on a trip to
Europe, had nearly his entire agency stolen out from under him.
The court decided that there was a conspiracy among the account
men and the clients. Heavy fines were assessed, and the practice
came to a halt. Now key executives are often made to sign contracts that prohibit their dealing with any client for from one to
three years after leaving. However, this did not interfere with an
almost-successful ploy staged recently by two creative men in a
small ad agency. The two men had already decided that they were
going to set up their shop, but were trying to get that first rent-
payer account. One day in the spring of 1971, while the president
was out of the office, the agency got one of those hoped-for calls.
An unsolicited bid to pitch their account. It was from a sizable
apparel account. The creative director (one of the pair planning
to leave) accepted the call, expressed enthusiastic interest, and
made an appointment for the following week. He and his co-con-
spirator kept everything under wraps. They quickly printed up their
own stationery, prepared a zingy campaign idea, and on the appointed day, quietly slipped out of the office. The meeting was a
success. At least to the point that they were entered as finalists.

A few days before the final decision, the president of the
agency, having heard elsewhere that the account was loose, made a
phone call to the head of the apparel company. He asked for a
chance to solicit the business. The conversation went like this:

"But, Mr. Brown, I don't know what to say," the president of
the apparel firm began. "I wonder if perhaps you have confused
your calls."

"I don't think I understand—er," the agency president fumbled.

"Well, you see, you people have already made your presentation. And it was a good one. You are being considered. That's why
I am mystified by your call now."

The mystery was shortly cleared up. The two creative people
were split from the shop before sundown.

The basic ad agency team must include an entrepreneur, a
man who can't be happy working for anyone else. It is best if the
several partners who start an ad agency have this entrepreneurial

spirit. Without it, chances of success are scant. It is more important than talent, contacts, assured billings, money in the bank. The good entrepreneur has such innate qualities as greed, egotism, self-confidence, hustle, and ballsiness. Of course, before an entrepreneur can start an ad agency, or start any business, he has to gain some experience, usually at somebody else's expense. He has to learn the basics, measure the odds, put some dough aside, learn to stand on his own feet. He is a take-charge guy, a go-it-alone guy, and often a son of a bitch to work with. He is scheming all the while he is on your payroll. Bosses know this, but in the meantime, they usually have a hard-working, productive employee. In advertising, it takes ten to fifteen years to learn the trade well, whether it's creative or account work. The best background is experience gained at several agencies, big and small. Also, experience on as many different kinds of accounts as possible. This will stand the man in good stead when he has his own shop and is seeking out any kind of account available to him. He could be an expert in, say, fashion and apparel, but then his new agency could only hope to specialize in these lines.

It is probably expecting too much for most of the top creative men to be good salesmen. Some have been. Dan Seymour of J. Walter Thompson has an evangelistic zeal. David Ogilvy only has to open his mouth and let go with the British accent. Mary Wells Lawrence, with her Pucci clothes and blonde hair, has the sale made as soon as she stands on her feet. Bill Bernbach used to be shy, but after years of platform experience, he is now poised and confident. So is George Lois, who comes by it naturally. Sometimes a creative man who is really a poor presenter comes on with such refreshing candor that he sells better than a glib salesman. Jesse Ellington, of the old Ellington Company, blushed red before an audience of five people. Leo Burnett always appeared uncomfortable in front of audiences. But these two sold themselves into some of the best accounts in the country. Carl Ally will never win prizes for public speaking, he's too apt to let fly with some of the salty expressions of his fighter-pilot days.

Then there are many creative men who start their own businesses overlooking one important ingredient. They have to be dogged doorknockers. Often this is definitely not their bag. Take these two, who were starving for business. A plush suite, a sexy receptionist who wore black leather hot pants to match the black leather furniture, but no business. So they called a trade paper editor, begging for a lead. The paper does not release news like this ordinarily, but since the issue for the next day was already at the printer's, it gave them half a day's lead on a prospect that would be appearing in print the next day. "Great!" "Thanks!" and they rang off. Ten minutes later they rang back. "Could you by any chance give us the name of the guy to call over there?" No chance, look it up yourself. They rang off again with a "Thanks, anyway." Another ten minutes. The same party again. "We got the right name. It's the marketing director. Yeah, but we wonder, maybe you could sort of break the ice by calling first." The editor's answer: "How the hell are you guys ever going to make it if you are afraid to knock on a door?"

It can get pretty hairy waiting for the first accounts. Some of these small new shops have run up debts of $100,000 in less than six months. Another got itself up to $400,000 in the hole in a year. Some of this comes from poor management, some from bad luck (they get a slow payer for their first account), some from spending too much on speculative presentations. One young shop blew $10,000 on a helicopter-filmed commercial of a "great idea" and never even got to show it to the prospect. He'd made his pick before they had a chance to pitch.

A track record is important for agency founders.

Here are the backgrounds of some recent beginners. George Lois came out of Papert, Koenig, Lois and Doyle Dane Bernbach. Bill Free came out of Marschalk; Foote, Cone & Belding; and others. Mary Wells Lawrence, out of Doyle Dane, Jack Tinker, and Macy's. Case and Krone came from both Tinker and Doyle Dane. Calderhead, Jackson, from Daniel & Charles and Wells, Rich, Greene. Sirowitz and Rosenfeld both came out of Doyle Dane Bernbach, with stops in between for Ron Rosenfeld. Scali McCabe, Sloves came out of Ally and PKL. Kurtz Kambanis Symon, from Jack Tinker. Della Femina and Travisano from Daniel & Charles, DKG, Bates and others. In Chicago, new owners are likely to come from Burnett or Ludgin. In Philadelphia, from

N. W. Ayer. In Los Angeles, from Carson/Roberts or the DDB office there.

What is the common denominator? The most successful of the new agencies were founded by people who had first gained experience with one or more of the top creative shops. Oddly enough, there have been practically no recent ad agencies formed by people from the big, safe, conservative shops like J. Walter Thompson, Young & Rubicam, BBDO, SSC and B, Lennen & Newell, or William Esty. Why? Either those shops don't breed the restless entrepreneurs, or they lock their people in so comfortably that they squash any desire to go it alone.

The growth of a new agency can be excruciatingly slow. No client wants to be the first one to gamble with the new outfit. And the new shop doesn't want to appear overly aggressive right off. In fact, most try desperately to look cool and confident. They are especially sensitive about first appearances. If they start off in their own offices, they are inordinately conscious of their furnishings and decorations. Rain or shine, George Lois, Ron Holland, and Jim Callaway marched all new guests out on the terrace of their windswept, yet-to-be-furnished penthouse, with its view of Central Park. Kurtz Kambanis Symon beamed as they stood under their glowing neon name display in their psychedelic reception room. Della Femina, Travisano stuffed their small front lobby with expensive antique advertising memorabilia. And one small agency, starting in the man's midtown apartment, boasted of a $12,000 painting and a $3,000 antique chest. He had borrowed these from a wealthy friend. There was a proviso, however; the agency founder had to have a picture-sitter at all times, since his apartment was not insured.

All this is supposed to make the prospective clients feel that the new shop is starting off well-heeled, blue-chip, rock-solid. It is sheer brass. Nearly all are underfinanced and understaffed, and the partners may even be undernourished. They are brown-bagging their lunches. They are paying themselves salaries that are perhaps only a third of what they had been earning. They won't buy a new suit for two years. They've sold their second car, motorcycle, or season ticket to pro football games; hocked their wives' jewelry; and wrung every drop of water out of their household budgets. When this isn't enough, they begin to make small loans from friends, from restaurant proprietors they know well, from bookies, and some, amazingly enough, get loans from their former bosses. Not a few have been helped by underworld money.

The new agency nearly always starts off with the pronouncement that they will only be interested in "top corporations." "No cat-and-dog stuff, no nickel-and-dime stuff, no Seventh Avenue shit." This policy lasts about two weeks. Sometimes three. Then they are ready to take anything. A dry cleaner in Queens, a pornographic book publisher, an ad for Yellow Pages insertion. Some begin their first assignments by accepting work from other ad agencies. One had to go back to work at a regular job, with an arrangement to dash out with his partners when they made a new business pitch.

Starting an ad agency is an alluring prospect for many ad people. It looks easy. There's the lovely 15 percent of billings hanging out in the open. That's $150,000 on a million-dollar account. A couple of good admen ought to be able to open shop with that kind of a take. But a closer look at the arithmetic reveals that an ad agency's financial pie chart splits up into something like this: payroll, 68 percent; rent, light, and so forth, 8 percent; promotion and operating expenses, 16 percent; all taxes, 5 percent; net profit, 3 percent. So how much is 3 percent of a million-dollar commission? A skimpy $4,500 after all the bills are paid. And this is assured only if the business is run in a businesslike manner. Many small new ad agencies are operated like candy stores. The money is spent as soon as it comes in. They don't project expenses out ahead for more than thirty days. They don't figure that the business is seasonal (a lot of billings are done in the first and fourth quarters) and that there is a long dry spell in between. They don't set aside a contingency fund, which may be needed to make a good presentation, to cover a media bill belonging to a slow payer, or to hire some good free-lance talent to pull them through a brush-fire project. This is when the young principals start hustling for hot cash. This is when the personality fuses begin to blow. If the cash flow runs out at this point, there is not a lot that can be done. There is no loan on inventory, no help from banks or savings and loan associations because there is nothing to put up for security. Once in a while a friendly banker will make an advance on a certified media contract, but rarely. There is no help anywhere except from friends, relatives, or the shadowy loan sources. After all, an ad agency is a service business, a risky, intangible, cotton-candy kind of operation.

Ill-advised financing and slim capital end up in friction between the partners. But there are other kinds of friction that can be bitter. When Dick Rich resigned from the new and highly successful Wells, Rich, Greene agency, there was much speculation over the reason. Many insiders felt part of the reason was because Dick neglected to delegate creative work until it was a serious problem. In any case, after Dick and Mary had their showdown— and Dick left with over $1 million plus shares of stock worth about twice that for less than three years' work—there was talk of bitterness. Mary had made Dick a millionaire. Now she was, at least temporarily, in a bind for creative work. Except for this previously unreported account, Mary's bitterness was never known to the public. Two of her former executives, however, remember this. They had gone to her office after work one evening and asked when a public announcement about Dick's resignation would be made. "The speculations are bad for our reputation," they advised. "Why not do it. Send out a release to the trade press tomorrow." Mary admitted she had put off the release because she was upset. However, she agreed to a release the following day. The two men left and returned to a discussion they were holding in an office far down the hall.

Ten minutes later, the two men, still working in the only lighted office, heard the solitary clicking of Mary's heels as she walked rapidly down the hall. When she arrived at the doorway, she stood there for a full minute. A gorgeous young lady, her face solemn and white, her eyes dark and snapping. She looked at the two men carefully and then said, "A year from now, nobody will even remember his name!"

Then she was gone in the darkness.

During its halcyon days as the hottest shop in town, Papert, Koenig, Lois was also known as Stillman's Gym East. One day George Lois and Carl Ally got into a loud, belly-to-belly confrontation. These two were well-known scrappers. George the

Greek and Carl the Turk. Just before blows were thrown, they were separated. After work, George decided that there was too much fighting going on at PKL, so he took the evening off and prowled Greenwich Village for hours looking for a special print he remembered. He finally found it, brought it back to the office, framed it nicely, and had it hung in Carl's office by nine the next morning. It was an enormous print of a battle scene from the Greek and Turkish war. At the bottom of the print, he had written, "The war's over." His signature was attached.

Creative people aren't the only ones who start ad agencies. In fact, this is a rather recent phenomenon. Over the past fifty years, most ad agencies have been founded (as indicated earlier) by the men who sold the advertising space. The Albert Laskers, the J. Walter Thompsons, and the like. This is still the practice in most small cities throughout the country. A newspaper or broadcast sales rep in a middle-sized city is servicing half a dozen good accounts, and he decides that he has enough contacts and assured billings to open his own agency. These are local accounts: banks, local restaurant chains, gas stations, a dairy, and so forth. In many cases, he has already been helping them prepare their ads or commercials. He simply gets this done now on a more organized basis. With a little luck and hard work, he may soon upgrade his clients to include a regional account or two: A meat-packer, a canner, a statewide chain of retail stores. At this point, he begins to add to staff: a full-time production man to make plates, set type, and so forth; a woman who can buy media; a couple of copywriters; an art director; one or two men to help him service the accounts; a bookkeeper; and a typing pool. His billings could be up around $1.5 to $2 million now. He can take home maybe $50,000 a year. In the United States today, there are perhaps two thousand ad agencies of this size, a dozen in any city of over a million people.

Without discrediting their importance, the mainstream of national advertising is not with these small ad agencies, whose billings are ordinarily less than $5 million and whose staffs are between a dozen and twenty people. The bulk of national advertising—75 percent of the nearly $10 billion placed through advertising agencies—evolves from about fifty of the large shops. These are concentrated in a handful of cities. New York represents perhaps 55 percent of all such national advertising; Chicago, perhaps 20 percent. Philadelphia, Los Angeles, Detroit, Cleveland, Houston, San Francisco, Atlanta, and Boston would account for much of the rest.

The average age of the fifty biggest agencies is about twenty-five years. That is, most of them were started in the post–World War II era. The ten largest agencies have roots that go back farther. J. Walter Thompson is 106 years old. McCann-Erickson; Foote, Cone & Belding; Young & Rubicam; BBDO; Benton & Bowles; N. W. Ayer & Son; Campbell-Ewald; MacManus John & Adams; William Esty; Compton Advertising; Kenyon & Eckhardt; Lennen & Newell; and Leo Burnett Company were started some thirty-five to fifty years ago. The biggest of the postwar agencies are Ogilvy & Mather, Ted Bates, Doyle Dane Bernbach, Grey Advertising, and SSC and B. Their average age is about twenty years. In other words, despite the flamboyance of the business, it takes a good while to reach the top ranks. The fastest-growing agency in the history of advertising is Wells, Rich, Greene, which has come from zero billings to $110 million in about five years. This ranks them about twenty-second. Others whose growth has been fast include Doyle Dane Bernbach, now seventh; Grey, tenth; and Ogilvy & Mather, now fifteenth. The four fastest growing in rank are, significantly, creatively oriented.

Is there a familiar pattern of growth for an ad agency? Probably only one pattern remains consistent. This is the growth that covers the life-span of the principal founder. Reviewing the longevity of agencies overall, most reflect the productive years of the founder. If he was able to bring it up to a fairly good size (say, $20 million or more), it probably survived into another generation. If he did not, it was sold, merged, or disappeared. Surprisingly few sons have followed in their father's footsteps. Some who did are Charles Adams, of MacManus John & Adams; John Warwick, of Warwick & Legler; Harry Hicks, Jr., of Hicks & Griest; Al Paul Lefton, Jr., of Al Paul Lefton; and a few others. The succession is more likely to occur in the small city agencies, which are always more of a family affair. Phil Voss, Jr., of Woodard, Voss & Hevenor in Albany, New York, is typical. Frequently, the sons follow in the business but with different ad agencies. Tom Ellington, now ad director of the Postal Service, was at Young & Rubicam for some years. Tony Weir is at Ogilvy & Mather; John Bernbach is at Gilbert Advertising. All are sons of agency presidents. Nepotism has never been much of a problem, perhaps because such a premium is placed upon talent and productivity rather than position and power.

The single-partner agency, typical of the formations started prior to the sixties, reflected the special expertise of the founder. If he was a creative man, the ad agency was likely to sell creative work as its prime product. Ted Bates's first reputation was based upon his copy skills. J. M. Mathes, which survived for some thirty years, until it was bought out this past year by its employees, was copy-oriented, like its founder. David Ogilvy, although originally a research executive with George Gallup, was also an exceptional writer. His agency grew on the strength of creativity. BBDO, Leo Burnett, Young & Rubicam, and Kenyon & Eckhardt owed much of their early growth to their reputations for excellence in copy and art. Others developed this image despite their noncreative founders. Conversely, others that were founded by creative men but were inherited by business types switched their emphasis toward research or services such as media and marketing. MacManus John & Adams, William Esty, and Ted Bates, founded by great copywriters, have long since lost their first-generation creative luster.

It was much harder in the early days of advertising for youngsters without background and education to get into the agency business. One exception was a kid from the Lower East Side of New York who was hired by Bruce Barton, head of the famous Batten, Barton, Durstine & Osborn agency. This was Jim Duffy, a fleet-footed messenger boy. One night when Bruce Barton returned from a trip, he found the offices nearly empty. It was late. Most of the lights were out. Except in his own office. When he got to the doorway, he saw the reason. Seated in his chair, behind his big desk, was little Jimmy Duffy. "Trying it out for size," he said smilingly. The size, as it turned out twenty-five years later, was exactly right. Jim Duffy was president for more than a decade.

Herbert Strauss, former chairman of Grey Advertising, a largely Jewish firm, was a keynote speaker at a Brotherhood banquet at the Waldorf Astoria during the years that the Interpublic Group of Companies was making so many mergers. Mr. Strauss's opening remark took the audience by surprise. "Tonight I have a special announcement. Grey Advertising agency is merging with BBDO [a notable Anglo-Saxon shop] and," Herb paused for effect, "the new agency will be called The Interfaith Group of Companies."

Here is an incident that shows how times have changed attitudes.

Albert Lasker, probably the richest of all advertising men, had a large estate on the North Shore of Chicago. One day back in the 1920s, while walking the boundary line of his enormous property, he came across his neighbor, a well-known tycoon and also very rich. The two estates were of nearly equal size and as expensively turned out. The two men chatted for a while, then Lasker said, "I don't mean to brag, but my estate is worth more money than yours."

The self-made tycoon was immediately ruffled. "What makes you think so?" He went on to elaborate treasures of his estate beyond eye range. "So," he concluded, "how can you say your place is worth more?"

"Because," Lasker replied, "you live next to a Jew."

Ad agency managements have an obsession with growth. "We've got to get off our goddamn asses and get some business in this shop!" "What the hell's the matter with us, are we lepers or something?" "Why didn't we know about the big switch last week?" They live this scenario day in and day out. Nothing is as important as jacking up the billings. As agency management sees it, it is grow, grow, grow or go down the drain. Getting a new account is the single most ecstatic, euphoric experience in top management's life. For example, take this president, sitting in his office late, waiting prayerfully for a phone call from a client prospect. He finally got the word at about 10:30 at night. It was "yes." He was so exuberant that he rushed out and shouted the news to the only people in sight, the squad of cleaning women. Since none of them spoke English, they could do little to share his enthusiasm.

Although the rate of growth depends largely upon the success of the agency's new business activities, the pattern of growth depends upon the agency's track record. The kind of ads they create, the type of case-history successes they can boast about. There is considerable luck involved in both these factors. A small, unknown ad agency might by luck or a tremendous burst of talent produce an outstanding ad or campaign.

Often a brilliant success, either for an agency or a creative man, can generate long mileage. The aura lasts for years. Currently, with so much more advertising everywhere, it is harder to stand out in this way. However, Geer, DuBois has done it with very bright work for Foster Grant and Dry Dock Savings Bank. Carl Ally, with Hertz; Scali, McCabe, Sloves, with Volvo. These are only a few examples.

The other magic ingredient of ad agency growth is something loosely known as being "hot." Every once in a while an ad agency will crank up a consistent winning streak. They'll land three, four, maybe a half dozen new accounts in a few months. In advertising nothing succeeds like success. Restless clients begin to pay attention. The appointments are easier to make when the shop is "hot," and more so if it's "hot" and "creative."

Ideally, ad agencies like to target their growth rate at about 15 percent or more per year. Most of the leaders have done this over the past decade. J. Walter Thompson grew from some $200 million to $700 million during the sixties. Doyle Dane Bernbach increased its size five times during the same period. Interpublic, despite its problems, added some $300 millions in billings. Ted Bates, SSC and B, Clinton E. Frank, Ogilvy & Mather, and Needham, Harper & Steers all exceeded the average growth rate of 4As agencies. Still, to listen to the top executives of any of these agencies, one gets the impression that this growth is far too slow. The old nervous panic is chronically there. As if they expect tomorrow morning to lose it all. It has happened. A giant ad agency, the Biow Company, rolled over and sank in a matter of months. The Jack Tinker shop disintegrated soon after the Alka-Seltzer loss and was only salvaged by merging with another Interpublic agency. The New York office of D'Arcy, one of the hottest agencies in the city during the sixties when it was under Pat Geyer's reign, literally collapsed in the year or so after his retirement. Momentum is easy to lose, and once the slide begins, it is almost impossible to stop.

An inverse growth trend for an agency is indeed something management must worry about. It becomes a sickness. Morale flags. Good creative people, always sensitive to being in the right place at the right time, begin to desert. Current clients begin to wonder what has happened. New prospects are suddenly too busy to come to the phone. The trade press, as is their custom, always loves a loser. The surmises and dire speculations begin to appear in print. The skid gets slicker. The run on the bank (clients leaving) steps up. Then to compound its troubles, the downhill agency finds it has more expenses than the ascending shop. Now senior partners decide to retire, taking away cash reserves. Salaries must often be raised to hold the now-restless people. Older agencies have more fringe benefits. Empty offices and unused floor space become financial drags. Dissembling is expensive. As Harold Strauss, a smart ad agency treasurer at Coordinated Communications, Inc., says, "Going up is lovely, going down is a bitch."

The first year is crucial. If an agency can simply survive this period, it will probably make it. Most fatalities occur within six months, although one agency lasted only a week in a hotel suite. It folded when the rent was due for the second week. Several others have folded almost as soon as they started because the clients who promised to come with them backed out. By this time, the young founders had quit their jobs, invested their savings, and found themselves high and dry. Very often the "absolutely positive" pieces of business new agencies count on are little more than remote possibilities. Agency founders overestimate their expected billings.

After the first year, and assuming the agency is on its way to solvency, several changes take place. One conspicuous one in the past year or so is the nature of the services offered. Many launch their shop with the firm announcement that they are going to be a creative-only agency. "We'll devote all our energies to getting out good ads and not get bogged down in media, research, and heavy housekeeping chores." Such an arrangement is entirely possible, and valid, with today's assortment of independent services. Something happens, however, with success. The partners, or their clients, begin to think a little bigger. They begin to accept addi tional responsibilities. Then a few more. And one day, they look around the shop that was going to limit itself to ad making only and find they have a media analyst, a merchandising expert, an account executive row. They are an agency. When this happens, they seldom fight it. Despite their protestations at the outset, it's more fun and more profitable to be an agency than a service.

Along about the fifth or sixth year, depending upon how fast growth has been, the partners begin to look out their corner offices at wider horizons. "Be pretty classy to have an office on the Coast," says the eastern agency, and opens a branch in Los Angeles. Some- times the client asks for service offices to handle local advertising for their dealer organizations. This results in "measles": Atlanta, St. Louis, Denver, Houston, Boston, and so forth. One- or two- man offices. In order to handle a Big Three auto account, a Detroit office is a must.

In the past two or three years, several dozen branch offices of major ad agencies have closed down because they were unprofit- able, growth was at a standstill, or the potential was negligible. The local ad agencies have won this battle in all but a few cases.

No matter what the location of the account, most ad agencies prefer to do all creative work at headquarters. Ted Bates, William Esty, and some other large shops have never had domestic branch offices. They insist that all creative work be done in the head office. N. W. Ayer maintained this rule for many years, even though it involved some long trips for account executives. In the days before planes, Ayer used to send a man to Cape Town twice a year to service the DeBeers diamond account. He spent some nine weeks of his year on shipboard.

Expanding overseas has been both a debacle and a boon to American ad agencies. Every conceivable mistake has been made. As one European ad executive puts it, "The Yanks have really been taken." Many of them indeed were innocents abroad. The D'Arcy agency for example, set up a hodgepodge network of shops all around Europe, reportedly making a different mistake in every city. In some cases, they bought controlling interest, which turned out to be a perfect excuse for the former owner, despite a management contract, to let the business go to seed. In another case, they would buy a minority interest. This often turned out worse because without control, the local agency owners simply pocketed the dollars and ran their businesses as they had before. Other ad agencies, such as Doyle Dane Bernbach and Wells, Rich, Greene, have tried to set up their own wholly owned agencies overseas. These have often been fountains of red ink. DDB lost money in Mexico City for years, although they did better in Germany. Norman, Craig & Kummel found a profitable handle. They followed the minority-purchase route with some success. They also inaugurated, at least for a time, a creative flying squad that jumped from country to country solving multilingual, multinational ad problems. Interpublic tried one of the most bizarre experiments. They took over a remote estate in Bavaria, where they set up a double-domed think tank. It was pleasant living for a group of high-priced executives for a while. The McCann-Erickson unit of Interpublic, however, has long been strong in West Germany. Founded shortly after World War I to handle the first Standard Oil advertising there, it prospered steadily. At a recent count, it was number one of all agencies in Germany.

The London scene has always been very attractive to Americans. Creative people especially love to work there even when salaries are only half of what they could earn in United States. All agency executives welcome the necessity to rush off to London for any excuse. Moreover, the American's special strength and expertise in TV advertising and in packaged-goods marketing were sought out by British advertisers. The special American brand of creativity was appealing to Britons, too. Doyle Dane Bernbach, although never big there, has added much to the creative standard raising. A score of top American creative men have enjoyed personal successes there.

Although there are underlying jealousies and tensions, American and British advertising people are very friendly. The London Creative Circle, a group of two hundred of the top creative people in Britain, have twice hosted a planeload of Americans brought over by a trade paper. The events held at the Royal College of Art were fabulous affairs, including costume parties, fashion shows, continuous performances of communicating arts and advertising, dramatic presentations, and lavish food and beverages, all from 6 P.M. to 6 A.M. The big American ad agencies that have been in Britain for years—such as J. Walter Thompson, Ted Bates (Hobson, Bates), Young & Rubicam, Compton, Grey, Mc-Cann-Erickson, Erwin Wasey, SSC and B, Lintas, Leo Burnett, LPE, Ogilvy & Mather—and half a dozen smaller ones have played a dominant role in British advertising in the postwar years. They have managed to overcome national chauvinism with outstanding creative work and sound marketing principles. J. Walter Thompson, the oldest, comfortably housed in nearly a full block of buildings on Berkeley Square, is the largest of all British ad agencies. It regularly has at least one member of Parliament on staff.

Despite the allure of setting up offices in exotic foreign cities, American ad agency executives have harbored many proper misgivings. The language barrier was obviously there. So were unfamiliarity with local marketing conditions and different rules and regulations regarding media buying. The creative approach that nationals in other countries apparently liked was dreadfully old-fashioned. The clients, however, pressured agencies into making the moves. When Colgate, for example, began to receive almost half of its profits from overseas, and when companies such as Pfizer, Sterling Drug, Nabisco, Gerber, H. J. Heinz, Ford, General Motors, and many other American firms began heavier investments in various parts of the world, the Americans had little choice. If they stayed out, these big clients, many of which they handled stateside, would go to other agencies for their advertising. Perhaps other agencies with American names. One lesson all American agencies eventually learned was that the local agency must be run almost entirely by nationals. J. Walter Thompson, with more than 2,000 overseas employees, has less than 200 Americans in all their fifty or so offices on five continents.

By 1970, most of the overseas expansion efforts of the top ten ad agencies had proved themselves profitable. In fact, many have been more profitable than the domestic offices. McCann-Erickson in recent years has made more from its overseas operations than from its United States office. Thompson, Young & Rubicam, Ted Bates, and Compton now count between 25 and 40 percent of their billings from their international operations. The countries

82

offering the most profits have been Canada, the United Kingdom, Mexico, Australia, and more recently, countries in the Far East. Grant International, originally a Chicago ad agency but early on the international scene, has long had some of the most exotic outposts. There are Grant offices in Ceylon, Thailand, West Pakistan, Chile, Malaysia, Zambia, Kenya, and Southern Rhodesia.

What other growth is possible? Profits from sources other than ordinary advertiser billings? Yes, ad agencies have experimented in many directions. Perhaps the broadest experiments have been in the area of additional services offered to clients on a fee basis. This move actually was bred of necessity. As the so-called full-service agency became difficult to operate profitably, agencies turned to the profit center concept of services. That is, they set up independent subsidiary operations for such traditionally unprofitable services as public relations, sales promotion, and market research. This arrangement, they discovered, made it somewhat easier to charge extra fees for these services than it had been under the previous system, when these functions were lumped together with general agency overhead. Success has been mixed. Often the public relations department will at least pay its way, but it seldom contributes very large profits. Marsteller, Gaynor & Ducas, and a few others have made decent profits on public relations. Almost none have done well on sales promotion or research. Nor have any done well on independent TV commercial production enterprises, such as Doyle Dane Bernbach tried and is still trying, with its independent unit. The problem with all these is the difficulty of competing favorably with the best outside sources. Too often, the ad agency has not been competitive either in price or in quality of work. There is a continuing drift in this direction, however, as more and more service departments are offered to clients on a modular basis.

Agencies have tried other outside investments. The obvious diversification would be in the direction of related communications and media, where agency executives could use their expertise. But not all agencies have done this. J. Walter Thompson's purchase of an insurance company in Puerto Rico a few years ago has turned out to be a bonanza. Profits of more than a million dollars annually are added to the JWT coffers. Other privately owned ad agencies have expanded into related communications services. Muller Jordan Herrick has a successful industrial film and show unit called Producers Row. Chalek & Dreyer own a profitable test marketing service. Henderson & Roll started Listfax, a public company. Ted Bates owns a successful data processing company. Warner, Bicking & Fenwick recently bought *Madison Avenue,* a trade magazine. Wells, Rich, Greene has a feature-film subsidiary operation that will soon be producing films for theater distribution. Campbell-Mithun owns a chain of fast food stores. Young & Rubicam bought a retail department store chain in the Northwest. There are many others. Doyle Dane Bernbach has made several investments that appear promising. They recently bought a group of Midwest discount chain stores, a plastic-boat company, and a chain of agencies in the south (the Cargill, Wilson & Acree firm). LaRoche, McCaffry and McCall, also a public agency, has a modest investment in an oyster farm. The first crop has yet to be harvested. J. Walter Thompson has used its reserves to set up profit center services. A new one, already successful, is an executive speech-training course. Wells, Rich, Greene, among other investments, plunged heavily into high risk oil-exploration firms. The profits from this exceeded the ad agency function income at one period. Mary Wells Lawrence does not make any gambles without the advice of her good friend Gus Levy, former president of the New York Stock Exchange. Nearly any ad agency of reasonable size that is more than ten years old has a cash-reserve fund that is invested somewhere. Usually it is in low-risk, stable securities or government bonds, but often it is in real estate. Ad agencies in smaller cities often own their own buildings. Hoefer, Dieterich & Brown own their own restored, prefire building on Jackson Square in San Francisco. Carson/Roberts owned nearly a block-long frontage on Beverly Boulevard in Los Angeles. Albert Frank-Guenther Law owned the multimillion-dollar piece of property in downtown Manhattan that had housed their agency for fifty years. They sold it to the Port Authority's new World Trade Center project.

The big agencies today would prefer to make investments in additional billings, that is, buy up other ad agencies. There is hardly an agency in the ranks of the top twenty-five that hasn't got an out-to-buy sign flying at all times. Presently, Needham,

Harper & Steers is seeking to buy anything up to the $50-million size. Ted Bates, Doyle Dane Bernbach, Grey Advertising, and Lennen & Newell have cash on the barrelhead for ad agencies of any reasonable size. Lennen & Newell, for example, will buy not only anything but anywhere. They recently have expanded into Alaska, Hawaii, and other places. Lennen & Newell itself is now the amalgamation of some dozen ad agencies. When it picked up Geyer/Oswald a year or two ago, it automatically inherited the antecedents of some six ad agencies. Typically, the merger, which at the time of consummation represented some $40 million in billings, has dropped nearly out of sight into the new parent company. This is the difficulty of mergers that swallow up or absorb the identity of the previous agency. Almost always, there is a sharp reduction of the staff because functions are duplicated. Before very long, there is a sharp attrition of the billings.*

The mistake most agencies make in acquisitions is the insistence on this loss of identity. When an agency is taken over lock, stock, and name, the morale and spirit evaporates. Power groups form quickly to take over the choice jobs and the choice accounts. Friction develops as job duties overlap. The clients of the old agency, now under new management, often do not feel comfortable and leave. There are bad feelings, too, among the survivors of the old agency who came along with the deal, because some of them got more money than others in the deal. For example, MacManus John & Adams recently acquired West Weir & Bartel and D'Arcy. The West Weir Bartel shop itself was a hybrid of the former Donahue & Coe Agency, the Walter Weir Agency and the old Ellington Company. The D'Arcy agency, too, had had previous mergers, one in New York with the old Federal Agency. MacManus itself had had mergers over the years. Their one office on Madison Avenue now houses the antecedents of at least twelve different shops. Amazingly, some clients, such as Gerber and Knox Gelatin, have survived through all these mergers.

Apparently, the best merger is the one that allows the acquired agency to preserve at least the outward signs of its identity. Ted Bates has had outstanding success with two acquisitions: the

* In the spring of 1972, after this book was set up in type, Lennen and Newell went into bankruptcy.

AC&R group and the Diener-Hauser-Greenthal Company. Both agencies retained their names and most of their officers and are housed in separate buildings. Interference is minimal; the use of all services of the parent company is there on an as-needed basis; economies are realized in centralizing many administrative services; and the big agency is always available to help the smaller ones when making new business pitches. Growth and progress have been remarkable. But oddly enough, few other agencies have copied the successful Bates formula. Their sense of pride and aggrandizement won't permit anything short of complete control. As a result, they find prospects only among those in hopeless financial straits or those who want to sell out and retire. Both bad risks.

5

The Mistakes Companies Make

IN THE SANCTUARY of their private luncheon clubs or the bar cars of their commuting trains, ad agency people have favorite labels to describe the stupidity of their clients. "Bubble heads," "sausage brains," "myopic bastards," "banana heads," "crackers," and worse. And sometimes the ad agency people are right.

For example, consider Procter & Gamble, a giant that can afford to be cited only because they generally do smart things. Procter & Gamble is the all-time pro of the packaged-goods arena. This is the company voted year in and year out by the various associations as the best-managed corporation in the nation. They are the uncontested leader in consumer-goods marketing. This is the story of one attempt to introduce a new product into a test market.

Everything was ready. The product, typical of P&G thoroughness, had been through three years of laboratory and consumer testing. The ads and TV commercials had been revised probably no less than a dozen times. The media schedules were pinpointed down to the most precise demographics. The test cities (usually three, for the sake of control) had been softened up with advance promotional efforts: coupon drops to households, special deals for retailers, in-store displays, overhead wire pennants, shelf talkers, you name it. Nothing was overlooked. And behind the whole introduction were the big dollars P&G throws into any of its promotions.

D day arrives, and everything goes into action precisely as planned. Saturation commercials begin to blink on the TV tubes; large-space newspaper ads with coupon offers scream the announcement; the stock is front and center on the store shelves. This is it. Now for the consumer response. The over-the-counter payoff. Sales.

And what happens? Practically nothing. A glacier. A negative feedback.

"What in the hell gives?" asked P&G top management.

The probable answer from the marketing executives on the spot: "It beats us. Some bastard out there is breaking up our ball game. Somebody big, somebody smart."

This is common practice among packaged-goods giants. Rival firms are always scouting the boondocks, searching out surprise competitive moves, such as the launching of a new product in a secret test market. They actually have hand-picked scouts who slip into towns like Bakersfield, California; Marion, Ohio; Syracuse, New York; scrounging for signs of an upcoming test market. They'll bribe a local radio or TV station to look over their advance bookings. They'll check out the stores to look for any unlikely new shipments of stock moving in. They'll watch for mail sampling or coupon drops. They'll get clubby with store managers over a few beers after closing. They'll do anything to find out what is in the wind. Some of these operators are tough, ruthless men. One company, an old hand in the packaged-goods battles, has a special outfit known as the "Flying Squad" to uncover competitors' plans. And once uncovered, they go into action fast.

Here are some typical moves by competitive spoilers. They'll jam in a special money-off price deal that is so attractive that the new product looks ridiculous. They'll offer premium deals, such as a comb rubber-banded onto a package of hair dressing, or a toothbrush on a pack of toothpaste. They'll double or triple local advertising campaigns. They'll offer free cases of merchandise to dealers to push their brand. They'll send in pretty store demonstrators who hand out hot goodies or free samples. They'll flood the mails with coupon offers.

They'll take other steps, too, that are not so open. For example, sending in salesmen who, while supposedly checking stock, will rearrange the new brand into bottom-shelf positions. Rearranging

88

gambits are varied. Some will see that his competitor has moved in a handsome new stand-up rack neatly stacked with his snack products. The wily competitor will, if unobserved, remove the top few rows of merchandise and put in his own. Or maybe it is a jumble display, a full bin of his competitor's products at a choice end-of-the-aisle location. The alert competitive salesman will sprinkle his own wares over the top of this bin. Another trick often used in the dairy cabinets is to rearrange a competitive milk brand so that the fresh milk is always up front. Customarily, when a driver salesman leaves off new milk in the morning, he will put yesterday's leftovers up front so that they will move out before turning bad. By pushing these to the back again, the competitor may succeed in getting some customers to buy sour milk under his rival's label. Another dairy-case trick: The competitive salesman will wear a special ring with a pin sticking out of the setting. As he stocks his own milk, his wrist will snap left and right as he punches tiny holes in the paper containers of his rival's brand. Grocers hate "leakers." The brand is dropped after a few such days.

One other illustration, just to show what P&G might have been up against in their problem case history. This happens when the rival scouts have discovered the test market, have looked it over closely, and have decided that the company is on its way to a "bomb out," a failure. When this happens, they move in, sometimes with heavy money, and quietly begin to give the test a boost. They'll buy up the product in sizable quantities all over the test area. After a week or so of this, the company begins to get fairly encouraged at the apparent results. Eventually, they call it a success. The next move is the big, expensive roll-out. Why not? Test results were great. So off they go nationally. Just what competition wanted. The company now has a big disaster when it might have had a small one.

Procter & Gamble, in the current example, was not outfoxed by any competitor. They are too savvy for that. After a few days of hard sleuthing, they came up with the answer.

"Well!" demanded top management. "Who is it?"

"Us," was the reluctant reply. "A P&G brand promotion in the same product class has been clobbering us behind the scenes."

Things like this happen. Perhaps a year and a half before, a heavy promotion that included the same cities was approved for a similar product. In trying to find out who the culprit was, Procter & Gamble overlooked their own brand until it was almost too late to save the introduction.

Bigness. Unwieldiness. Inefficient communications. They all contribute to the apparent stupidity of large corporations. The errors spring from lack of coordination. Here are some typical results. Companies send out ads to newspapers with the bottom third of the ads reading, in bold type, "local dealer's name and address go here." Or the place for the price says "$00.00." Nobody informs the dealer, and the ad runs just like that. Or large companies send out tons of store displays that salesmen are supposed to distribute to stores. When the salesmen get them, they are too big to go in the trunks of their cars. So hundreds of salesmen throw them away. Or the company sends Confederate flags as part of a promotion to dealers in New England. Others don't tell their field people that they are phasing out a product, cutting off its advertising and support, so that the salesman will get rid of his stock. Others fail or ignore telling their men that the private-label brand of merchandise in the chain store they are selling to is actually made by their own company. There are others who come out with a new brand of a product that is not identified by the company name and sell against their own salesmen without their knowledge.

How big is big? ITT has bought over one hundred companies in the past few years. The products and services range all the way from bread and rolls (Continental Baking) to rental cars (Avis). General Mills, in addition to cereal and bakery products, owns toy companies, highway restaurants, and jewelry and apparel companies. Procter & Gamble embraces laundry products, foods, cosmetics, and paper products. General Foods sells its products under some four hundred different labels and uses some forty advertising agencies and untold numbers of independent creative services. The big tobacco companies have diversified into a score of unrelated fields, including liquor, pet foods, and hotels. The conglomerate development in the past five years has brought together the most unlikely of partners. Greyhound owns a meat-packer. Coca-Cola makes coffee. Hershey makes spaghetti. The Brown & Williamson Tobacco company sells seafood. CBS makes Creative Playthings. And so it goes, ever bigger, ever more complex.

Enormous size and wide diversification can, of course, bring many advantages to corporations: huge cash reserves for development and expansion, sophisticated management techniques, a cross-fertilization of experience that can be helpful to many smaller companies. And it can encourage competition that is essentially good for the consumer. It can, however, lead to confusion and a wide margin for errors. Literally, the left hand may not know what the right hand is doing in many major corporations. The only semblance of order and cohesion is based upon the fact that the executives and employees supposedly have a system to follow. Every major corporation has a way of operating. It has its own set of disciplines, rules, regulations, red lights and green lights, methods, and methodologies. If it didn't, it couldn't work. The sheer size and scope of modern companies is beyond the management capabilities of one man or even a top executive team. These men, capable as they may be, can only implement the system.

How did the systems get there? How did they inherit their built-in strengths and weaknesses? Basically, the systems were needed to control bigness. To make sprawling, expanding companies with more volume and more products manageable. The systems also became necessary because as any business grows, its suppliers and distributors proliferate. It has to depend upon more and more assistance from outside the home office. Wholesalers, brokers, jobbers, freight forwarders, and a dozen other services are needed to move merchandise from the factory to the warehouses to the stores to the eventual consumer. Most major American corporations were started by one man: H. J. Heinz in Pittsburgh, H. K. Kellogg in Battle Creek, Sara Lee's father in Chicago, Henry Ford in Detroit, and so forth. These were strong, independent-spirited men. They would have preferred to do everything for themselves from making the product to serving it over the counter to customers.

But growth caught up with the successful companies. Especially growth in the marketing areas, the selling and distribution of their products. These were the very areas where entrepreneurs were weakest. Most founders of companies were inventors or production wizards. They knew how to make things but not how to sell them. Their companies, as they grew, tended to prize the production end of things and neglect the sales operations. They turned these problems over to wholesalers and jobbers. Or they set up dealerships who became independent businessmen on their own with the company products. They let salesmen in distant territories run private fiefdoms. Anything, so long as the reorders came in. They paid almost no attention to the actual retail outlets, except to guarantee freshness and quality of their products.

At the turn of the century, more than 75 percent of the major corporations in America were family-owned and family-dominated. Even as late as a decade ago, the Ford family owned and ran the Ford Motor Company, and at least a hundred breweries were still managed by descendants of the founders. Many of the big distilleries, watch companies, publishers, and regional food companies were family-owned. But again size took over. There weren't enough sons-in-law or distant cousins to step in. Then another change took place. More and more of the major companies went public. When this happened, the family domination was no longer significant; the stockholders owned the company. And stockholders began to exert their influence. "Why isn't our company growing faster, taking advantage of more opportunities, making bigger profits and paying bigger dividends?"

One of the first of the structural changes that took place in big companies was a decentralization of authority. Big companies broke up into divisions, subsidiaries, satellite operations. The antitrust laws made some of this necessary when a concentration looked too big, too monopolistic. Eventually, even the divisions were giants in themselves. The splitting-up processes took another step. The various brands within a division were looked upon as separate profit centers. Each had to pull its own weight, prove itself, or go under. Under this system, brands within the same company began to compete with each other. As top management saw it, it was better to have one of their own new brands win out over one of their old brands than to have a competitive brand win the field.

In a nutshell, then, this is the present basic system. It's called

the *brand manager system* and is practiced by most larger consumer-goods companies with multiple lines of products. The
M.B.A.s out of Harvard, Wharton, NYU, and other top graduate
schools of business have been trained to fit into this mold. After a
few years of experience in basic company functions such as sales,
merchandising, advertising, and perhaps a stint in an advertising
agency, the young man earns his stripes. He becomes a brand
manager. It's not easy. At a firm like Procter & Gamble or General
Foods, only one of a class of twenty-five trainees reaches the position. When he does, however, his responsibilities are formidable.
He is virtually a "little president." In theory, he runs his brand
just as if it were his own company. He determines the market,
plans the strategy, directs the packaging, pricing, and merchandising of the product. He orders and approves the advertising. Sets
the advertising and promotion budgets. Works with the sales force
to estimate quantities of goods needed and orders them from production. His final responsibility is to project the profits the company can expect from the marketing plan he has set up for his
brand.

This is the theory. But like many theories in business, actual
practice is something quite different. The biggest handicap to the
brand manager system is that the job expects too much of the man.
How can a young M.B.A. out of school, with maybe three years
on the job, know about product production, pricing, packaging,
promotion, test marketing, media buying and scheduling, TV commercial production, market research, computer models, concept
testing, Nielsen share-of-market reports, warehouse-withdrawal
studies, store audits, piggybacking commercials, syndicate time sales,
radio barter, cents-off deals, blister-pack premiums, Siamese-pack
offers, shelf talkers, jumble-display promotions, Latin squares,
demographics, psychographics, focus-group testing, pupil-dilation
studies, paired-attribute tests, share-of-mind studies, eye traffic on a
page layout, sustained interest patterns of a TV commercial, the
difference between A counties and B counties, costs of prime time
versus fringe time in the twenty-five major markets, how a chain
buying office operates, what is a good Starch report for a black and
white half page in women's service books, how many rating points
is good for a late-night talk show in Chicago or a morning news

program in Atlanta, whether the model in the commercial should look twenty-five or twenty-seven, what weight paper for a free-standing newspaper insert, and so forth?

Ridiculous? No. Routine. The brand manager is nothing if not a walking encyclopedia of market mishmash. And that's the trouble. He knows a little about a fantastic number of things, but he is an expert at none. He'd better sound like one, though, or he'll be needing an executive recruiter in a hurry. The result is that a lot of decisions get made that are stupid beyond belief.

For example, an advertising campaign breaks in a Hartford, Connecticut, test market. The works. Saturation TV, newspaper coupon ads, store displays, drive time radio commercials, bus-card showings, direct-mail support, maybe even a Goodyear blimp overhead. Nothing is overlooked. Only one thing. There is no merchandise in the stores.

Think this is crazy? It happens again and again to enormous companies.

Or take another classic blooper. A new product is tested. Maybe in Phoenix, Arizona; Indianapolis, Indiana; or Syracuse, New York. Something like eighteen months to two years have gone into the preliminaries: testing various shapes, flavors, packages of the product; testing a dozen versions of the advertising message. Hundreds of hours are spent listening behind one-way mirrors to housewives yatter in panel sessions. Squads of executives put in weeks of time revising, reshaping, and restructuring the market plan. Finally everything is ready. The product goes into the test markets with salesmen pep talks, well-wishing from top management, a real kick-in-the-ass send off. And what happens? A jackpot! Everything worked. Click, click, click right down the line. The stuff actually sold. The dealers loved it. The customers came back for more. The share-of-market studies showed that competition was hurting. Success with a capital S.

So the next move. "Take it national! We've got a winner. Roll it out." And this is where the mistake comes in. The cost of the test market introduction in two cities was roughly $1 million. Now the company is going to launch the product across the country. Somebody hurriedly sets up a budget. How about $3 million? $4 million? Hell, give it some support, say, $5 million. Sounds like a lot of long green, especially when everyone agrees the product is a shoo-in. But wait a minute, here is where the arithmetic really kills: $1 million in support was ideal for the two cities, but how good is $5 million for fifty cities? Nobody questioned this. Out goes the product. The pipelines are filled to clogging. The store managers have stock up to their armpits when the advertising breaks. What happens? The national roll-out bombs. The stuff just sits there. The dealers begin to chuck it back. The price gets slashed. After a while, you can't give it away.

In the enthusiasm of the success no one really cared about the nitty-gritty of projecting advertising weights nationwide on a scientific basis. The product might have succeeded if maybe $12 or $14 million was spent, enough to give it the same kind of razzle-dazzle it got in the test markets. The final outcome: The whole two-year, multimillion-dollar project is a cropper. Heads roll; an ad agency may get fired; the annual report fudges over the mistake with something like "we are continuing to evaluate and test the opportunities for new products, with the normal occasional setback."

There are a lot of little bloopers that can cost millions. Here are some examples.

Procter & Gamble—almost always a leader—however has sometimes been a follower. Once this was not a complete success. To meet the competition of Lever Bros. who had come out with a heavy duty liquid detergent called Vim, Procter & Gamble rushed into test markets with a rival called Biz. It was a strong and effective detergent—but apparently too powerful a mixture to be contained in the cans. The stores soon reported corrosion and rotting of the cans. The product had to be recalled. Another disaster for Procter & Gamble happened nearly a generation ago with a liquid toothpaste called Teel. It was a first ever product with great promise. Unfortunately, however, due to varying water conditions throughout the country users in some areas found their teeth turning shades of grey and mottled color. The experience was so impressive on other marketers that ever since liquid toothpastes have been avoided like a plague.

Several beer companies had trouble with a container. One of the major can companies came up with what they thought was a great idea: gallon kegs of beer. Pabst, Schlitz, and several other brewers bought the idea. It looked good in the stores, but later when housewives began to juggle the space in their refrigerators, they decided that the damn thing took up more room than a turkey. It never took off as a product.

Another brilliant marketer got the bright idea of inserting a toy premium right inside the screw-top bottle. Nifty, except the product was liquid glue.

Bristol Myers attached a comb premium somewhat loosely to packages of hair dressing. Customers, seeing the word *free*, pilfered the comb by the thousands.

Ovaltine, once considered old and stuffy, broke out of its traces a few years ago and began introducing wild new products. One was called Screaming Yellow Zonkers! That's breaking out of traces all right. The only hitch, this snack product was a mystery to people in the stores. All they could see was the name and the wildly designed package. What the hell was inside? Customers opened the packages in the stores when their curiosity got the best of them. The thousands of open packs in stores across the country made a nice free snack for passersby. Not enough people, however, took them home for the product to be a big success.

Pepsi-Cola put huge ad budgets into a soft drink that had a brief popularity in the South but washed out when they tried to introduce it in northern markets. It was called Mountain Dew. A towering flop.

Beech-Nut also had a recent disaster with a new soft drink with a Life Saver flavor. It billed itself as the "only drink with a hole in it." The hole, unfortunately, was in the marketing plan. It never got out of its test market.

Pillsbury thought it had a good idea with a new frozen biscuit dough packed in a tube. But sometimes the package popped the uncooked globs in a flight that could clear the width of the kitchen or stick to the ceiling. The same thing happened at a press conference demonstration.

Schick came up with the bright thought that hot shaving lather would be a nifty idea for men. Their problem: You had to heat the stuff under a hot-water faucet first. If you have that much hot water, who needs a hot lather? Down the drain. Since then, however, Schick has developed a successful hair lather product.

Ken-L Ration, a pet-food maker, added chlorophyll to its dog food to deodorize it. The bright green color in the dog droppings was too much for the dog owners.

These are only a fraction of the miscalculations that occur every day of the week. This year it is estimated that perhaps three thousand new or newly improved products will fail. The average is about six losers out of ten tries. Translated into dollars, the cost of failure is astronomical. Billions of dollars. Hundreds of thousands of man-hours. Enormous inconveniences to retail store personnel who are required to stock, display, and promote the new hopefuls. To the advertising agencies involved, the disasters have been so frequent and costly that they are shell shocked. Many simply refuse to handle new products for their clients. They would rather lose the business or see the new product be assigned to another agency.

It would seem that common sense alone would tell companies that many of these bright wunderkind products are certain to fail. But this is the rub. Common sense is not always a prized commodity around corporations these days. Neither are good hunches, experienced personal judgment, or the use of a sure gut feeling. Instead, there is an almost total dependence upon research and the readout from scientific market analysis. Survival in the executive jungle demands that everyone have research data or a perfect alibi for any move or decision he makes. It's called *accountability*. And it is the current sine qua non of executive suites. No product can be launched, no marketing program initiated, no single simple action (even as small as the flap on a package) can be undertaken without tests, research, computer models, statistical backup, or some kind of nonhuman, objective evaluation.

Companies like this kind of reasoning in theory because it is modern and scientific. No guesswork, no flying by the seat of the pants, no shots in the dark. "Let's get all the facts and figures before we move." It is hard to quarrel with this approach. Companies, as custodians of stockholders' investments, ought to act responsibly, ought to use every tool possible to remove the risks from their major actions. They like to think that dependence upon their modern scientific resources can assure them of success. But they forget that tools are only as good as the men who use them. Research has to be planned by people. Questionnaires have to be written by people. Field surveys have to be made by people. Evaluation of results and projections of the findings are jobs that people must do. Then, too, every good marketing project should provide options, different logical plans that can be used if needed. Somebody, a person, has to decide which of several good options to choose. So in the long run, human decisions have to be made, rightly or wrongly.

In effect, many of the so-called scientific explanations used by the companies are often nothing less than alibis or excuses for failures. They can always say, "The research must have been wrong." "The computer gave out the wrong data." "The market must have changed." Or the perfect alibi: "The ad agency should have told us we were on the wrong track."

Despite the fact that many ad agencies have lost a great deal of the marketing leadership they once had, many do indeed warn their clients of impending disasters. Bill Bernbach repeatedly told the Miles Laboratory people that their new product Alka-Seltzer Plus was going to cannibalize the sales of regular Alka-Seltzer. It did, and they lost the account. Foote, Cone & Belding voiced many misgivings to Ford over the prospects for the Edsel. J. Walter Thompson told the Johnson outboard motor people not to get in a horsepower race with its motors because speed on the waterways was dangerous. Benton & Bowles warned American Motors against trying to compete with a full line of cars.

There are many other cases where the agency's advice goes unheeded. The usual reason is that the agency does not have an impressive array of statistics behind its recommendations. These days, the heavy market research is done by the client, and often he alone is privy to the results.

The swing of authority from ad agencies to the clients has led to an arrogance over assumed advertising expertise. Since companies believe they know more about the marketing of their products than their advertising agencies, they assume that they also know exactly what kind of advertising is needed. This leads to a vast amount of boring, sterile, unimaginative advertising. The product manager who has so much to say about advertising is poorly equipped to judge good advertising, much less to create it. Yet many try. Many succeed in intimidating the agency into preparing advertising that it knows is ineffectual. "The son of a bitch is ramming it down our throat," says the account executive. "But Christ, we want to eat don't we? Give him what he wants. It's his money." This accounts for so many campaigns like these: "now from Colgate, an all-new"; "now compare Plymouth to any other four door under $2,300"; "only Lark cigarettes have the gas-trap filter." When you see campaigns like that, you almost always assume it is client-dominated advertising. Ad agencies usually know better. Creative people can do better. Consumers deserve better.

The most arrogant clients are, almost without exception, the ones with the worst-looking, most tasteless, most annoying, and most overbearing advertising. American Home, with its Anacin, its Dristan, its Easy-Off line, its denture cleaners; J. B. Williams, with its Geritol and other proprietaries; Bristol Myers, with Bufferin; Carter-Wallace, with its "little" pills; Warner-Lambert; General Foods; and Procter & Gamble often use their heavy hand of authority and intimidation to force their ad agencies to create irritating, obnoxious advertising. And in the case of American Home, J. B. Williams, and Carter-Wallace it is frequently legally questionable advertising too, for these three companies are often cited by the Washington watchdogs and charged with unfair or misleading advertising. Perhaps some of these companies, notably American Home, are smart in their ability to make profits. But profits alone are **not**, and in the future will not be, the only measure of successful companies. Consumers will have their say about this. Moreover, it must be remembered that the companies mentioned here have products with some of the lowest costs per goods and the highest allowances for advertising of nearly any product in the marketplace. It does not take an abundance of intelligence to market a product that sells for $1 yet costs less than 10 cents to make. You can make a lot of mistakes with that kind of a margin and still come out ahead.

Stupidity on the part of companies could be laughed off if only the companies suffered because of their faults. But this isn't the case. When a major company introduces one failure after another, the costs have to be amortized over other profitable operations. There are many ways of doing this. A company may, without any notice, reduce the quantity of actual product in some of its other brands. A major soap company, for example, found that it had spent more than it had budgeted for a new-product introduction. The product was a success. That is, it stayed on the market, but shortly after the introduction, when consumers supposedly had tried and liked the product and were familiar with the package, a slight shift in quantity was made. One ounce less went into the same container. The price was unchanged. Who would notice? Another means of amortizing mistakes is simply to raise the price of other brands the company makes. Borrow from Peter to pay Paul. A third method is to reduce quality without reducing price. Fortunately, there are limits to this kind of manipulating. Consumers soon catch up with the best bargains.

A closer look at the company method of operation will help to explain why companies make mistakes.

Gillette wished to capitalize on its experience in toiletries by moving into higher-priced, prestige products. It introduced an expensive line of products called Nine Flags, nine different exotic cologne fragrances for men. After several years and several million dollars, the line was dropped. Mistakes: men don't want nine fragrances; some were liked, others were untouched. Also, Gillette was knowledgeable in mass-selling impulse-type products but inexperienced in this area. Then to compound their trouble, they also introduced a high-priced, prestige line for women called Eve of Roma. This firm they had purchased, along with Eve. They put heavy expenses into promotions, including a private plane for Eve to visit stores. Unfortunately, among their other troubles, Eve died, and stores were never receptive to the line. Two bombs, by a very big and smart marketer.

Or take Alberto Culver, who watched Mennen successfully introduce a new product called Protein 21. Mennen did everything right; they had a good product and knew precisely what it was good for: for split-end hairs and hair conditioning. Alberto Culver did what many companies do; they rushed in with a similar product. It was too late and never a success.

Or Procter & Gamble, aware that hair sprays were suddenly taking off for other companies, came out with a version of their own called Sudden Magic. For all the expertise and savvy of this company, it was a multimillion-dollar failure.

And Bristol Myers, long a company supposedly smart in the mouthwash and dentifrice field, introduced two extravagant disasters in toothpaste in two short years: Vote, which got no vote from consumers; and Fact, which was both a literal and factual failure.

Kellogg and several other cereal makers all bombed together in the freeze-dried-fruit fiasco a few years back. They were all so eager to be first that they failed to get a perfected product ready before they went into distribution. The small, hard pellets of real fruit took too long to reconstitute in the bowl. Millions of bowls of cereal went into garbage cans.

You ask company people why these mistakes happen. Why didn't somebody see the futility of the project before it was launched? Was it the fault of the system? The product manager? The marketing director? The head of the company? The philosophy of the company? The ad agency might be inclined to blame the client organization. "The product manager wanted to have his own way." "The marketing director is new, and he wanted to do everything the way it was done in his old company." "They wanted to play it safe." "They never want to innovate, they wait for somebody else to come up with a winner, then they copy." "They chickened out and pulled back the budgets. It didn't have a chance after that." "They are always too slow. It takes them two years to make any decision." Or the opposite: "They rush in too fast before they know where they are going." "There's too much politics over there. If one camp doesn't like it, they will pull the rug out from the other camp."

In many cases, these are the reasons so many projects fail. They would account for mistakes, miscalculations and errors like these. A product is tested successfully and is ready for national roll-out. Supposedly everything done in the test market program was successful. The ads were right. The product was right. The whole program clicked. The sensible thing to do now would be to duplicate every step exactly when going national. But no. The product manager is tired of the commercials. He wants some new ones. The marketing director decides the product could be improved. He makes some changes. The design department would like a few improvements in the package. The finance committee decides the margin is too low and asks for a price boost. So then the product goes out across the country—and fails. Should anybody be surprised? The company in effect has thrown away everything it learned in the test market.

Another common mistake. Slavish adherence to market research results. Research is not infallible. Especially when companies are inclined to look for "bargain" research. Many things can go wrong. The questionnaire asked the wrong questions. The validity of the answers is dubious because field supervision of the interviews was weak. Then interpretations of the research are often faulty. The research firm and many executives in the company read in a favorable outlook because they wish to give top management the answers they want. Research results are like the answers of the Delphic oracle; they can predict success and failure at the same time. Research, especially in the area of creative advertising, has faults. The bright new idea often suffers because respondents find it too different, too alien; and when answering questions about creative work, the housewife tries to be an expert. She is inclined to say that the best ad or commercial is the one she is familiar with. Or the creative research simply proves which of three bad ideas is least bad.

Another reason for errors. Some companies never learn from experience. For example, in picking test towns, it has long been known that the place must be typical of the average American town, should never be too close to the maker's hometown, and should not be too large. Yet big companies go right ahead and make the same mistakes. Campbell Soup tested a product recently right next door in Philadelphia. Colgate used New York City as a test for a mouthwash. And another company discovered too late that it was testing in the hometown of one of its rivals. Also, and this is typical of the way big companies copy each other in nearly every marketing move, some cities are used so often for testing that the consumers there are no longer typical. A waste of money.

Hesitation, delays, procrastination are the causes of many other company failures. Here's an example. An ad agency executive called into a client meeting in the summer of 1971 was handed a plan for a new-product test. As he began reading, he noticed that the first important date was for September. Since it was already midsummer, he asked if this was realistic. He was told to look at the date at the top of the page. It was 1969. Some companies are notoriously slow. Colgate-Palmolive has time and again arrived on the scene long after the original excitement of a new product has gone. Bristol Myers has also frequently been late. Companies like Procter & Gamble and S. C. Johnson will spend a great deal of time preparing to introduce a new kind of a product. S. C. Johnson tested its Edge shaving cream for four years before going national. Procter & Gamble spent nearly as long with Pampers disposable diapers. Both are successes. Sometimes it pays to hold back and watch a new product prove itself before attempting to copy it. The giants were cautious about the quick success of little Texize cleaner spray. And they waited so long that it took heavy investments to catch up. The same thing happened with the original Lestoil. This was introduced by a small chemical company. Only when it was an assured success did the other big soap companies copy it. Anderson Clayton, another small company, was first with a soft margarine, which they called Chiffon. It cost the giants a great deal of money to catch up. Some didn't. Lever lost $10 million with its late entry called Golden Glow. A flop.

In the recent flap over phosphates and other polluting detergents, it was the small, fast-on-their-feet companies who rushed in with the new nonpolluting products, catching the ponderous giants flat-footed. But then some giants are faster than others. General Foods, often slow and careful, lost out to quicker Kellogg. Kellogg, watching and reading carefully the results of General Foods test marketing of toaster pastries, rushed in and beat out GF in many sections of the country with their toaster product. Carnation also beat out General Foods in the instant-breakfast field. They watched GF try and fail with a product called Brim. Carnation, however, studied the General Foods test carefully and found out where they went wrong. Profiting by these mistakes, Carnation then came out with their very successful Instant Breakfast. Alberto Culver, a company run by a decisive marketing man, Leonard Lavin, often steals a march on competitors. When Lavin saw that there was a fast-growing market for feminine hygiene products, he rushed in ahead of a dawdling Warner-Lambert product called Pristeen and scored a quick success with FDS.

Are these mistakes, or simply the ups and downs of a highly competitive marketplace? Mostly, they are mistakes. Or at least they were projects that shouldn't have failed. Nobody can win them all, obviously; but no big, experienced company should have so many costly disasters. In addition to largeness and unwieldiness, there is another, more common cause of errors: bad chemistry among executives. Things like: "I knew the product was a bomb, but it was Mr. Big's private baby, so why should I stick my neck out?" "They promoted him over me, why should I give the bastard any help?" "He's the new man, let him learn the ropes on his own." Or, "Confidentially, I saw he was going wrong with the product, but what the hell, if he failed, I figured I might get a chance at his job. Doesn't everyone look at it that way?" Alas, corporations are jungles. Executives are seldom the team-spirited, cooperative gentlemen management would like people to think.

There are several reasons for the bad chemistry in companies. Some of them seem ridiculous on the surface. Would you believe that it makes a difference whether an executive's hobby is sailboats or powerboats? It does. The sailboat enthusiast is a purist snob to the powerboat owner. And conversely, to the sailboat man the other guy is a "stinkpot" owner. Disparity in golf scores can make a big difference. Bob Neuser, a top marketing executive recruiter in New York City, recently was looking for a 12-to-14 handicap golfer. When offered one with a 3 handicap, he replied, "No way, we can't have a good golfer in that crowd." This same recruiter, who has placed hundreds of men with top corporations, also points out some of the other chemistry problems. For example, for weeks he had been sending top applicants to one of the major packaged-goods firms in New Jersey. No dice. Everyone was turned down for no apparent reason. He finally asked to have lunch with the marketing director who was rejecting his men. The moment he met the five-foot-six executive in the doorway of the restaurant, he saw his mistake. All the men he had sent out to the company happened to be over six feet tall.

Here are some other examples of how companies make mistakes because their people don't get along with each other. Some top executives prefer to work only with older men. Young men make them uneasy. Some corporations like a certain kind of outdoorsman, a sports fan, a man not too smart but congenial and hardworking. Others are more intellectual and political as a group. The new man in all these cases either fits or doesn't fit. On the surface perhaps he does, but underneath the tensions grow, the rugs begin to slip, the rapier thrusts move invisibly but surely. Company meetings turn into what someone aptly labels "conversational karate." Also, there is an occasional old-fashioned tyrant, a man who apparently gets his way by brute bullying. Even their bosses are afraid of some of these arrogant weight throwers. They have one thing going for them. Way up on top, the management likes the idea that they have a couple of "rough, tough bastards" in the ranks. "Keeps the rest of them on their toes." Maybe it does, but those toes turn outward after a while and march off to more agreeable companies.

Loyalty to one's company is perhaps the clearest evidence of good morale, just as bad chemistry is the best evidence of disloyalty. Some companies—big, successful giants—have almost no executive loyalty at all. These people are insensitive, impersonal money players straight down the line. Some of them literally hate their companies, yet stay on pulling down enormous salaries. The marketing director of a toiletries company was earning over $100,000 a year and so disliked his company that he deliberately sent out lists of key executives in his firm to management recruiters inviting them to "pirate" anyone they wished. Or another executive, who had already arranged to take a new job, set about firing three of the most valuable men on his staff, just so his company would be weakened after he left. Others will deliberately withhold key information about a weak territory, a failing product, a wrongly interpreted market research report because they would just as soon see the "shitheads upstairs" suffer, as long as they personally aren't pinned with the troubles. Do these actions sound fantastic? Men who are earning big salaries, have full fringe benefits, are even stockholders? Maybe they do, but the corporation executive of today is in many cases a different breed. He is no Horatio Alger, no "stick with the company, the company will stick with me" idealist. He believes he is paid for what he does, and the minute he stops doing it, he considers the trapdoor will snap open. If he likes his job, it is less because he is working for a "nice" company than because he feels he is productive, meeting his own concepts of success, accepting a stimulating challenge. These personal goals may or may not fit in with the company's goals. The average executive couldn't care less.

This is all part of the broad sea change in attitudes toward business and society today. Most able young executives are success-oriented, salary-conscious, self-confident, and well-trained. An M.B.A. degree is a must. But there are other important considerations. The new young men are seeking more quality in their lives, more meaning in their professions, more overall satisfactions and gratifications. If they don't find them in one corporation, they'll switch to another and another. Or to a smaller company. Or they'll switch out of the field entirely. Life is too short. They believe in bucking the system. In fact, they may not even respect the system. The trappings of big business (the executive dining room, the privileged parking place, the special "perks" or perquisites) are considered mickey mouse or chicken shit by the modern executive. "Respect me for my talent, pay me what I deserve, but leave my private life outside your goddamn system."

If companies are so big, so smart, and so successful, why don't they know about such attitudes? Most of them do. In fact, some are actually proud of their reputations for being "ball-breaking" places to work. In effect they are saying, "We are pros here, no coddling, no wet nursing. We're interested in the bottom line. Profits. Fuck everything else." American Home might be considered one of these. And they consistently post the best bottom line in American industry. They also have a high turnover of executives and much bad mouthing throughout the business world. Are they worried? Not at all. There are enough tough pros to fill their ranks for the top salaries they pay. Revlon is another and is also a leader in its field of cosmetics. Executive attrition there is high.

On the other hand, there are companies that are generally regarded as good places to work for either because they are respected as smart marketers or because they have good morale. The following impressions and opinions—and that is precisely what they are—were gathered from conversations with top executive recruiters. These men often know more about what goes on inside major corporations than the chief executive officers do. This is because they are constantly talking to the new executives who go in and to the old ones who come out.

When the interrelationships of executives working together are bad, along with other failings mentioned earlier, it is easy to see why some companies are indeed stupid-looking to the ad agency executive or to any businessman. But, then, maybe things are improving; one major corporation recently offered to pay psychiatric bills not only for husbands but for wives *and* children

6

Why Agencies and Clients Don't Get Along

AFTER SEVERAL FUMBLING STARTS in the business, a young agency man finally landed his first account. Full of hope and enthusiasm, he arrived at the offices with his first campaign. "It was just like in the movies about advertising," he reported later. "They actually stomped on the ads, kicked them, walked up and down on them, and threw them across the room."

Debonair David Ogilvy has known some bad days. This one occurred in San Francisco, where David had gone to make an important presentation to a large group of Shell dealers. In order of their occurrence, these are the things that went wrong. The meeting opened with David seated on the floor trying to open the tripod legs of the movie screen. The first act—presentation of color slides—was interrupted when the thumb-punch advancer stalled. The slides had to be forwarded manually, which upset David's rhythm. Next, the fuses on the entire floor blew out. A coffee break was declared, and the sixty-five dealers were served Danish and ice-cold coffee. The catered coffee dispenser didn't heat. The next portion of the show—the presentation of the filmed commercials—was delayed for forty-five minutes because the reel of films was left back in Ogilvy's hotel room. It took a secretary an inordinate amount of time to find these because the reel was tucked inside a bag of David's laundry. When the film finally arrived and was strung up, with some difficulty, the projector failed. A bulb burned out and was hard to replace from nearby stores because the projector was an English model David had brought along. Then when the new bulb was in and the film began to run, it was out of focus. A frantic Ogilvy & Mather man, trying to find the right focus, pulled the lens completely out of the projector. Finally, the meeting over, they all adjourned to a famous Japanese restaurant for luncheon. The food tasted good, but David reported that all the way back to New York, he was "running to the loo." After all his other problems, he worried that all sixty-five Shell executives had the same bowel trouble.

An ad agency concerned about its new client's fussiness over costs and expenses entered the first meeting with him. A memorandum prepared by the ad agency was distributed as the first move of the meeting. The client—a square-jawed, shrewd-eyed older man—picked up his copy. He hefted it gently in his hand, held it up to the light, removed his glasses for a closer look, then began reading. The president of the agency scribbled a note to the account supervisor, "Now you know how he feels about *costs*."

Joe Weiner, a San Francisco adman, sold his Rainier Brewery client on the first use of a sweatshirt with a portrait of Beethoven printed across the front. The client agreed to the idea only if Weiner would assume the full financial risk of the sweatshirts, which were offered as an inexpensive, self-liquidating premium. Joe did. He made $110,000 during the first six weeks of the promotion.

The president of a big agency had a young wife. His major client also had a young wife. The two women were great friends. One day the wife of the client left her husband to live with another man. The client rushed to the agency president and asked if he knew who his wife had run off with. He didn't. The client said, "Your wife must know. They're close friends." The president answered, "She probably does, but I won't ask her." He didn't, and the president lost the account.

Creative people are sensitive about reactions to their handiwork. When it is not applauded or bought with enthusiasm, they are likely to describe the outcome in special terminology: "It was shot down in flames." "They pissed all over it." "Ran into some flak." "They cut it to ribbons." "The stupid account man crapped on it." "They walked all over it." "They shot it full of holes." "Threw darts at it." "Cut the gonads off it." "Took all the zing out of it." "Cut the legs off." "Bombed it out of the water." Or the worst that could possibly happen: "They let the client rewrite it."

The bad news about an account loss can come in many ways. Maybe it is a confidential memo hand delivered from the client to the agency president. It could come over the phone, chief executive officer to chief executive officer. Sometimes it's a telegram dispatched to the agency head's home on a Saturday morning. Another method is over a private lunch at a private club. Dan Seymour, of J. Walter Thompson, was called away from his summer cottage at Cape Cod to a hotel in Boston by the people from Ford Motor. There have also been occasions—a shattering experience—when the agency president learns the news for the first time when he reads it in the *New York Times* as he is seated on his commuting train. It makes no difference really; whenever it comes, however it comes, the agency-client split is a jolting blow. There is no way to soften it.

An agency president, explaining this shock, said that he stood behind the closed doors of his office for five full minutes trying to decide who among his two thousand people in the office to tell first. "I finally called my wife. Isn't that silly?"

The "resignation," as it is charitably called in the business (the client can afford to be generous), is the ultimate misunderstanding. The last and final disagreement, usually coming after many months of unpleasantness. Yet it always comes as a surprise. There is always the last frantic hope that maybe it can still be saved. "Let's call them back again. Tell them we've just had a terrific idea. Tell them—" Futile. Hopeless. Nothing in the world of business is as final as an agency-client split.

The break is seldom because the ad agency could not do the work. Interpublic, with 4,500 people, is not fired because they lack capability. Doyle Dane Bernbach, the most creative ad agency in a generation, is not fired because it is not creative. Young & Rubicam cannot be faulted because of specific failings in media, creativity, or research. They have perhaps the best overall strength in the business. Yet these, and all agencies, get fired regularly. Some 10 to 15 percent of the billings will be lost in any given year. Altogether, a billion dollars' worth of accounts will change agencies this year. Each time it happens, with a multimillion-dollar account anyway, the business is rocked. Agency people feel it deep in the gut. It is that god-awful basic insecurity of the business again. Nothing is safe; nothing is permanent. What the hell next?

The postmortems are usually stupid. "The president missed a big meeting." "They zigged when they should have zagged." "They tried to ram a bad idea down the client's throat." "Somebody was screwing the client's wife." (Maybe that one's not so stupid. Some time ago, it actually was the cause of a loss of a major account.) In general, however, none of these reasons are the real ones. The official statement from the client usually reads: "A basic disagreement in strategy—" Vague and unspecific as that sounds, it is, however, the closest to the truth that is ever likely to emerge from these major or minor account turnovers. It is all there in the tragically true words "basic disagreement."

Why the disagreements? Why so many of them? Why are they so irreconcilable? It doesn't happen this way with clients in other business service organizations, such as law firms, accountants, designers, architects, and tax consultants. Why advertising? Why only advertising? The pat answer would seem to be: "It's the intangible nature of the service offered." After all, what else is being sold or offered but promises? An ad or a commercial can never deliver guaranteed results. Advertising is not a science. Even with modern research techniques, predictions of outcome are mostly uncertain. This is all true, but it is only part of the truth. The main thing is that clients and agency people do not understand each other. They do not read each other clearly enough to maintain a workable relationship. Perhaps they do at the beginning of the marriage, perhaps for many years they do, but the time finally comes when no more dialogue is possible. Nothing further can be said or done. The sky falls.

To understand why this happens, it is necessary to look back, to a period when these relationships were first formed. There was a time when the advertising agency or agent served his client in an astonishingly comprehensive fashion. He told him literally everything about making and selling his products. After decades of great sales successes, the adman became a demigod to his client. He was the keeper of the great mystique, the man with "the big idea," the man who had some fabulous truths secreted about his person, things clients could never hope to know. They would look at some of the great campaigns of the time (which don't look so great now) and say, "God, I wish I could have thought up that idea!" "Our advertising man is a *genius!*" Or they would ask, with profound wonder, "How *do* you do it?" This was heady stuff to the admen. They began to feel and act like geniuses. If it was a myth, they certainly were not the ones who would disprove it. Then to add to the stature came the huge personal fortunes these early admen made. To substantiate their greatness, they lived high, dressed in the finest clothes, entertained their clients in the most famous eateries, took them to the most popular Broadway shows, often introduced them to movie stars and other celebrities.

Bruce Barton, one of the early giants and a founder of BBDO was a very wealthy man. As reported, he hated to pay income taxes. Toward the end of his career, in order to avoid high inheritance taxes, he systematically began giving money away to all his relatives and to numerous charities. One day, his partner Alex Osborn said, "Bruce, if you die and leave practically no estate the Internal Revenue Service will search every bank in the country for some hidden-away safety deposit box of yours. They'll be convinced that you've stashed a fortune away somewhere."

Bruce Barton, as Alex told it, replied: "You are right. I've thought of that. I'm sure they will search the banks. And some day they will find a safety deposit box in my name. They'll get a court order to open it. Inside they will find an envelope. They'll open the envelope and they'll find a piece of paper. On it will be written, in my own hand writing, these words: 'Kiss my ass.'"

Adding to this already-towering position of the adman came another development: the take-over of the business by a new class of well-bred, Eastern Establishment gentlemen. The born-rich, impeccably dressed, smooth-mannered men. The combination of the great mystique, plus great wealth, plus the high-class posture gave the advertising man an enormous advantage over his client.

It must be remembered that for many years, clients were mill owners, manufacturers, makers and peddlers of drugs and pills. They usually lived in small manufacturing cities. Some may have been college educated, but few could match the poise, assurance, confidence, and big-city sophistication of the "agency boys."

The president of a big midwestern manufacturing plant showed up in the reception room of Cunningham & Walsh, an old-line, blue-chip agency on Madison Avenue. This was in the early fifties, and in those days C&W handled such accounts as Texaco, Liggett & Myers, and Lever Brothers. The manufacturer, however, was no small operator. His advertising account was in the multimillion-dollar category.

"What can we do for you?" the receptionist asked in her finest Radcliffe accent.

"I want to see the president."

"May I ask what it is about, Mr. Jones?"

"It's about advertising," the manufacturer snapped.

"Please take a seat for just a moment. I'll be right back."

Since she would not ordinarily lead every stranger to the president's office, the receptionist soon returned with a young, handsome, Ivy League account executive, who greeted the man in a polite, friendly manner. The young man, however, was given no opportunity to speak. As soon as the manufacturer learned that he was not the president, he practically shouted: "I was going to *give* my business to your agency, but after treatment like this, I wouldn't think of it."

"Well, sir, I'm certain you can see the president immediately. Please come in."

"I'll come, but it won't make a damn bit of difference."

A few moments later, in the oak-paneled, deep-carpeted office of John Cunningham, the agency's chairman, the manufacturer repeated his tirade. Mr. Cunningham, tall, urbane, darkly handsome, listened politely, nodding occasionally. The potential client

113

wound up at length, "So you see, you might have had all my business. But now you won't get a red cent. I'm going to take it elsewhere."

Mr. Cunningham got up, walked around the desk, shook hands with elaborate graciousness, and said, "Thank you *very* much, Mr. Jones, for stopping by. I think you will be doing exactly the right thing by taking your business elsewhere. Good day."

Arrogance? An excess of self-confidence? Or just simply the way the business was transacted in those days? For years on end, the big agencies bragged that they never made a speculative presentation, never aggressively solicited business. "They will come to us, if they want us." The big agencies, the pacesetters (who scorned the "noisy little second-raters" on the fringe of the business), maintained this imposing façade, this dignified, taken-for-granted stance of authority and superiority. Sometimes they did it unwittingly. J. Walter Thompson had just taken over Johnson Motors of Waukegan, Illinois. A group of people from the agency visited the plant shortly after the contract signing. The agency and client people, after a morning of inspecting the plant, adjourned to Racine's finest chop house and tavern, which was next to a railroad siding. Simply as a conversation starter the Thompson account executive asked the executive vice-president a question: "By the way, how many people do you employ now?"

"Glad you asked. We were just adding them up yesterday," the man replied proudly, "1,341—that includes a few part-time men in the boatyard."

"Say, that's quite a lot of people. I didn't realize."

In the short pause that followed, the account man realized his mistake. He knew the question he hadn't meant to prompt was coming up. It did.

"And how many men do you have in that ad agency of yours?"

There was no way to avoid a direct answer.

"Well—er—officially—let's see, worldwide—we have just a few over 5,000."

Here's another example, a recent one, to show how the myth persists.

Two ad agency executives—young, barely out of office training programs—arrive at a small, grassy airfield in the Piedmont section of North Carolina. They are on a routine visit to their client, a fine furniture maker. It is 6:30 A.M., but the ad manager is there to meet the two-engine plane as it lands. The ad manager —a vice-president, a principal in the company, college educated— owns a comfortable home on a lake. His new car, his yacht on the nearby lake, his obviously substantial income all mark him as a successful executive. He is nearly twice the age of the young agency people. Here is the conversation that took place on the grassy apron of the tiny airport.

"Well, it's mighty nice to see you boys."

"Nice to see you, Mr. James."

"First thing Ah want to do is to apologize for this dreadful dew on the grass here. It should be burned off by this time. Now your shoes are going to get all wet." He stamped on the ground to emphasize his disapproval.

Why such deference, almost demeaning respect? Maybe one explanation is that glib-talking admen have perpetrated the biggest snow job of the century. Certainly ad agencies have done their best to perpetuate the myths. Why else do they have such extravagant offices, dine their clients in the finest restaurants, wine them in exclusive old clubs, meet them in limousines? Many times they literally cannot afford such nonsense. Jerry Della Femina can now admit that his first client party was on borrowed cash. Another agency held a fancy buffet for a client at a top New York hotel and then took the leftovers home in doggie bags. Why else do ad agencies have so many vice-presidents: 300 at BBDO, 400 at McCann-Erickson, 165 at Ted Bates. There was a time there for a while when ad agency presidents were a race of giants. Physical stature apparently was an absolute requisite for the chief executive officer. Mix Dancer, of Dancer-Fitzgerald-Sample, was six-feet-five. President David Steward, of Kenyon & Eckhardt, was six-three. Terrance Clyne, of Clyne Maxon, was six-two. Norman Straus, of J. Walter Thompson, was six-two. Also, appropriately, John Creighton, head of the 4As, was six-four. Although a creative wag called some of these men "tall people with no stature," size did often command additional clout with clients or prospects.

For example, John Anderson, then president of Anderson Davis & Platte (a shop that eventually sank out of sight in the

Interpublic pool of companies) was six-five, a former Princeton tackle, with snow-white hair. Whether by chance or design, John had many accounts in the apparel and garment industry. On one occasion, he attended a convention of apparel makers in Atlantic City. Most of these manufacturers were from New York's Seventh Avenue garment center. As a group they run somewhat on the short side. John, moving among these potential clients during the three-day session, looked like Gulliver among the Lilliputians. When someone shook his hand, they looked like they were pulling a light cord. A few days later, he was asked how he made out with new business prospects.

"Quite well, as a matter of fact," he replied. "I think I have at least three live ones lined up." Then he added modestly, "Small ones."

Add it all up; add in the number of years it has gone on; and you will see the basic reason admen and clients are never quite comfortable together. Surely, advertising today is not the prestige profession it once was. Gone, long gone, is much of the mystique and secret knowledge. And gone, too, is much of the arrogance, snobbishness, and superior airs. But enough of the residual is still there. Enough to put a strain on relationships. Enough for many a client, on the junior level especially, to say, "We'll fix those wise-ass bastards from the agency." "We'll cut their tires every chance we get." And they do. Often with a vengeance. There are many documented cases of clients tearing ads to shreds, turning over chairs, stomping ads into the carpet, ripping them from conference room walls, throwing water carafes, and using unbelievably foul language. One client-agency melee started in a twentieth-floor conference room, continued as a jostling match down the corridor and into the elevator, where blows were exchanged and a nose bloodied, and out onto the street, where the client's limousine waited. The agency man got in the last licks. He dented the rear fender with a powerful kick as the car moved away.

Some clients love to make whipping boys of their ad agencies. When Philip Courtney was president of Coty cosmetics, he used to call sudden staff meetings attended by all the key executives. The meetings had no planned agenda. The only purpose seemed to be how much heat Mr. Courtney could bring to bear on each of the key executives. The aim: to keep them all on their toes. No matter how well any man acquitted himself under the barrage of questions thrown at him by Courtney, he was nonetheless berated. On one occasion, Courtney took out after the ad manager, Gene Judd, and as Judd remembers it, the berating went something like this:

"Why don't you whip those agency people more often? Why don't you take issue with them more often?" Courtney demanded of Judd.

Judd explained that he was well aware of the capabilities of the agency (it was BBDO) and that in his opinion he was able to get more out of them by cooperation and joint decision making.

"Then you are more loyal to them than you are to Coty!" Courtney snapped.

"Not at all, I want the best advertising possible for Coty."

Courtney wouldn't accept this. As usual, he did his best to embarrass Judd. Judd listened for a few minutes, then submitted his resignation on the spot.

"What's the matter, Judd, can't stand the heat?" Courtney asked.

"It's not the heat, Mr. Courtney," Judd replied evenly, "it's the humility."

Gene Judd is now president of a successful management consulting firm.

Other clients have established long-term reputations for being rough on their agencies. The Revson brothers at Revlon. The American Home executives. Seagram Distillers and National Distillers. John Toigo, when he was marketing director of Joseph Schlitz Brewing. John's face could turn so stark white with rage that it looked like a death mask with black fire for eyes. His language reverted to his youthful coal-mining days. J. B. Williams Company. The product managers at Colgate. Procter & Gamble executives, although the weight they throw is an overwhelming superiority of facts and figures. Ford Motor, with John Iaccoca at the head, have been tough taskmasters. So have the marketing executives at Gillette, Mennen, and at times, Bristol Myers. Some of the smaller advertisers, often run by family executives, have built up solid reputations for acerbity and impetuous demands.

The Lazrus brothers at Benrus Watch, years ago, barked at their agencies. One brother sat at meetings with an open bottle of bourbon at his elbow. Probably the toughest customers of all are the heads or committee members of dealer organizations. RCA distributors are well known for their roughshod treatment of ads and ad people. Chevrolet dealers are a hard-nosed crowd. Citgo gas dealers have been known to welcome a new campaign with a chorus of cusswords. The dealer groups come on with a double whammy. They don't like the ad agency because usually they didn't pick it (it was inherited with the national account), and they are constantly fighting with headquarters anyway. They don't want to have any ads shoved down their throats by the factory or the factory's ad agency, especially since they will have to pay for all or most of the cost.

In recent years, the differences between clients and agencies have narrowed. Ad making is not all that mysterious. Clients know it. Agency people are not the great marketing wizards they were once thought to be. At the same time, clients have become vastly more sophisticated. Agencies no longer possess the advantages they once held in areas of research, strategy, planning, even media savvy. Now clients know these things, too, and all too often know them in greater depth and scope than the agencies. This is the era of client organizations staffed with rank upon rank of bright young men with M.B.A.s. Then, too, all the trappings of wealth, breeding, and social poise count for very little today. Especially when the hottest, brightest new agencies are often manned on the top by clever youngsters from Brooklyn or the Bronx. The salary differences have leveled out. Paul Harper, chairman of Needham, Harper & Steers explained this problem. "We lost ten good young men to the client side last year. Men we wanted, men we had trained. The biggest reason: salaries. We simply couldn't match the offers they were getting."

The balance is no longer weighted on the agency side. If anything, it has tipped clearly and definitely to the other side of the desk. This is especially true of the agency-client relationships in the packaged-goods areas.

How would this operate in a hypothetical agency-client meet-

118

ing? The agency executive has arrived in the client's office with some new ads·

Agency: Got some great new stuff for you, Fred. Breakthrough stuff. Very creative.

Client: We can use it. The last SAMI report was pretty sick. [SAMI is an expensive share-of-market sales report. The client gets it. The agency doesn't.]

Agency: This new approach will goose up sales. Wait'll you see it. Ties in with the new ecology kick, too.

Client: So we are polluters now? Do we have to get in that bag?

Agency: Oh, that's not the main thrust, it's just to set us up with the consumer groups. Don't worry, the hard sell is right in there with brass knuckles. We're hitting the "works faster" proposition loud and clear.

Client: Works faster? Not so sure that's it. I think our R and D boys have come up with something else. Guess we didn't tell you. By the way, did you test your ads?

Agency: Absolutely! Focus groups. The housewives loved it. Terrific feedback!

Client: That's nice. Of course we'll have to run it through our system. By the way, I see you didn't bring the creative people along today. Got them locked up in cages, ha? By the way, how's that Adam and Eve team. [Reference is to a boy-girl unit that has been working on the account.]

Agency: Well, they were pretty busy today. Thought just us boys would get the feel of the stuff first. You know how sensitive they are sometimes. [The agency man avoids a direct answer about the creative team. They have left the agency.]

Client: Before you unwrap the work, I want to get Joe and Charlie in here. Too bad Big Al is out of town. It's probably too early for him at this stage anyway.

The client excuses himself. He is back in a few moments with Joe and Charlie. Charlie is friendly to the agency man. Joe simply nods and takes a seat.

Client: Well, here goes. Let's see what buster has in his bag—

The agency man has the floor. He is ready to give his pitch. Good luck. He has ten strikes against him. Exactly ten. Count them. (1) He comes on strong with a promise of great new creative stuff. An indication that previous creative work was weak. (2) He is hit immediately by the fact that the client has bad news about the sales of the product (SAMI reports) that he doesn't know about. How can an agency perform its job properly if it is not privy to such important information as sales? (3) The agency man now tips his hand by mentioning the "ecology" tie in. His people had thought this would please the client. It turns out unfortunately to be a sensitive subject. (4) He also mentions the fact that the main selling theme is based upon "works faster." Now he learns that the client's research department has something new. The agency hadn't been informed. (5) Testing the ads. The agency does only preliminary tests. The client's more extensive tests will be decisive eventually. (6) The client asks why the creative people are not on hand. He is disappointed. (7) He'll be more disappointed later to find that his favorite creative team has left the agency. (8) He then calls in Joe and Charlie, which means that this will be a group decision. Another handicap. (9) The key man, Big Al, won't be brought into it until later. And (10) the client man, Joe, does not like the agency man. That old problem of chemistry among personalities.

Selling against handicaps like this day in and day out is the job of the ad agency account executive. Perhaps a passing introduction to his position in the agency-client operation is needed here. The account man (Clark Gable's role in the movie *The Hucksters*) is the most fabled and maligned of all ad agency people. He is the man eternally in the middle. He lives a damned-if-I-do, damned-if-I-don't existence. One half of his job is to please the client, and the other half is to please the agency, particularly the creative people who make the ads he has to sell to the client. It is a cul-de-sac. The opposite nature of the people involved makes it theoretically impossible to please both. He usually ends up being a son of a bitch to one and a bastard to the other. How even seasoned account executives manage to play this no-win game year in and year out without losing their aplomb or going out of their minds is astonishing.

The status of the account executive in ad agencies is currently in double jeopardy. He is not only a man in the middle; he is also a man in a nutcracker. The economic squeeze, the changing nature of the business from full service to specialized creative service, and the general malaise of the ad agency business have questioned the very existence of his job. "Who needs him?" "He is just another stumbling block." "He's obsolete." "An overpriced messenger boy." And some say, "The account man is what's wrong with this whole business." These are indeed trying times for the account man. It is true that his role as a marketing advisor to the client has diminished in recent years. To smaller accounts and unsophisticated advertisers, perhaps he can make some contributions in this area. On the large accounts, the multimillion-dollar spenders, he is seldom listened to. In fact, a recent survey showed that some 75 percent of a group of large companies preferred not to show their agency account men an important type of sales-intelligence reports. Yet this kind of information ought to be fundamental to an account executive's job. Another study made among a representative sample of account men showed that the majority of them could not pass a simple twenty-question test on marketing that was designed for college business students.

There is a problem of obsolescence in the account executive hierarchy in many of the larger ad agencies. Many of these men, now in their late forties and fifties, were products of the earlier era when ad agencies commanded more power and respect in the areas of market research, test marketing, media strategy, and overall client sales problems. Those were the days when ad agencies operated powerful backup services. It was possible then to tell the client things he didn't know, things he should do, and have the weight of authority behind the recommendations. Now the research departments are shells; the media departments have often been replaced by outside media services; the new-product development has slipped out of their hands into outside new-product workshops or has been given as special projects to creative teams and small creative-emphasis agencies. The result is a group of superfluous account men, especially on the levels of group account supervisors and management supervisors of client services. Scores of these men have been dropped by ad agencies in the past few years. Their severance caused much hardship. They could not find work in other ad agencies, nor could they, as many had anticipated, find jobs on the client side, proof certainly that they were not the marketing men they believed themselves to be. Young account men with a few years of agency experience could make the move to the client side (as indicated by Mr. Harper's comments). Their brief experience in agencies stands them in good stead when they move to the client organizations. It teaches them what they can and cannot expect from an agency. The older account men are stranded like whales on a beach.

Client-agency misunderstandings are often based upon different concepts of the kind and quality of service expected from an agency. Client organizations today often have far more advanced management systems. They are better planners, expediters, followuppers. The large corporations now have information management systems that are simply beyond the ken of many ad agencies, who do not have the computer capability and data processing equipment. As a result, although the ad agency may be doing its best, it may be far from adequate. "Where the hell is that job?" "Why haven't you found the answer to that question we gave you last week?" "Don't you people know what's going on in the marketplace?" "Christ almighty, we can't wait forever for you guys." These are typical client comments. They hurt the relationship, badly. Agencies are supposed to lead their clients. They are supposed to know about fast-moving new marketing trends, new areas of opportunity, new communication techniques, new developments concerning the client's competitors. They should be their client's eyes and ears in the marketplace.

The account man, again, is the key to this whole interrelationship. He's the two-way transmitter of information, the man who has to interpret his client's needs, translate them to his agency work forces, bring it back correct. It is unfair to call him just a messenger boy. He has to know his client intimately, his foibles, hang-ups, the white elephants, the hidden power groups, the skeletons in the closets, the shifts in strengths and weaknesses within the organization. He has to know the short- and long-range aims of the company. He has to know how much money they make, how much they can afford to spend on advertising, how much return they can expect if all goes well. Then back at the shop, he has to know his agency's strengths and weaknesses, what the creative people are capable of, how much time it takes people to do things. How much money? How much needling and encouragement is necessary? He must answer also to his own top management. Is the account handled profitably? Is it run smoothly? Is it happy?

When the account man fails on any of these functions, small or big, the score begins to build up against him and against the account at the agency. If he is reading his client accurately, they should not happen. But this is idealistic thinking. Few account men are so skilled that they can anticipate all problems, especially in a service business that has so many nonspecific functions and subjective decisions. "Is this ad too far out for the client? Will he laugh me out of the meeting?" "Or if I take it back to the creative people, will they shout, 'You yellow-bellied bastard, you're afraid to show them anything fresh and different. You're a square, a reactionary old fart. What do you know about good creative work?' " Exaggerated? Not at all. The conflicts between account and creative people are legendary. The names account people are called by the writers and art directors are endless. "Banana head." "Accountniks." "Client suckers." "Double-crossing shitheads."

The breakdowns in communications and understanding, however, are not always the fault of the account man. After all, others at the agency also see the client. Theoretically, the president and top management executives are at least in touch with the client and his problems. But this is an area of often shameful neglect. Some clients of the large ad agencies don't see the agency president more than once or twice a year. One client had been with Interpublic for seven years, and he had never met the president. Some small clients in big agencies actually do not have a permanent, full-time account executive. A small client was overheard asking at a reception desk at a large agency to see "his account man"; he was told that they had no record of his business. He had been spending more than $500,000 per year. Amazingly enough, he did not take his business away. This had happened before. He came around about twice a year, and after a half hour or so in the reception room, someone would come out. It would be a new account man every time. He would be invited in, given a cup of coffee, talked with for about a half hour. A short while later, an art director and a copywriter would join the meeting. Ads would be planned, schedules set, and away he'd go. A few weeks later, ads would be presented to the client at his office, approved with a few changes, and he would be set for another six months. That kind of service would flabbergast a typical client, but this one said, "I never liked a bunch of flunkies bothering me all through the year. When I was ready, I went over and told them my needs. They always did a good job."

There are not many clients like that. Most are incessantly demanding a rush of ongoing services hour by hour, day after day. And some of these are well beyond the call of duty. Theater and sports tickets, luncheons at top restaurants, personal stationery or calling cards, dates with models, freebies of all kinds (liquor, gifts, trips).

Client bullying has intensified in the past few years. The economic recession put a tight cash-flow squeeze on many companies. They, in turn, have applied the squeeze to ad agencies. Many major companies have delayed paying bills way beyond the 30-day net allowance. Many are taking three months, six months, nearly a year. Yet, incredibly, when they do pay, they nearly all deduct the 2 percent allowance for 30-day cash payment. Foreign companies dealing with American ad agencies are notoriously slow payers. Japanese, Swiss, and Caribbean companies are especially bad. At least five ad agencies have been forced directly into bankruptcy by such slow payers. Many of the others force agencies to factor their bills. This means raising the money to pay their obligations from factors who may charge as high as 12 to 15 percent for short-term loans. Another bullying tactic is actually to ask ad agencies to loan them money. Reportedly, cash-rich Ted Bates has extended amounts into the millions for clients who could not meet their media obligations. It is a safe way to hold an account but an unfair business tactic.

Every business has its scoundrels and scalawags. If they differ in advertising it is because, after all, it is a creative business. You would expect a certain amount of imagination and innovation in the kinds of politics played and the ways advertising executives outmaneuver their competitors. Here is a brief look at some of the charlatans and fakers you might run into.

The kickbackers. The agency business was founded on the fair and reasonable commission system. All media offer all legitimate agents a 15 percent commission on advertising time or space that they sell for the media. Sometimes the 15 percent is not enough to cover the cost of preparing the ads and handling the account. Agencies then charge an extra fee or retainer. So far, no problem. However, sometimes the 15 percent commission looks a little large. If, for example, the advertiser is a large packaged-goods manufacturer who may spend $10 million a year but who needs no more than say five or six TV commercials, then the 15 percent, or $1.5 million, begins to loom very large indeed. The advertiser is well aware that the agency doesn't need all that money to make just a few commercials. So the squeeze is on. Sometimes the client asks for maybe just 1 percent of the 15 percent as a kickback. Or 2 percent or 3 percent.

The commission system permits other evils to creep into agency-client relationships. Often the kickback becomes a solicitation device. The agency that promises to give back the most gets the business. Or another evil. The commissions are paid by media to any organization that calls itself an agency. This may be no more than a business card or a letterhead. Or in the case of the "house" agency (the client is in effect his own agency), the commissions are really little more than a discount to the advertiser, an unfair one because the house agency is often only a cubbyhole office with a name on the door, down the hall from the advertising manager.

Shenanigans over commissions have taken many forms, too numerous to mention. The agency business is not proud of this, but to date, there seems to be no way to exert effective control. It is one of the reasons many in the business hope that eventually there will be no commissions. Instead, all advertisers will pay for all services performed. The higher fees would go to those offering the best services.

On the heels of the commission system, and treading lightly, is another ancient and much-abused practice: buried costs and payoffs. Advertising agencies buy a great deal of advertising supplies: printing, engraving, artwork, photography, TV commercials, music and jingles, and so forth. Standard practice permits the agencies to mark up these expenses by a set 17.75 percent that in theory covers the costs of purchasing them on behalf of the clients. Again, like the system of commissions from media, the percentage can look small or big. It can look mighty small for a messy catalog with dozens of photographs, tiny type blocks, and detailed copy. Or it can look quite large with a single outdoor poster that will be reproduced identically for tens of thousands of boards. So again, the squeeze comes in. In many agencies the costs are spread around among accounts. The easy commissions cover for the hard ones. Many clients do not realize that they are covering the costs of losers at the agency. A Harvard study recently showed that among a hundred ad agencies, some 30 percent of the accounts were carried at a loss. That is, they were carried by the grace of the other clients. The supplier payoffs to ad agencies are perhaps not much different from those in many businesses. In advertising, they are accomplished by the supplier rendering bills that are jacked up. The agency passes these on to his client with his usual markup. Then, eventually, and, of course, quietly, the supplier "refunds" the agency in the form of paid vacations, a leased car, a club membership, or cash in an outside bank. Over the years clients have become wary of these bills and have asked for competitive bids and careful rechecking, and in many cases they have fired their agencies when disclosures were made. Today, this is less easy to get away with.

In the early days of television, when nobody knew how much things cost, there was a great deal of this sort of swindling and overcharging. A single $75,000 TV commercial could involve literally hundreds of incidental expenses. Hundreds of chances for markups that were almost impossible to check or compare. Agencies, however, were not the only guilty parties. Lesser executives in the client's organization were notorious for receiving kickbacks of various forms. Typical was their acquisition of props used in the filming of commercials. When the set was knocked down after the filming, it was a grab-bag operation. Speedboats, sports cars, suites of living room furniture, evening clothes, and so forth "disappeared." The clients, however, finally learned firsthand what it actually cost to make a TV commercial. No longer are budgets of $100,000 and even $200,000 per minute permitted. The average cost today is more like $15,000 to $20,000.

Kraft Foods once complained to J. Walter Thompson over the price charged them for a dozen brownies baked in the J. Walter Thompson test kitchen. At $500, it costed out at $41.60 each.

Secrecy is a crucial element of ad agency-client relationships. Many campaign ideas have been stolen, many new-product ideas adopted, and many major accounts lost over the years because of unguarded actions or loose words. No matter how gravely employees are warned, the slips occur. For example, again and again, ad agency people will use a popular TV studio to shoot a commercial, which is always confidential, and leave the studio scattered with storyboards, scripts, lyrics, and layouts for the next agency to pick up. This happened on one occasion when Chase & Sanborn followed Maxwell House into a studio. Another common security leak happens every week at the big photostat shops in midtown New York that are used by half a dozen big agencies in the neighborhood. In the Grand Central area, for example, agencies using some of the same photostat houses often send junior account executives with good eyesight to pick up stats when they are ready. Kenyon & Eckhardt may not know to this day that their Mercury car layouts are carefully reported from spies watching the stat shop in the Pan Am Building.

Overheard words and sentences have caused many a disaster. Supplier salesmen and publication representatives pick up many of their newsworthy tidbits during rides in trains and elevators. One of the most foolish mistakes happens this way, either on a commuting train or in an elevator of a building housing many agencies. Two agency execs are complaining about an unnamed client. They are very careful to use code words like "our friends in New Jersey" or "those s.o.b.s in White Plains." What they are forgetting is their own identity. It is relatively easy for an eavesdropper to recognize one or both of the talkers. Or if it is a commuting train with many admen on it, it is permissible to ask your fellow passenger if he recognizes one of the talkers. "Oh yes, that's Joe Brown, he works at Smith/Jones agency." The next step is to look the man up in directories or simply phone the agency and ask the telephone operator which account Mr. Joe Brown works on. She'll be happy to oblige.

Sometimes the overheard comments are picked up by the client himself. Once, a Foote, Cone & Belding client, moving through a crowded New Jersey commuting train, passed a seated copywriter from that agency whom he recognized. The copywriter was harmlessly reading a headline from a newspaper ad aloud to his seat companion. The words said in part, "the richest man in the cemetery." These words reached the client just as he passed by. He wheeled on the young man, shouting, "Listen to me, buster, I know you lazy bastards at the agency think I work too hard, but if you don't like it, keep it to yourself!" The copywriter never got a chance to explain the mistaken impression. The agency lost the account.

Another time, a Young & Rubicam copywriter left a whole Goodyear campaign package of ads, including strategy, client call reports, and layouts, in a Lexington Avenue subway. The person who picked it up and returned it to Y&R after carefully looking it over, just happened to be an advertising trade reporter. The story broke into print well ahead of the release date. So many important papers, portfolios, and presentations are left on New Haven railroad cars that the conductors no longer hold them at the Stamford end of the line. They bring them back to Grand Central every morning. The conductors also report that the ad crowd is especially generous with their left-behind bundles of flowers, boxes of cream puffs and goodies, and often perfume and gifts. The trainmen speculate that these were hastily purchased before late train departures by admen who were feeling guilty about something. In any case, the trainmen buy containers of coffee at the end of the line and every night sit down to a hearty snack of left-behind goodies. Since they are seldom called for, the trainmen take the flowers and gifts home to *their* wives.

Some agencies are stricter about security than others. When Marion Harper headed Interpublic, he had a network of spies who reported employees' loose talk. A TV writer was rapped by Marion one day about this. He had mentioned something about a new business prospect to a friend in an adjoining stall in a railroad station men's room. Marion got the word within hours. Herb Davidson recalls that during his working years at Benton & Bowles, printed warnings about security used to come with his monthly paycheck.

Betrayal of new-product secrets can cause serious losses to many manufacturers. In order to prevent this, the company often takes the whole project out of the normal operations and puts it into a venture group, an isolated subsidiary, or keeps it in the hands of an independent new-product workshop for as long as possible. The need for secrecy often becomes a morale problem for people who are left out of the plans. Salesmen, for example, are irritated to find a product made by their company already on the shelves in a test market before they are told about it. The product is being sold in by a special sales force. A promotion executive, for example, at Carter-Wallace laments the fact that he is always the last to know about new products. The reason is obvious: The instant he begins to order promotional material, the word is out.

Using the client's product can sometimes cause trouble. One account executive brought home several samples of a new product, a dessert he wanted his wife to try out. He failed to tell her that it should be kept quiet. The wife, with so much on hand, tried it out on her bridge club. They liked it. One of them asked for the brand name. The wife told this person, not remembering that her husband worked for a rival ad agency. The first husband was on the mat within twenty-four hours.

Clients are often sensitive about the use of their product by the ad agency. Obviously, they are flattered when they see their brand of cigarettes, chewing gum, or candy in the reception room of the agency. Obviously, also, they are irked when they see an agency person using a different brand of cigarettes, beer, or liquor when that person is handling the account. There are many stories of admen caught in embarrassing situations of this kind. One is told by Carl Johnson, recently president of Tinker Pritchard Wood. Carl and Emerson Foote (believed to be the model, in some respects, for the original huckster in the movie), along with two other executives from McCann-Erickson (where they all worked) were entertaining the advertising director of the Spanish Olive Council at the University Club in Chicago. When it was time to order drinks, the client ordered a Spanish sherry, and the agency people, to a man, ordered martinis. Carl glanced toward Emerson, reputedly one of the suave executives in the business, for instructions about what would go in his martini. When it was obvious that neither Emerson nor the other McCann executives were ordering anything but a plain, very dry martini, Carl leaped in and saved the day: "And bring the olives on the side!"

Another story concerns the account executive holding a party in his suburban home; one of the guests was his liquor client. It was a large party, and typical of such bashes, he had bought a case of moderate-priced Scotch, forgetting that his client's famous brand was high-priced Scotch. At the last hour, since it was too late to rush a new order from the liquor store, he sent his youngsters scouring the neighborhood for empty bottles of the well-known brand. He got together five bottles. The contents were quickly switched. The client's brand was prominently on display the entire evening. Nobody, including the client, was the wiser.

Are such things important? They are indeed. At Doyle Dane Bernbach, no creative person is allowed to work on the Volkswagen account unless he really likes the car and approves of the German car maker. Also, none of the ad agencies currently handling cigarette advertising assign people to the account if they are nonsmokers. There are few nonsmoking presidents of agencies with cigarette accounts. Archie Foster (Bates and Brown & Williamson) is a chain smoker. So is Dan Seymour, of Thompson. But Al Seaman (SSC and B and Pall Mall) abstains.

Clients are always disturbed when they see competitive advertising that seems more creative than their own. Recently, the worldwide managers of giant Unilever voiced this complaint and demanded a meeting with their agency, SSC and B-Lintas in London. All fourteen Unilever ad managers were on hand when George Plante, Lintas creative director, presided over the meeting. In the center of the table, before the meeting started, George had set up an enormous red balloon, the biggest he could buy. He then spent an hour telling the ad managers how the agency tried its best to sell creative advertising to Unilever. "The trouble," George said, "is right here in this room. Let me demonstrate what happens to the 'big idea' when all you men are the critics. He reached over and released the mouth of the balloon. George had expected the balloon to deflate, but he wasn't prepared for the long, moist raspberry sound that burst loudly as the last air expired. "It was a frightfully rude noise," says Plante.

Since *creativity* has become a big word in the advertising business, many clients have demanded more and more of it, even when they don't really want it or don't know good creative work when they see it. The cost has been high to ad agencies. Many have rushed out to hire fabulously expensive superstars at the insistence of their clients. The star, and perhaps a team of co-workers, is hired. A fresh batch of new creative work is prepared. The client looks at it and throws it aside. He likes what he has been getting. It was just a whim. This happened to J. Walter Thompson when they hired Ron Rosenfeld and a group of cohorts at a total price of perhaps $200,000. RCA was one of the clients demanding "new creativity." Nothing this top-flight creative team ever prepared for them satisfied RCA. Thompson finally had to give up the Rosenfeld experiment. Somehow the same thing happened at Papert, Koenig, Lois. Clients such as Procter & Gamble and Quaker Oats wanted all kinds of fresh ideas. When they got them, they changed their minds and went back to the safe, square work they had before.

Clients are frequently unreasonable. They will set mad rush deadlines, club and clobber the account man to meet them. Then, the completed work will sit on the client's desk for days, maybe weeks. Or they will ask the agency for "experimental," "standby," "backup" campaigns that are usually little more than make-work exercises. They aren't needed or really wanted. The agency wastes many great creative ideas this way. Not to mention money and the loss of enthusiasm on the part of creative people. Recently, eighty-seven versions of one print ad for a Mustang car were prepared, every one completely done up in finished, comprehensive form. A single TV commercial went through thirty-six new and different storyboards and then six different film variations for International Playtex. For something like fourteen years running, the creative people at Ted Bates prepared a half-dozen new campaign ideas each year for Wonder Bread, only to see them junked every time. And the campaign that ran unchanged for years was recently challenged by the FTC, which alleged (with some truth) that the claims made were unwarranted. An explanation for much of this wasteful, wheel-spinning work is found in the questionable commission system, which gives the client a feeling that the agency is making too much money. "Ought to make them sweat for it."

Clients can also be devious, misleading, and actually untruthful in many of their agency relationships. Not a few have been known to promise ad budgets far in excess of what they intend to spend, in the hope of getting more work out of the agency. Invariably, when an account is being solicited, the budget is 25 to 50 percent more than it turns out to be. Sometimes they end up spending no money at all. Another ploy is to ask the ad agency to work for a year or two on a new product with the assurances that when it goes national, the agency will get all this extra billing and commissions. For many years ad agencies were hoodwinked into this arrangement until it became clear that five out of six new products failed or were never taken into national distribution. Still another gambit used by many clients is the estimated-cost trick. They will insist that the ad agency set a fixed price for a TV commercial or an advertisement before work is started. It must be low, of course. Then throughout the development of the work, the client will constantly change the signals, make costly revisions, reshoot big segments of the film footage, maybe change the model. After all this, when it's time to settle the bill—you guessed it—the agency must stick to the original estimate.

Sadly, one cause for client-agency disagreements is outright lying on the part of both parties. It seems incredible that chief executive officers of major companies and major ad agencies can lie so brazenly. Here is an example of two men lying about the same subject. An editor learned that a certain account was considering a change. He called the company president. "Absolutely no truth in it. We are perfectly happy with our present ad agency." He then called the agency president. "No sir, we are not losing the account. Everything is fine." As it turned out, both parties knew that the account was changing. The agency was resigning it to take a bigger account in the field that would conflict. The company was indeed interviewing new agencies, some at the suggestion of the former agency. Lying to the press is perhaps understandable, but lying directly to one's client or one's agency is inexcusable. A typical lie is when an account is looking for a new agency but does not tell its present shop. Instead, while it is talking to new agencies, as quietly as possible, they are told that the company is planning a new product that will require a new agency. If the old agency learns about the solicitations (as it sooner or later does), it is also told this same story. It is, of course, a lie. There is no new product. The company is talking about the whole advertising account, as the losing agency learns to its surprise and chagrin when it is announced.

An underhanded, if not actually deceitful, practice engaged in by clients is known as "building a case against the agency." Sometimes it is the middle management staff of the client that does not like the agency. Perhaps they inherited it and have another favorite they prefer. The case is built up thusly. Every time the agency makes any error, no matter how small, it is duly noted and recorded by the conspirators. The agency, however, is not informed. They are allowed to proceed as if nothing had happened. After months of this, the evidence is sufficiently strong for the middle management people to take the story to top management and get the agency fired. Had the agency known it was making mistakes, it might well have been able to rectify them and produce good work. It didn't know. It was deceived into thinking it was doing the job correctly.

Agencies play games, too. And the rules are slippery. Some shortchange their accounts in a dozen different ways that eventually, if detected, lead to misunderstandings, disagreements, battles, and final breakups. Many of these have to do with costs and charges. Agencies are often guilty of sloppy accounting, improper billing, fuzzy charges, and overcharges. Who knows how long it takes a creative man to create an ad? Who knows whether so many stats were needed? Who can tell for sure that time wasn't wasted or lost in shooting the commercial? Often the faults are the result of sheer inefficiency. Media bills are not checked for errors. The cost of an engraving or plate might have been much less if someone had used another process. Competitive bids might have reduced the price of a TV commercial. A creative team preferred to shoot a commercial on location when it might have done it cheaper and just as effectively in a studio. Agencies, in defense of these charges, may say that the client's unreasonable demands force them to find ways to make up for lost profits. Whatever, it all adds up to additional causes for disagreements.

In order to balance out this report on agency-client relationships, it should be mentioned that agencies are not always poisoning the clients' wells, that clients are not always slashing the agencies' tires. There are many long and happy relationships. Many friendly give-and-take, fair-is-fair relationships. Coca-Cola stood by Interpublic through long, desperate years of reorganization and rebuilding. Had it left at any time between 1965 and 1970, it is doubtful that Interpublic could have survived. For more than half a century, Kodak and J. Walter Thompson have meshed their interests closely as both have grown. Procter & Gamble—a tough-minded, no-nonsense giant—has nonetheless shown great loyalty to its ad agencies. Firings have been few and far between. Green Giant and the Leo Burnett agency have had a relationship that grew from the time both were tiny midwestern firms. Many clients have gone out of their way to recommend their ad agencies to other companies, thereby helping the agencies to grow. Many agencies have helped their clients in personal, confidential matters such as recommending tax lawyers or Washington contacts. Some big agencies have actually loaned money to promising young companies.

But the fact still remains: There is too much disagreement. Too many breakdowns in communications. Too many divorces between clients and ad agencies. Every loss of an account is serious. A small one of, say, $1 million may be huge to a small ad agency. When a big one of, say, $10 or $20 million plus falls out of bed with its ad agency, the entire business is rocked. When a client the size of Ford, Eastern Airlines, Atlantic Richfield, or anything over $15 million springs loose, the word jumps from phone to phone, local and long distance. It goes from office to office, down corridors, into elevators, out into the streets of Manhattan. Bartenders serve the news with each drink. Taxi drivers often tell it to perfect strangers. The suburbs learn it long before the commuting trains roll homeward. Liquor consumption goes up. Evening meals go untouched. Social events are canceled. A panic cloud settles over the advertising dormitory towns of Westport, Greenwich, Rye,

Scarsdale, and so forth. The repercussions will be widespread, and not only for the people who will lose their jobs swiftly. Agencies cannot afford to retain employees for long after a big loss. But hundreds, even thousands, of other people in the advertising business will be affected shortly. Printers, engravers, media reps, network people, publications, TV production studios, management consultants, research firms, all who have been locked into the previous arrangements. Now they will lose fees, commissions, or other income, as well as close friendships. The dislocations are fantastically wide. In the past several years, these $10-million-plus accounts have switched: Ford Motor, Alberto Culver, Quaker Oats, Falstaff beer, Rheingold (twice), Monsanto, Bristol Myers, American Home, Menley & James, TWA, American Brands, Hunt Wesson, H. J. Heinz, Firestone, Beech-Nut, International Playtex, Chesebrough-Ponds, Gillette, Seagram, Warner-Lambert, Braniff, Miles Laboratories, Pepsi International, Mennen, Clorox, Ralston Purina, and a score of other giants.

Maybe there is no certain hope that agency-client relationships will ever improve to the extent that these traumatic breakups will diminish.

7

How Ad Agencies Get New Business

Fire Island is reached by ferry from the South Shore of Long Island. The boat is a small, open-deck affair. On Friday evening during the summer season, it is so loaded down that passengers expect to be swamped by every wave. Many of these riders are ad people, men and women, mostly singles. They will spend the weekend shacking up in co-ed cottages, sharing sleeping bags on the dunes, or moving in on friends of friends. One particular Friday evening several years ago, there were more than the usual number of ad people aboard the ferry. They were not fun seekers, sun seekers, or sin seekers. They were new-business hustlers. Their quarry: a $5-million liquor account. Or, specifically, a certain Mr. Big who was believed to be the "button," who could say yes or no to ad agency presentations. The liquor account had been loose for weeks. No less than seventy-five ad agencies had been actively pursuing the business.

The lead about Mr. Big spending the weekend at Fire Island with friends came over the Madison Avenue rumor network, toward the tail end of the lunch hour. Actually a few crafty account executives had a fifteen-minute tip-off from their favorite bartenders. No matter, it was an awkward time for most of the agencies concerned with the account. Here it was Friday afternoon, summertime, when some of their best contact men had cut out at noon or were lingering over frosted daiquiris, cold salmon, and cucumber salad, perhaps in the patio dining area of a hard-to-

136

reach bistro. A hell of a time to organize a task force. Yet the rumor was growing. It was now ascertained that Mr. Big would positively be on the Long Island Rail Road's Cannonball Express (an absurd name for one of the slowest trains in America), which was departing the city at 4:19.

The top executive, who had broken off his luncheon at the Yale Club in the middle of a lobster salad to rush back to his office nearby, was not an easy man to get along with under any circumstance. His name was Coxe, and his staff was called Coxe's army. He had already screened his troops and now had two candidates standing in front of him in his enormous corner office.

"Now boys, you've got to get cracking. There's no time to chase your asses out to Westchester to get your luggage. So get over to Abercrombie and Fitch or Brooks Brothers and charge up what you need. Slacks, sports jackets, summer tux, sandals, sunglasses, tennis racket—whatever! But fast—goddamnit—what are you waiting for!"

The two young men barreled out for their equipment. None too soon either, for as one of them reported later, they spotted men from BBDO and Foote, Cone & Belding already there hastily selecting weekend gear. "I recognized the sly bastards right off," he said. "They had that cool, furtive look. You know, the scared-shitless look. They knew the meter was running. You bet your ass they knew."

What happened at Fire Island that weekend? Most of the ad agency hustlers managed to make some contact with Mr. Big during the weekend. One exchanged pleasantries with him on the sun deck of his host's cottage. The adman had just happened by. Another talked briefly with him at a house party. A third reported speaking to him on Sunday morning as he walked his host's dogs on the beach. A fourth faked it out completely. He met a cute chick and never left her side. He reported to his bosses that Mr. Big was using a disguise. A fifth man worried his way through the weekend until finally on Sunday night he spotted Mr. Big in the waiting line for the homebound ferry. He claims that he managed to slip a business card in the pocket of Mr. Big's seersucker jacket. The sixth man, however, scored a hit. He got himself invited to a cocktail party at the cottage where Mr. Big was staying and came away with an appointment for his agency to make a presentation. Although his agency was a late entry into the race, they did get to make a presentation.

Another boat rider, however, had better luck. He was an executive with Ogilvy & Mather en route to England on the old *Queen Mary*. The man was an accomplished bird watcher who knew sea birds as well as land birds. Every day he spent a great deal of time spotting birds and discussing them with his fellow passengers. During the final two days, as they neared England, there were more birds. At this point, the account executive struck up a friendship with another bird-watching enthusiast. The Ogilvy & Mather man was very helpful. "Ah see, an Irish tern—an English black-tipped gull—a Welsh bittern," and so forth. The acquaintanceship ripened over Scotches at the bar. When the *Queen* arrived at Southampton, the account executive had a brand-new account. It was the Mars candy company, with a $3-million budget.

Sound like movie scenarios? They actually happened. And they are tame examples of the efforts ad agencies make to bag new accounts. Many are far more elaborate and take much more time. It is not unusual, for example, for an ad agency to take years pursuing a particular account. J. Walter Thompson spent fourteen years soliciting Schlitz beer and finally got it. McCann-Erickson wooed Miller beer for six years and finally got it by buying up the agency that had it. At a whopping price, too. Charlie Goldschmidt of Daniel & Charles first called on Bristol Myers twelve years ago and got his first assignment only last year. Sometimes it takes years for an ad agency to wangle a membership in a certain exclusive club so they can close in on a few prized members. One young executive had excellent success with this club gambit. Separated from his wife, he discovered that he had a Dutch uncle who was a member of the very posh Knickerbocker Club on upper Fifth Avenue. Since he carried the same family name and the generations of credentials, he moved in. "It was spooky living," he said. "The rooms were like college dormitories, except that they were furnished with expensive antiques and funky pictures. But the big thing was—man!—every member there was on the board of directors of some top corporation. Somebody said over three hundred companies were represented. I discovered that lonely weekends were best for scoring hits. Always found someone dying to chat," he reminisced. Then he added, "We got some beautiful contacts out of that place. Beautiful."

Many hustlers like football weekends and the station wagon tailgate parties in stadium parking lots. "You amble around with a thermos of martinis. It's great hunting." Others prefer the winter resorts. The gambling casinos in the Bahamas are popular now for admen seeking out prospects. Country clubs are getting too crowded. They also tend to be family affairs these days. Yacht clubs are excellent, especially along the Rye, New York–Old Greenwich gold coast. There are others who are true believers in holding offices in charitable, social, or hospital fund-raising organizations. The relationships developed are supposedly more "sincere." Political clubs are no good. Nor school boards. Too much bad blood. Luncheon clubs in Manhattan are fine up to a point, but to be effective, you should change memberships often. For example, the Pinnacle Club on top of the Mobil Building at Forty-second Street invariably will bring together the same crowd (American Home, Lorillard, J. Walter Thompson, Tatham-Laird & Kudner). The Stratosphere Club on top of the Time & Life Building used to be popular with Interpublic executives until that company went public and put the squeeze on expense accounts. The Canadian Club at the Waldorf has long been a haunt of BBDO and SSC and B chiefs. The impressive new Board Room on the top of Three Hundred Park is frequented by Ogilvy & Mather, Bristol Myers, and neighborhood bankers. Benton & Bowles, as befitting an old-line firm, likes the elegant University Club on Fifth Avenue, which is nice on cold winter days when the enormous fireplace in the lobby is blazing brightly. The college clubs are supposed to be genteel places to woo prospects. But there is some risk: The food is apt to be poor; the service, slow.

Haunting certain good restaurants can be fruitful, too. David Ogilvy likes the Côte Basque. The Ted Bates people favor the Baroque and the Twenty One Club. Needham, Harper people in Chicago stake out the International Club in the Drake Hotel. In Washington, D.C., many admen manage to get memberships in the National Press Club, which is nice for entertaining but not so easy for meeting new prospects. This restaurant bit takes a certain amount of patience and tact. You can't simply table-hop to meet someone you'd like to put the arm on. You have to watch for a chance meeting.

Peter Geer, president of the Geer, DuBois agency, got a phone call one Sunday morning at breakfast. It was from one of his clients, Foster Grant sunglasses. Obviously, the president of the firm, Joseph Foster, was worried about something to be calling at this odd hour. As Geer recalls the conversation:

"What is it, Joe?" Peter asked.

"Peter, can you promise me a 10 percent increase in sales this coming year?"

"Well, gosh, Joe, we certainly predict sales will be up. After all, we've just finished all the new advertising. David Hemmings, Leslie Caron, and all the others in the TV commercials. You know, we all thought it's the greatest—"

"Yes, I know, but tell me, can you promise a 10 percent increase in sales? Guarantee it?"

Peter thought over his reply carefully. "Why exactly 10 percent, have you been talking to somebody, Joe?"

There was a slight hesitation on the other end. Then Peter said, "Have you been talking to Marion Harper?"

"As a matter of fact, yes. How did you guess?"

"That's an old ploy of Marion's. He tries it on everyone."

Geer, DuBois still has the account.

New-business hustlers have many private gambits. Jim Henderson, the shrewd and successful president of Henderson Advertising, one of the top shops in the South, swears that the best new-business investment he ever made was to attend a summer executive seminar at Harvard University. "Made contacts that lasted for years," he states. Obviously, the conventions and meetings of the Association of National Advertisers, the American Management Association, the American Marketing Association, and the National Association of Manufacturers are all attended by client types in large numbers. Obviously, too, there will be a sizable pack of agency hustlers on hand. "The trick," says one expert, "is to stand out." He has used such devices as bringing a stunning model along as an escort. She is introduced as "the star in one of our commercials." In an all-male room this works quite well. Another trick is to purloin a press badge (these can be found discarded on a table near the exit). Put this on one of the younger men in your group and let him range around asking questions. Another gambit used by cost-conscious hustlers is to check out all the "hospitality suites" at a convention. These are the ongoing parties with free booze and canapés thrown by publications or media people. They afford you a cozy opportunity to bend elbows with prospects while, of course, freeloading the goodies.

One nifty gambit along these lines was practiced by an old pro, who has since retired. He concentrated on trade shows at the New York Coliseum. Every winter there are about six industry-wide shows that bring to town some of the best prospects. Here's how this pro operated one day at the New York Hardware Show, which attracts a choice gathering of prospects who sell hundreds of nationally advertised products from power lawn mowers to snowmobiles. As he described the situation, "There they are like sitting ducks, right in front of their booths, often the president, the marketing director, and usually the advertising manager. All smiles, all with their mitts out ready to greet you. I never figured out why I didn't have more competition." His modus operandi was simple. He would endeavor to lure as many of these prime prospects as possible into accepting an invitation to a meal at the nearby Essex House, where he had a standby table reserved throughout the show period. "My only problem," he reported, "some days I was too successful." On the day in question, he had eaten three breakfasts, two luncheons, and a five-course dinner.

If this constant search for new business sounds like a drag, you can believe it; it is. Actually, it is more than one man in an agency can do full time. For this reason, most agencies try to impress upon all their senior executives the need to share the responsibility. "Everybody here has to be a salesman, all of the time," says one agency president. He means it, too. An alert executive staff can pick up hot leads in the most unlikely places. Of course, it helps to have long ears to pick up bad news about some account on a train platform. Or it is useful to be skilled at over-the-shoulder speed reading. Many a tip has leaped from the opened briefcase of an unwary commuter to a fellow traveler in the seat behind. The aim is to find trouble in a client-agency relationship before the word gets out. There are many ways this can be detected. The agency is putting in a lot of extra hours of night work. They must be having trouble getting work approved. The agency is hiring a lot of extra free-lancers and moonlighters. Again, the ads aren't acceptable. Friendly media salesmen often bring bad tidings. They spot troubles in the cancellation of ads, deadlines missed, schedules overhauled. Discharged employees are likely to be steeped in venomous reports about client-agency relationships. This is one reason why many agencies grant interviews to all job seekers. It is hoped they will shed some interesting light on the more vulnerable of their former agency's accounts. Employment agents and executive recruiters learn a great deal about accounts in trouble. But if they are pros, they keep closemouthed. The trade press, which is highly competitive in the advertising field, is probing for trouble all day long. And when they find it, it is headline stuff.

Sometimes, though, a client-agency relationship can disintegrate under sudden and seemingly unavoidable circumstances. For example, Ballantine beer, then handled by J. Walter Thompson, came up with a remarkably successful campaign built around the theme "Ballantine watches your beltline." It seemed to have everything going for it. The reduced-calories story could be substantiated. The creative work was bright and pertinent. Sales began to pick up almost immediately. Everything was dandy until the then-president of Ballantine headed off to New Orleans for the national brewery convention. The brewing industry has always been made up of many family-owned companies, most of them German. They are a closely knit clan. The annual convention was always a cordial, convivial reunion of old friends. The Ballantine president, Joseph Brodenhauser, was looking forward to this particular convention. As an old patriarch of the brewing industry, he numbered among his friends several generations of brewers and brewmeisters. Imagine, then, his surprise and dismay when he arrived in the lobby of his New Orleans hotel and was immediately snubbed by a group of brewers from Milwaukee. Not a word of greeting. Cut dead. And this was to go on for the entire three days and nights of the convention. The poor old gentleman was ignored, left out, literally ostracized by friends of thirty- and forty-years' standing. He was hurt to the quick. And he couldn't understand it. No one

142

would talk to him long enough to explain. Until the final day; then one old friend told him, "Mr. Brodenhauser, you see, it's that advertising you are running. It says beer makes people fat. It's not good. Not good for the business. For you maybe—" Mr. Brodenhauser didn't wait for the rest of the sentence. Within minutes, he was on the long-distance phone to New York, firing the agency. A $10-million account zapped in an instant. How would an agency know beforehand that old-family, old-country ties were far more important to their client than sales?

This story indicates why it is important for ad agencies to pursue new accounts so relentlessly. It is that god-awful attrition, the in-and-out, swinging-door hassle of getting and losing billings. At any given week, in almost any season of the year, between a dozen and a score of major accounts are loose. These may range in size from $250,000 to $5 million and more. They will include generally several food accounts, toiletries and cosmetics, proprietary drugs, transportation, and many others who, for whatever reason, change agencies frequently. Additionally in recent years, since companies have restructured into diversified operations, portions of big advertisers may be assigned to agencies separately. There may well be twenty or thirty such projects available at any one time. The loose accounts remain on the make for a period of about two weeks to two months. The shorter period indicates that the advertiser, when leaving his old agency, perhaps had several agencies in mind and will review these only. The longer period means that the field is open. The advertiser then may make a preliminary screening of fifteen or twenty agencies, finally narrowing it down to perhaps five or six finalists who will put on full-scale presentations. Once the word is public, the account is like a bitch in heat. The pack of agencies goes wild.

Some of the less-than-scrupulous advertisers take advantage of this excess of eagerness. They deliberately let scores of agencies pitch them, entertain them, woo them shamelessly. Often their ulterior motive is to learn as much as they can, not about the capabilities of the agencies, but about solutions to their marketing and advertising problems. Agencies are frequently overly generous in giving away ideas and strategies for free. A recent example comes to mind. Perdue Foods, a comparatively new advertiser (which may explain its behavior) accepted at least forty-six presentations by ad agencies over a period of seven months. At one point in this long siege, a new-business executive who had made his agency's pitch and was then given time off for a vacation elected to take his wife to Mexico. In an effort to get away from it all, they trekked far off into the western mountain area of Mexico. One evening, they found themselves in a tiny hamlet where there was only one restaurant. This was crowded, but the proprietor asked another American couple to allow them to share their table. After introductions, they were told that the restaurant had no menu. Chicken was the only meal served. The wife of the newly arrived couple cried out, "Oh God, anything but chicken!" The husband then turned to the other couple and explained. "It is a private joke. I'm in the advertising business, and I have just finished soliciting a poultry account. We've talked about nothing else for a week."

The other couple looked at each other, then broke up. "You, too?" said the man. "Not by any chance Perdue Foods? I've just finished my pitch with them this week."

Advertising is a small world.

Is it really necessary, all this mad scramble for accounts? It is indeed. Avarice is only part of it. Survival is the larger part. In a five-year period, the typical ad agency can expect to lose some 50 percent of its accounts. Replacement alone, then, is enough to keep an ad agency on a permanent panic footing. If, however, they are really cranked up and shooting for the big ball—to acquire the coveted label of "hot shop"—then they really have to bushwhack the boondocks.

Selling the services of an advertising agency has to be one of the most difficult jobs in modern business. If there ever was a more intangible commodity to sell than advertising, it would have to be tied down. Literally, the agency is selling promises. It has no specific evidence that it can produce better advertising for a new prospect than he has been getting. No concrete assets or capabilities that assure the prospect that his qualifications are better than his competitors'. He has only people, and people are available to any agency. "We'll hire whatever you need." Obviously, the agency will try to persuade new prospects on the basis of special expertise

144

in his product field or the success of advertising done for other clients. "Okay, but our problem is different," most companies feel.

You would think that advertising agencies, purveyors of selling and advertising expertise themselves, would be good salesmen and good self-advertisers. Oddly enough, many are hopelessly inept when it comes to promoting themselves. As Pogo put it, "We have met the enemy, and he is us." Unfortunately, some of the most talented agencies, those whose principals are top creative men, are the worst salesmen. They are afraid to make blind phone calls, are uncomfortable in stand-up selling, are likely to become surly and arrogant in the solicitation, and are poor planners. One bright team managed, after a long series of calls, to get itself a very promising invitation to pitch a client. At the appointed hour of their arrival, they discovered that no one had remembered to bring along their presentation material. "We couldn't go on. Without something to show, we were helpless." They simply slipped out of the client's reception room and disappeared. Another agency arrived at its presentation with all of the color slides that were to be used in their carefully rehearsed pitch completely disassembled. They were not only upside-down but backward. After ten minutes, they retired from the field.

On the other hand, some agencies are too aggressive. Just recently, Papert, Koenig, Lois's London office, seeking a meeting with an account that was loose, used this technique. They learned exactly which suburb the key man lived in and his route from his house to his commuting train. They then bought up all available billboard space along this route. The resulting exposure of the man's name displayed so prominently, day after day, irritated him so much that he got the community officials to put a stop to it. PKL got no invitation to pitch. Another aggressive move was made by the Barickman agency in seeking an interview with the Western Union officials when their account was up for solicitations. The creative director sent a crate containing a carrier pigeon whose role was to bring back the invitation for a meeting. It brought back instead a turndown but congratulations for imagination. Other typical showmanship techniques involved sending a team of chorus girls who performed a brief routine for the prospect. This worked once. As did the gimmick used by an agency that sent a plane over a prospect's hometown, trailing a banner asking Mr. Important Man to call the agency's phone number.

Since getting business is so important to ad agencies, perhaps a quick review of the best methods is in order.

1. *Making good ads* that get seen, that get talked about, that produce results, and in doing this, that stimulate prospects into finding out who made them. "Maybe we should call them in." This is, unquestionably, the number-one business getter.

2. *Making news* about yourself. This takes many forms: news about good work you have done for your clients, new services you have developed, new awards you have received, new talent you have hired, studies you have made, new facilities, and so forth. It doesn't take much to get in print in the trade magazines.

3. *Making speeches* and writing articles. It depends upon how good they are, what audiences hear them, how much pickup they get in the trade. The best of these are made to industry groups in which the agency has a special capability. This can lead to accounts right from the crowd.

4. *Making house ads*. Results have always been sketchy, mostly because ads have been self-conscious and written by committees. Good ones, like Burnett's, can help your image.

5. *Making promotion pieces* and mailings. Some of these are excellent and get response. Success depends upon having something important to say, these should not be just a loose collection of ads. Some shops send out newsletters or regular bulletins. These can be effective if they provide a real service. At least they have the advantage of continuity and pave the way for a call.

6. *Making an exclusive study* of a particular product field and coming up with really new findings. Most companies in the field will nibble at this lead. But it had better be good.

7. *Making a study* of a problem company. If you call on the dealers, customers, and so forth and come up with new insights, you may well get a hearing.

8. *Making speculative campaigns*. A costly procedure and pretty much a gamble. Unless you know the client's problem in depth, the spec stuff will probably be off target. Also the type of

prospect that listens to an unsolicited pitch is hardly worth coveting. This belongs way down on the new-business-tactics list.

9. *Hiring a new-business bird dog.* Sounds like an admission of inadequacy, but don't knock it. He is probably a better salesman than any you have in the shop, and a good one can cover a lot of territory. You have to pay him 2 to 3 percent of the first year's net, but for you this might be "found" money. Many service firms (such as designers) depend heavily on these salesmen.

10. *Hire a P.R. man or P.R. firm.* Besides flakking for you, these people can direct business your way. And don't sell the flakking short. Nearly every agency is shortchanging themselves in this area. Let's face it, companies don't do business with agencies they've never heard of. A P.R. person can get your name around, and you need this.

11. *Get a gimmick.* Maybe it is a new kind of research, a new marketing method, a new service such as a TV studio, a media-buying method, a new-product workshop, a corporate-image service, or a product-testing lab. An investment? Yes, but you've got an edge.

12. *Hire some creative stars.* This is more useful in holding business than getting new business, although it adds luster to your name, and prospects buy this. They may claim no interest in awards, but a good man with awards is better than just a good man.

13. *Cultivate referrals.* This means keeping up friendships in the business and making lots of new agency friends. Most good shops have a lot of business they are forced to turn down every year. Who gets it? Respected friends. How many friends have you made this year?

14. *Keep in circulation.* Have people in your shop attend as many trade, business, and advertising events as possible. You need all the contacts you can get, not only among marketing people but among your own agency peers (see referral suggestion above).

15. *Throw a party* once in a while. You and your top executives should get to know the press. The ad press corps is not large, and it's very agreeable to meeting agency people. It may not be worth an immediate story, but it may help you next time you have

news (good or bad). The press, by the way, limited in authority as it may be, is often asked for agency recommendations. If they've never heard of you, how much can you expect?

16. *Do your homework* (or, rather, fieldwork). It's too late to bone up on a field when word comes to you that an account is loose. You've got to know your markets well beforehand.

17. *Keep morale up* in your agency. Enthusiastic, happy workers carry a lot of good will for you throughout the business. Contrariwise, bad mouthers are bad for new business.

18. *Hustle. Hustle. Hustle.* The eager new shops do a lot of this, and often cold-turkey solicitation, just like insurance men or encyclopedia sellers. And it works.

The stories about landing big new accounts are plentiful. Most of these have been overdramatized in the retelling as the years go by. A few recent examples have not been too embellished. The $2-million Virgin Islands tourist bureau account chose Grey Advertising, whose retired chairman Herb Strauss owned a $500,000 property on the Island, over at least two dozen competitors. Or the Cunard steamship line (no longer a giant account but prestigious) moved to Ogilvy & Mather which is headed by ex-Englishman David Ogilvy. Ogilvy today is something of an international figure, with honors from the queen and a château in France, and would be a regular passenger himself on the Cunard ships. He truly abhors flying. Another: The Georg Jensen account is reportedly at the Gilbert Advertising Agency because Doyle Dane Bernbach could not accept it because of a similar account. It was referred to Gilbert, where it happens Bill Bernbach's son works. The Irving Trust bank's advertising is handled by J. Walter Thompson, where, coincidentally, an Irving Trust man is on the agency's board of directors. There are many other liaisons and links involved in getting and holding accounts. This does not, however, imply that these fortuitous arrangements are shady or illegal. All business selling is aided and abetted through friendships and associations of one sort or another. Moreover, in today's competitive marketplace, and with the fishbowl disclosures of the public companies, few relationships survive a dip in sales or profits.

The Benton & Bowles agency, representing the big American Motors account, was in Detroit for a presentation of a new campaign. The meeting was attended by dozens of key executives of the automaker. The advertising was well received. Cheers. Congratulations. Leaving the hall together were the two chief executive officers, Bill Hesse of Benton & Bowles and Bill Blassingame of American Motors, arms over each other's shoulders. Two tough, burly males who saw things eye to eye, man to man. They were laughing. A Benton & Bowles executive directly behind the pair overheard their private joke and remembers the conversation as follows: Blassingame was talking, "Let me tell you a funny thing that happened at the board of directors meeting yesterday. We were talking about advertising and someone got up and said, 'I think we ought to look up a girl called Mary Wells in New York.' Can you imagine that—a girl!" The two men laughed. "Ever hear of her?" Blassingame asked Hesse. "Never!" said Hesse. They went out of the building, chuckling.

Two years later, the front pages of the Detroit newspapers carried the story of the appointment by American Motors of the Wells, Rich, Greene agency. As an indication of how the advertising business goes, Wells, Rich, Greene has just lost the American Motors account to Cunningham and Walsh.

Several recent changes in advertising have made the solicitation of business a more exciting free-for-all. In the past, the big national advertisers almost always assigned their advertising to the handful of big, solid ad agencies. It was a closed, exclusive circle. Unless the ad agency could offer a full range of services, boast of a large staff of creative people, and carry the extra clout with media that only the enormous buying power of the big shops could carry, the chances of even opening a door of a big corporation were slim indeed. The creative revolution, the birth of the media services, and the growth of the brand or product manager system in the big multibrand companies all contributed to a new opportunity for good ad agencies of any size to get a hearing with the big advertisers. This has happened because big companies have become far more resourceful themselves. Today, they no longer need many of the services ad agencies once supplied. They do most of their own market research, write their marketing plans, create their own new products, and test the effectiveness of their own ads; and many are now much more expert at media planning and negotiating. Thus, they look to their advertising agencies primarily for ad making. That is, for creativity. And this is where the creative revolution has made such a profound difference in the advertising business. No longer do the big, blue-chip agencies have a corner on the best creative people. Now they can be found in the small, bright new agencies who offer their creative talents as their foremost product. Many of these smaller shops are run by well-known creative superstars. They can promise not only fine talents but also a closer working relationship with the clients, which is another new desire on the part of the big companies today. This is part of the brand manager system, which places more responsibility on the brand manager to produce sales for his brand. Often these men can pick and choose their own ad agencies without the necessity of the entire company getting involved.

The growth of the independent media services has also made it easier for these smaller, creative-emphasis agencies to get into the big-time solicitations. They are not expected to provide expert media services, which can now be obtained from the independent media-buying services. Nor do they have to supply research or marketing services. In short, they can line up side by side with the biggest ad agencies and be given an equal chance to win the account. Here are some typical recent examples. Small, new Kurtz Kambanis Symon took the $5-million Bic pen account away from Ted Bates. Young and new Rosenfeld, Sirowitz & Lawson took the John Hancock account from big McCann-Erickson. The Project Group, then only ninety days old, took giant Pepsi International ($10 million in billings) from J. Walter Thompson, the world's largest agency. And then there is Kelly, Nason, an agency that limped along for twenty-five years at the $5-million mark until they added a bright creative team and took off. In a year, they nailed five big blue-chip accounts: Campbell Soup, Scott Paper, Johnson & Johnson, Gillette, and Church and Dwight.

You may wonder how companies can stand the pressure of so many solicitations. They really don't mind the attention. It is flattering and sometimes quite pleasant. Invitations to luncheons at fine restaurants, tickets to the theater or sports events; and once the word reaches the trade press, there are continuing stories about the progress of the solicitations. Basking in such a limelight every couple of years at agency-switch time isn't all that hard to take. The actual presentation of the pitch, however, is something else. The field is eventually narrowed down to perhaps six agencies. They will be invited into the company's offices to put on their presentations. The meetings will be attended on the prospect's side by about half a dozen people, top management, marketing, and advertising executives. The running time: between one and two hours. Sometimes the agencies are actually lined up in the reception room, ready to follow each other's acts. Even with a few new gimmicks added, nearly every agency's new-business pitch is excruciatingly alike, a repetitive parroting of old clichés, old promises; and sometimes even the flip charts are dog-eared. A ballet in tedium.

The spiel is so pat that any presenter could pitch it with a lip-sync tape recorder. It generally goes like this: "First, we are only interested in *one* thing, *selling your* product." Hurrah. "Before we start anything, we study your product thoroughly." How else can you start? "We want to know your product better than you do yourself. Then we want to study *your* market *in depth*." Or it could be "with all its parameters." "We want to be your *partners*. Your problems are our problems. If you get rich, we'll get rich." Smile. "Now, about *creativity*. We are considered a very creative agency, even '*hot*,' *but* we aren't ego trippers. We couldn't care less about awards." The prospect couldn't have missed the awards on display in the agency's foyer. "Our creative men love to make ads that *sell*. In fact they are damn good businessmen in their own right." When it comes to salary. "Everybody here likes hard work. Why, we have to kick them out at night." Try reaching someone at 4:30 any day. "They even work on weekends on their own time." The creative men are shooting home movies against the time when they can chuck the business and go to Hollywood. The account men are making important contacts at the country club. "We are considered very strong in *marketing*. Quite possibly one of the strongest marketing agencies for our size in the business." Actually this means they have one client who gets Nielsen Reports and an account executive who visited a shopping plaza last spring. Plus, of course, the valuable experience of food shopping with their wives a couple of times a year. "We also believe in research. We research everything." That is, if the client will pay the tab for the outside research firm. "Even our creative people love research. They don't fight it." Ha. "We also consider ourselves a *full-service agency.*" They may have only twenty people on staff, but they'll say this with a straight face. "We meet *all* your needs no matter what." They will get tickets to *Jesus Christ, Superstar!* "And, another thing, we love to do sales promotional crap"—slip—"we mean sales promotional material. Every bit of it." At 33 percent markup. "And we love new products. We're inventing them all the time." Like a candy bar in the shape of an astronaut. Then, rushing on, since enthusiasm is supposed to count more than anything else. "We think there is too much *superficial* advertising these days, stuff done just to please other creative people. Not here. No, sir. We stick to *basics.*" Good old brass knuckles.

These platitudes use up the first hour. It was supposed to have knocked off competitive agencies. Now it's time to flash a few things. New presenters take over. Wrappers come off. "We've been looking over *your* problem." Which means they've collected a batch of competitive ads and commercials. "The trouble with all the advertising in your field is it all looks alike." Great new insight. "And none of it *sells hard* enough." Hard sell means stretched claims, black type, spurious demos. "Why? Because they don't *understand* Mrs. Middle Majority Consumer with two and half kids. *We* do. In fact, we just made a focus-group study of your product field." They got together a handful of housewives and taped the session. Every agency does this. "And we've done a little preliminary research." The library got together a few trade articles, and somebody called the industry association, whose latest figures are at least two years old. "And"—get ready, Mr. Prospect —"we think you need a *whole new approach.*"

The creative act that comes on now is given with almost blushing modesty: "Nothing but a few very rough ideas. Just to show you how we think." Actually the work is very slick and may even include full-blown commercials. Of course, it is way off target but apologies are made. "Just very preliminary thinking, you understand." Then comes the agency reel, as the lights go down. This will include every award winner, no matter how remote in time or geography (Dublin, Ireland, Honorable Mention, 1959; West Texas Art Directors Festival, 1964; and so forth). The reel is played a few decibels too loud, so that with the final curtain and stiff good-byes, the agency team can barely hear the words, "We'll let you know."

This implies that there is an attempt at least toward order and purpose in a new-business pitch. Actually, there seldom is. There are last-minute changes or the appearance of a ringer in the audience (often a management consultant hired by the client "just to listen"), or perhaps someone has learned that the agency which pitched the day before used a sex-pot fashion coordinator in their show who apparently scored points. Or things go wrong. One ad agency arrived in Houston, Texas, ready for a scheduled appointment to pitch Braniff International, and found that the whole presentation was lost. Actually lost by Braniff itself on the flight down.

Ad agencies have always deplored the cost of speculative presentations. Actually, everything about a pitch is speculative, but it is the cost of elaborate dog-and-pony shows that rankles. Some of these do get fantastic. Now that color TV is almost a standard media unit, it is hard to show a creative idea without the expensive filming, editing, and production of commercials. This can be $5,000 to $10,000 for a single "quick and dirty" as the trade calls these first-run epics. Some presentations have cost ad agencies over $100,000 in time and materials. Only to lose out. Are these presentations necessary? Perhaps they are in some cases. But surely they do not have to be as expensive as some of them have been. The prospect does find it useful in making his decision to see what approaches the new agencies will take with his problem. He can learn a great deal, which accounts for the furious note-taking at these meetings.

There has been a trend in recent years among responsible advertisers to offer a presentation budget of, say, $5,000 to cover the costs of "seeing ideas." It is a fair and hopeful beginning because the high cost of solicitations in the long run must be deducted from the agency's operating costs. This might well be a detriment to other clients in the agency. On the other hand, some advertisers explicitly state that they do not want any of the soliciting ad agencies to show speculative creative work. Some, in fact (like Menley & James, when recently reviewing agencies for its

$10-million Contac account), point with great pride to the fact that "no presentations were expected, none were made!" The president of this firm, Peter Godfrey, received much praise throughout the trade for his stand. However, one trade paper pointed out that the agency which landed the account did indeed "present." They had actually prepared filmed commercials of a "for instance" nature, as well as selling lines and strategies. The revelation of this by the trade paper greatly annoyed the president. He denied it totally until the trade paper editor carefully reconstructed the full minutes of the meeting.

At some point in the courtship of an account, the prospect visits the agency premises. This is a sort of meeting-the-family ritual. It is always done with elaborate protestations of informality. "We don't care if you work out of a loft, as long as the work is good." The visit, however, is crucial, or it is regarded as such by the nervous ad agency. It's akin to the strip-down physical exam before getting hired. And it has, on occasion, been just as humiliating. Such as the time when the word had not been passed around to the typing pool that the prospect was coming through one agency's offices during the noon hour. Everything was in great shape throughout the general office tour until the party got to the president's office. When the door was opened, out poured a crash of acid rock music, a chorus of laughs and shouts, and the heady smell of hot pizza pies. The typing pool and some of the boys from the art department were enjoying their lunch hour.

The right impression is so hard to create legitimately that a pattern of permissible fake-outs has evolved. For example, all agencies, but especially young ones, place great store on head counts. The more employees in sight, the more successful you supposedly are. To accomplish this effect when the prospect is due to arrive, there are several time-honored ploys. First, the office temps who can be hired by the hour. (Better screen them first, some of the temps look like they came from a computerized dating bureau.) Next, friends, relatives, printing salesmen, free-lancers, and space reps can be called in to occupy desks, dash through corridors, or poke heads into the meeting room. One sensible agency has a more permanent arrangement. It rents out the center well of its office to a nearby CPA firm. The clutch of girls busily working on their tax forms are coached to smile at visitors. Another up-scale shop hires only model agency temps for client visiting days. The regulars are told to take the day off, copy test some ads in Grand Central, or do some research at the library while the models try to act out their roles behind the desks. This is all permissible. Hell, many can remember the pleasant telephone receptionist at Wells, Rich, Greene during their incubation stage. She sounded too good to be true. She was. She was Mary Wells's mother, in from Ohio.

Another familiar fake-out is the office itself. Often it doesn't exist. One executive suite at a posh midtown address houses five "offices" of ad agencies. These really are slender reeds. One switchboard operator sings out the name of the desired agency and informs callers that Mr. Big can't be called out of a meeting. Another, more deluxe, arrangement features an ultrachic reception room (thick pile wall-to-wall, funky oil paintings of Cutty Sark ships, muted lighting, deep-seated crinkle leather sofas and chairs), and this adjoins an equally atmospheric book-lined conference room. The books are not fakes, they are real Zane Greys. Somewhere in back is a warren of cubbyholes from which the agency principals sweep out to greet the prospect and usher him into the conference room. There is only one hang-up: You have to book a week in advance for the conference room. Along the same lines is the Chinese puzzle office. Basically, this is the company within the company within the company. One such operation houses three agencies, a trade magazine, a travel agent, several itinerant creative men, and a tax consultant. The phone is answered by a number. In effect, you are asked, "What agency do you want? We have a nice assortment."

The fake executive office is another ploy. Some agencies have one superchic standby office that is called the *floating executive's* office. By prior arrangement, the new-business contact man, who might ordinarily sit in the Xerox room, meets his prospect in this plush stakeout. He gets in early, puts suitable ads on the corkboard wall, spreads out his material, spots an office "temp" at the desk outside, and usually has a happy and successful meeting. But one such arrangement boomeranged. An incoming phone call for the prospect was inadvertently switched into the office. The new-business exec politely left the room, during which time the prospect began searching for a pencil and paper to write down a message. Everything—desk, file cabinets, chests—was totally empty. Nobody knew what happened actually. The prospect left at the end of his phone call and was never seen again.

Moving up to more sophisticated levels of permissible fake-outs is the one called the *missing partners*. Many a prospect who became a client may have often wondered whatever happened to those smart, persuasive gentlemen that sold him on the agency in the first place. He might well suspect that they are working on some other account—a typical ruse. But he would be wrong. They never worked for the agency at all. They were executive temps. These are available on short notice. They are noted for their fast pickup of your agency pitch, eager team spirit, and great stand-up salesmanship. As long as you are in this bag, you might as well staff up. Some good exec temps, including one stunning woman P.R. director, can show up in ten minutes.

At other times, the location of new-business pitches is at the client's. Some have been made in hotel suites, Pullman drawing rooms, stadiums, company cafeterias, and small theaters rented for the occasion. Ab White, a copy pro, tells of a couple of pitches out West that set a sort of precedent. Ab and his team, from an agency named Mogge-Privett, arrived in Las Vegas late one evening to pitch the New Frontier Hotel account. There were six finalists, and all were on hand at the hotel. The client laid down the ground rules. Each agency was to make its presentation in the hotel's Little Church, a chapel on the New Frontier's property that specialized in quick marriages. Ab remembers that his was the fourth of six presentations, all using the church altar for the lecture. After each presentation, the agency team would head for the hotel's casino. It seemed the logical place to await the decision that was to be handed down after 2 A.M. Naturally, they gambled. Naturally, they lost. All of them, even Ab's agency, which, however, won the client's hand.

Another unique new-business presentation was for the Wenatchee Apple Growers Association of Washington State. The agencies were all asked to make their presentations on a Saturday afternoon. It seemed like an odd time, but that was explained when the competing agencies arrived, complete with charts and flip sheets. The four agencies were shepherded to a grove outside Wenatchee, where several hundred apple growers and their families were having an annual picnic. "There they are," the representative said. "Pitch your stories to them. They pay the bills." Each agency in turn presented his case to the eating, drinking, horseshoe-pitching crowd from the bandstand. The account went to the agency whose presenter, they said, had a voice like an evangelist.

The large conference room was nearly full when David Ogilvy, the principal speaker, arrived. It was a new-business pitch. About half the people in the room were agency people; the other half were from the client organization. Before taking over the pitch, David discreetly asked one of his subordinates who the key individuals in the client group were. A few whispered suggestions were made, "a man in a mustache," "the one in the glasses," and so forth. David nodded and began his spiel. Almost immediately the Ogilvy men present saw that something was wrong. Notes were passed. Tugs at David's sleeve. But Ogilvy would permit no interruption. He had by this time fastened his full attention to one of the several men present with mustaches. "You'll agree with me, I'm sure," he says pointedly to his target listener. "Your problems will be our problems—" The listener squirms uncomfortably. David bears down harder. There is no diverting him until the end of the meeting.

David spends as much time as possible at his French château. He is not altogether familiar with the people in his large office. He has, then, just spent nearly an hour of persuasive selling addressing a distinguished man in a mustache, who, it turns out, works in his own research department.

8

How to Get Ahead in Advertising

IT WAS A TYPICAL Friday evening cocktail party, one of those spontaneous get-togethers of young ad people at an Upper East Side Manhattan apartment. Among the young group, there was a bright, good-looking girl, graduate of a good New England college. She was already well on her way to a successful career as an agency copywriter. The conversation got around to how hard it had been for the various people there to break into advertising. The young lady, without meaning to be dramatic, simply asked, "Did any of you ever eat a pigeon?"

If advertising is such a rip-off racket, such a god-awful rat race, a prostitution of talents, why does it still fascinate, still attract an eager, almost desperate group of applicants?

It has always been hard to get a job in advertising, especially a creative job. And especially in an ad agency. For one thing, there simply aren't that many openings available. It is a far smaller business than is generally supposed. The world's largest ad agency, J. Walter Thompson, employs about 400 creative people in its New York office. The next ten largest agencies average about 250 creative people each. The next fifty may employ perhaps 5 to 10 each. Many of the others are literally 1-man shops. So all told, perhaps there are 5,000 creative people working in American ad agencies. Counting all the other jobs in ad agencies, right down to the retired fireman who works in the mail room, the whole business may add up to 50,000 people. Hell, there are four times that many computer programmers. Remarkably, this small group of people is responsible for the creation and placing of some $10-billion worth of national advertising annually.

The scarcity of openings in ad agency creative departments always comes as a special surprise to young people who have spent a few years doing something they consider valuable experience for advertising. Teaching English, instructing in fine arts, working in a publishing firm, or teaching creative writing at a university. They and their friends apparently have been telling themselves, "Well, we can always get a job in advertising. It's a complete sellout, of course, but it would be an easy way to pick up some big money for a few years." The confrontation, should they deign to make this move, is an enlightening experience. One young man with a master's in fine arts had just come from an interview with an ad agency. "They asked me if I wanted to be a paste-up boy in the bullpen, for God's sake!" Later, when he conceded that he might have to take this demeaning position, he lost out to someone else who had previous paste-up experience.

The right attitude has a lot to do with getting a job and holding it. The candidate ought at least to believe that the business has a legitimate place in the economic scheme of things. At least suffer a certain tolerance for its existence. But maybe this is more than the typical young college graduate today will concede. To nine out of ten young people today, advertising is a great con game, a big baloney business, a complete fake-out. You even hear this among those who are studying the business. The editor of a trade paper was asked to lecture to a graduating class of students at a top-ranking New York art school recently. During the question-and-answer period, he heard comments like: "You've got to be kidding, who believes all that horseshit!" "You've got to be out of your skull to take it seriously." You listen to these kids, then you look at the applicants backed up in the reception rooms of ad agencies. A Woodstock scene. What gives? Well, maybe they ran into ex-classmate Joe the other day, just back from the Coast, where he was shooting commercials. Or they see Al, who used to get only a few bucks for writing long articles in the *Village Voice* and who now earns $30,000 a year in a high-rise office building uptown. Or they bump into old friend Jim, who also moved uptown. He's on his way into Charley O's saloon wearing a London-cut double-breasted suit, a Cardin shirt, with a Bill Blass tie, and Italian blocked half boots. On his arm is a lissome model. It gets to them. A kind of gut feeling.

Actually, the conversion is not that easy. Not all who get into the business like it or stay with it. Some of them do indeed take the bread for a while and then chuck it. Israel Horowitz, a writer, did very well in a top agency for a while, but his heart was in playwriting. He quit and turned out some good stuff, including *The Indian Wants the Bronx*, and *The Strawberry Statement*. Norman Wexler stayed in quite a few years and then chucked it to freelance. His latest success is the movie *Joe*. Helen Gurley Brown, now successful editor of *Cosmopolitan* magazine, was one of the top ad writers on the West Coast for many years. Some ad people, seemingly without conflict, combine their job with an outside interest. Stan Ragoti, a top TV commercial maker, really prefers movie making, but he is so valuable to his firm, Wells, Rich, Greene, that his boss Mary Wells Lawrence set up an arrangement where he can do both. His feature movie *Dirty Little Billy*, based on the Billy the Kid saga, will be released through Warner Bros.

The smart advertising agencies hire some of these youngsters knowing full well that many of them are anti-Establishment, anti-business, and anti-advertising. The agency, however, is interested in talent, not ideology. Moreover, ad agencies have always been hotbeds of independent and liberal thinkers. Creative people, especially, are generally Democrats and often New Left advocates, so much so that during election years, it is always hard to find an ad agency to handle campaigns for Republican or Conservative candidates. Often, in fact, the creative people working on these campaigns are somewhat less than enthusiastic about the candidate or the party. Norman Herwood, the copywriter who wrote the Nixon line "This time vote like your whole world depended on it" was and still is a liberal Democrat. On the other hand, however, Leo Burnett, agency president and midwestern Conservative, was true to his feelings when he wrote the line for Goldwater, "In your heart, you know he's right." Actually, for those people in ad agencies who are dedicated to social causes, there are plenty of opportunities to work on volunteer campaigns for the some 250 organizations handled by agencies through the Advertising Council. These causes range all the way from help for the handicapped to drug addiction. The zeal and spirit they put into these public service campaigns is remarkable. Milt Gossett, the young president of Compton Advertising, recently talked about their campaign to stem drug addiction among young people. "The guys worked day and night, weekends on their own time, and often at their own expense. They visited ghettos, schoolyards, rehabilitation centers. They talked with parents, teachers, public-health officials. All before they sat down to write the ads and commercials." Their dedication and the resulting advertising won the group a White House citation and personal congratulations from President Nixon.

Two other creative people at Doyle Dane Bernbach found time on the job and encouragement from their bosses to accomplish a notable public service. The two, Charles Kollewe and Bert Steinhauser, were so upset by Congress's refusal to appropriate money for rat control in ghettos that they did something about it themselves. They sat down and prepared a full-page ad with the provocative headline, "Cut this rat out and put it on your child's pillow tonight." The enormous, ugly rat (life-size) was surrounded by a dotted border to suggest clipping it out. The copy urged people to write to their congressmen. Thousands did, and the bill was returned to the floor and passed overwhelmingly. The two young men paid for the ad's placement in the newspapers themselves, some $6,000 out of their own pockets. Carl Ally and his people did the same kind of thing when they got sick and tired of air pollution in New York City. They also prepared their own advertising and paid $40,000 for running it. The result was the formation of a group of active citizens who started things moving to control pollution in the city. There are so many cases like these that it would take pages to enumerate them. The fact is, advertising agencies afford plenty of chances for dedicated activists to apply their talents and concerns toward helping solve social problems.

Aside from the right attitude, job getting requires more specific evidence. "What have you got to show?" "How do we know you are any good?" "What have you done lately?" It's the same old hang-up, true in show business, true in a lot of businesses. "Get some experience first, then we'll hire you." The advertising business is tougher on this than many other fields. First, because only the few top agencies have anything resembling a training program. And even these big companies are having second thoughts about them. They've discovered over the years that they have been training people for jobs somewhere else. Second, advertising is a highly specialized field. Everyone is some kind of a pro. A media pro, copy, art, marketing, and so forth. And third, it is a service business. Ad agencies spend somebody else's money, the advertiser's.

They can't legitimately train young people at their clients' expense. It's too important. Too costly at $55,000 for a page in *Life* magazine. You can't let some kid practice on these jobs. In times past, there was the old mail room launching pad for young male tyros. The cream of the Ivy League crop assembled here every June and waited their chance to move into an opening, wherever it happened in the agency. There were some pretty classy mail rooms for a while there. They included scions of great families, independently wealthy young yachtsmen and polo players, maybe a ringer occasionally who was merely class president from the University of Michigan. But this is long gone. The elite mail room graduates didn't have the right feel for the business.

Many of the successful men and women in advertising today came from entirely different fields. Dan Seymour, head of J. Walter Thompson, was a top-ranked radio and TV announcer. David Ogilvy earned cordon bleu credentials as assistant chef in a famous Paris hotel. (Recently, when David Ogilvy applied for citizenship papers in France, the millionaire adman listed his occupation as "cook.") George Lois was a semipro basketball player and magazine-cover illustrator. Dolf Toigo worked in the southern Illinois coal fields. Mary Wells Lawrence, now the highest-paid woman exec in the United States ($325,000 per year) worked in a Columbus, Ohio, department store. Paul Chusid, president of Grey Medical Advertising, was a jazz musician. Dick Gilbert was a radio time salesman. Bob Healy was a corporation lawyer. Stan Tannenbaum worked for six years in the Philadelphia post office. All these people are now presidents or chief executive officers of leading ad agencies. In general, the creative people come into their first job with ad agencies after some previous working experience. Many of them have had retail advertising experience with department stores. Others, with sales promotion departments of companies. Some of the copywriters have journalism or publishing backgrounds. Among the art directors and writers are many who tried to make it on their own. Gene Case, now a partner in the successful Case and Krone agency, spent two unfruitful years in Rome trying to write novels. Alex Kroll, creative director of Young & Rubicam, played pro football and tried writing on the side. Carl Spielvogel, now a top man with Interpublic, was a columnist for the *New York Times*. Arnold Grisman, creative director of J. Walter Thompson, wrote novels with moderate success before coming into advertising. Bill Free, head of his own agency, also spent some years abroad trying to become a successful artist. Warren Pfaff, now head of his own firm, was once a Broadway set designer.

Recommendations count a lot in landing jobs. Creative directors who know each other well seldom mislead each other. They know how important it is to get a reading on someone before hiring. It's that pig-in-a-poke thing. Here are some not-so-good recommendations passed along by creative directors.

"He's fine if you keep your eye on him. We never had much trouble, except that one time out in Detroit when he barfed all over an ad manager. He had too many stingers at lunch. Otherwise, you know, he can write."

"He's a nosy bastard. Reads everything he sees on other people's desks. Got caught one day when the copywriter came in on him. The guy was so mad he decked him."

"It's up to you . . . he's tough on account men. Hates them on sight. He's been known to throw containers of coffee."

"A damn fine art director. Good design. Good concepts. Works hard. Maybe not so good in meetings. He farts a lot."

Obviously, personality tidbits such as these are worth knowing ahead of time. It doesn't, however, mean that the man won't get the job. The barfer and the farter above both got the jobs they were seeking. After all, good creative men are expected to have a few hang-ups.

In theory, creative people are hired mainly on the basis of their proof book of ads and sample reels of commercials. Artists, on the basis of their portfolios. It would hardly be fair to judge them on appearances. Often the boys arrive for their interview in faded blue denim work clothes, field boots, and shoulder-length hair. The girls might appear in gingham pioneer dresses and walk around the office in bare feet. Neither boy nor girl will come on strong in personal salesmanship. They are usually shy, nearly always sensitive, and often utterly inarticulate. So the samples they have to show are everything. Never mind if the beginner's portfolio contains little more than a batch of poems, some unsold short stories, and yellowed clips from a college or underground newspaper. Often this is enough if the interviewer knows talent and can see promise. It is actually harder to judge the more experienced applicants. They have by this time learned to present themselves with more flair. Their garb might still be somewhat freakish, but it is hip and proper for ad agency environments. They have also learned a few of the current buzz words and phrases that demonstrate their knowledge of the contemporary ad scene. Now their samples are far less modest, in fact, not modest at all. And here is where the hitch comes. How can the interviewer be sure that all the impressive four-color ads, the brilliant reel of TV commercials, and the samples are truly the work of the applicant. The plain fact is, probably half the stuff shown is "borrowed," faked, or swiped from work done by others in the applicant's previous agency associations. Everybody knows this, but nobody knows how much. Occasionally, an interviewer actually runs into his own ads or commercials. Still, the sample book is the only thing aside from personal recommendations that the person doing the hiring has to go on. Counterfeit or not, it counts.

The importance of the sample book has grown so much over the years that one enterprising creative director, Bill Casey, decided to go into the business of helping people put together sample books and portfolios—for a price. A nifty price, too: $350 each. Bill figured it ought to be worth the high fee. And he figured right. He ran a regular mill for several years, turning out top youngsters with reliable sample books. BBDO and several other agencies hired his graduates straightaway. Casey was the right man for this kind of operation. As a creative man who had waltzed through fourteen jobs in sixteen years, each one better than the last (he was then in the $80,000-a-year bracket), he had seen a lot of faked books in his day. He was also aware that the situation had gotten so out of hand that star copywriters, including several from Doyle Dane Bernbach, were peddling proof books around town in the hands of their wives. The men made up the books, the wives got the jobs. They held them, too, if they were smart. That is, if they just looked smart during the daytime and brought home the assignments for their husbands to do at night. It was a neat fiddle. Two salaries. Two damn good salaries.

Bill Casey's Copy Course (or proof-book mill) doesn't exist any longer. Bill is off running his own creative service now for a group of blue-chip clients. His last graduation exercises, however, are worth recounting.

In addition to being a brilliant creative man, Bill Casey is also a hot-tempered Irishman. This got him into nany knockdown fights throughout his years in the business. One of these came on the night of the last graduation exercises. It should have been a nice evening for Bill. The June weather was balmy. He was all primed for his graduation speech, and he had picked a well-known creative executive, John Nelson, to help him pass out the diplomas. The two of them in fact passed a pleasant half hour in a Third Avenue saloon while waiting for the graduates and friends to assemble in the school headquarters a block away on East Forty-eighth Street. When it was time to go, they ambled down the sidewalk ready for the exercises. About a hundred yards away they came in sight of a busy figure blocking the school entrance. A gardener was trimming the hedges right at the front door. Incensed, Casey ordered the man to leave.

The gardener, who didn't understand English very well, didn't respond fast enough to satisfy Bill. Cusswords and, soon, fists began to fly. John Nelson, prime witness to this, later reported, "Bill might have won his point except that the gardener began swishing the air around Bill's ears with his long-bladed clippers. Bill took off, heading west on Forty-eighth Street, with the gardener hot on his heels. Every ten feet or so Bill would toss a garbage can or a flower pot under the gardener's feet to slow him down. But the clippers were swiping closer. Bill was saved by a brace of police cars that stopped the fight at the end of the block. He and the gardener were packed off to the local precinct house to cool off." Nelson, the guest, got stuck with running the whole graduation ceremony.

Job applicants have some other problems. Many times they get no farther than the reception rooms, where they are handed an application blank and told to mail it in. That is the end of that. Other times, if they have a sample book, they are told to leave it for a few days, then call back. This is dandy for the poor guy who has to sit in a YMCA or on a park bench while his book is being considered. Usually it is returned to him with no comment, not a word at all. Others are often victims of the old tests-of-ability gambit. The agency's position is, "We don't know how good you are, would you mind taking a little test on creativity?" Some of these are not little; they look like college entrance exams. Others are hypothetical assignments to prepare ads on make-believe products. It is a ridiculous way to test a person because no good ads can ever be written without full information about the selling problem. And some of these, the tricky ones, are not hypothetical at all. They are real assignments for real products that the agency handles. The young applicant, obviously eager to prove himself, may spend days working up new ideas on these products. Once in a while some of them are real winners. He doesn't get the job, but sometime in the future he may note a curious coincidence. His ideas, which weren't good enough to get a job, are nevertheless good enough to appear in print or on the air. Not a few ad agencies have been bilking applicants with this gambit for years.

Ben Colarossi, when creative director at Ketchum, MacLeod & Grove, turned down a copywriter's headline. Months later, the copywriter saw the same words in an ad Ben was taking complete credit for. When he pointed it out Ben replied, "What the hell are you talking about? You only had the headline!"

A new wrinkle to this brain-picking ploy showed up recently. A new research firm thought it had discovered a brilliant way to sell new-product ideas to major companies. The system: advertise in the *New York Times*, "Top Positions for Copywriters." When the letters of application came in—and many came because it was a soft market—the firm picked a dozen or so of the best candidates and invited them in for interviews. In the course of the interview, the applicants were told that in order to qualify they were expected to produce a bunch of new-product ideas, "maybe twenty or thirty" each. The various chosen candidates were given different product assignments: cosmetics, snacks, and the like. As the ideas came back—and there were excellent ones because these jobless people were top pros—the research firm began to inform major companies that they had a wealth of ideas they were ready to sell. Major companies, always needful of new-product concepts, began to sign up with the research firm. Everything looked peachy for the firm.

They had an inexhaustible supply of free talent. They ran a new ad each week. They had clients. They were very much in business. Until a trade paper, learning of the fraud through one of the unhappy copywriters, printed the full story. The bubble popped quickly.

Applicants also are often the victims of unscrupulous employment agency practices. A few examples will suffice. Often these employment agencies advertise jobs they don't actually have. The objective: to bring in highly qualified applicants whom they hope to sell once they have them signed up on their application contract. Other times, they get a call from a person who is unhappy in his job but hasn't told his bosses. He is trusting the employment agency to keep an eye open for something better. The agent, however, misusing this trust, immediately calls the applicant's boss and tells him that he will soon be needing a new person, "Joe is leaving." Joe gets axed fast. The agent gets a job to fill. Another gimmick: Employment agents make deals with supervisors who hire people. They may, for example, split the fee. "You hire my man, and I will share the fee the applicant pays me." The person getting the job may find that he loses it just as soon as the time period for refunds elapses. Then the agent and the supervisor bring in another sucker. It would be unfair to leave the impression that these practices are prevalent. They happen, but rarely. The ad agency field has many really dedicated placement agents who not only have helped individuals throughout their careers but have helped many ad agencies solve extremely difficult and important personnel problems.

A hard-working but relatively poorly paid woman in one employment agency interviewed an aging executive one day. The man, who had once held top jobs, was literally so down and out that he simply didn't have money in his pocket to go out to Connecticut for an interview the woman had set up for him. She gave him $10 of her own money and went without lunches for a few days. She didn't expect to hear from the man again, and since he didn't get the job, she forgot about it. A few years went by. Then she heard not from the man she befriended but from a law firm. Her $10 had grown to $10,000, paid to her by the man's estate. He had gone on to Texas and done quite well before he died. He didn't forget.

The early years in advertising can be frustrating. The beginner finds that no one has time to guide or instruct him. The assignments he gets are typically the tedious, boring, full-of-detail jobs. Catalog pages, brochures, radio commercials, package inserts, or a trade ad in *Pit and Quarry* or *Dog World*. He also finds that he doesn't have much clout with the various departments whose help he needs to get his job done. Art directors are always busy on bigger things, the production department puts off his typesetting or engravings till last. He has trouble getting his creative supervisor to sit still long enough to approve or disapprove his copy. He seldom gets in on the big meetings with clients or in conferences where strategy and plans are set. Typically, he finds a fourth carbon on his desk with little more than the briefest of information. (Size of the ad, publication, client, brand, and due date.) The junior creative people don't have secretaries, often don't have offices (desks out in the open or cubbyholes are typical), are seldom known by name to any but few of their immediate associates. They get paper and desk supplies from the office manager or supply room, change their own typewriter ribbons. It is a lonely, solitary existence. It is also quietly and intensely competitive. The other junior creative people are fighting hard to survive and advance. They are not likely to be friendly or cooperative. He also learns early in the game that many of his early contributions go unnoticed or, worse, that his superiors or peers grab the credit for them. This is a constant and shameful practice in ad agencies. You would think that when creative men advance up the ladder into positions of authority and power, they would not feel the need for stealing credit from juniors. But they do. Perhaps the reasons are vanity, aggressive drive, or lack of self-confidence. Often the executive creative man is frustrated. He now spends so much time in meetings and away from his typewriter or drawing board that he becomes uneasy, unsure of his talent. To cover himself in management's eyes, he appropriates credit for the ideas of his underlings.

One creative director did this so consistently that he finally did himself in. He had been telling management that all the good ideas that came out of his staff of twenty people were his, entirely his, from origination to full concept. This went on for a year or so until a business recession came on the scene. Top management called a meeting of the department heads in view of taking some stringent economy steps. They began with the creative director. "Michael," the chief executive officer said, "well, this ought to be easy with your department. Since you are the one who thinks up all the good ideas anyway, we ought to be able to wipe out nearly your whole staff. Apparently they are a bunch of drones back there. Can't imagine why you hired them in the first place. But, anyway, starting Monday, cut the staff 50 percent." The creative director had no choice. He himself was cut within three months.

The early satisfactions and gratifications come slowly. An account executive comes by the cubbyhole one day and says, "Say, Bob, that little brochure you did a while back. You remember?" You bet your butt Bob remembers; it took him three weeks of hard work. "Well," the account man continues, "the client says it's doing a pretty good job. I think it pulled a few thousand inquiries or something like that." Then he's gone. But Bob feels a little better. Sometimes success comes a little faster. A junior copywriter was working for Emerson Foote at Foote, Cone & Belding on the horrendous American Tobacco account then dominated by the legendary George Washington Hill. (Sidney Greenstreet played that role in the movie *The Hucksters,* which was based in part on these same real-life people.) The young writer, Carter Jones, was part of a large task force of writers working practically around the clock to come up with a knockout new campaign Mr. Hill was demanding. One night Carter dragged out of the offices on Park Avenue and barely managed to catch the 11:20 train out of Penn Station for his home in New Jersey. The train was a through express with a club car in the rear. Young Jones parked himself in this and ordered a bottle of beer. In the seat next to him, he found a sympathetic passenger. "Christ almighty," Jones said, "I just can't get this idea I need." He poured out his story to the man. He then took out a package of Lucky Strikes, the brand so much in need of a new campaign. "That's it!" Jones said. "Just a simple package of cigarettes, and I only need maybe five words to describe it, five words that will sound good on radio." The friendly gentleman took the pack of cigarettes from Carter and held it out at arm's length. They both looked at it silently for a few long minutes as the express roared through the night across the Jersey swamplands. Finally, Carter said, "Just look at it, what the hell can you say about a plain, ordinary package of cigarettes. Go ahead, make believe you are an adman, what the hell would you say?" The man replied sympathetically, "I just don't know what I would say. It must be tough being a copywriter. I always wondered how you get ideas." Carter, sipping his beer, looked again at the package still held out in front of them. The center of the package contained a large red circle, like the center of a target. Then he said, "Well, it's tough all right. I'll get it somehow. I've just got to keep my eye on that red bull's-eye, and maybe it will come." The man handed back the package and said, "Maybe I don't know much about advertising, but those words you just said—what were they, 'Keep your eye on the red bull's-eye'?—they sound pretty catchy to me."

George Washington Hill was sometimes called the inventor of advertising repetition ad nauseam. In any event, the slogan "Keep your eye on the red bull's-eye" was hammered into America's consciousness at the rate of hundreds of times per week for the next six months. And to the junior writer, this chance meeting on a late-night train brought him earlier success than he had expected. When he introduced the slogan into an open meeting in the Foote Cone & Belding offices the next morning, Emerson Foote, the head man, got out of his chair, picked up the phone, and asked for the treasurer. While he was waiting for the connection, he turned to ask, "What did you say your name was?" Carter told him. The phone now had the treasurer on the other end. "Write out a check right now for $5,000. Yes, that's right, to Jones, Carter Jones. He's won his way back to your office."

Young people have another handicap during the early years in advertising. It is generally supposed—a myth, really—that young people have the newest, brightest ideas. In reality, they seldom do. They have energy, drive, curiosity, spontaneity, a certain use- ful contentiousness, and fierce independence. None of these, how- ever, actually add up to innovation, original thinking, or really new creative approaches. During their early developing years, they produce a fantastic volume of hackneyed, old-hat ideas. It is almost as if they have to get these out of their systems before they move into new fields. How many young art directors come up with the Statue of Liberty holding a can of peas or a Whistler's Mother plugging a product? They honestly think they are original. Writers, too, come up with the same clichés. Uncle Sam wants you! with a twist. Or a takeoff from Lincoln's Gettysburg Address, lines bor- rowed from *Oklahoma!,* or puns on old political campaigns. Sooner or later, they discover the hard truth: You can't do something new until you know what's been done before. But this comes, and the good creative men start blooming early. In fact, if they are going to bloom at all, they show their brilliance usually before they are twenty-five or twenty-eight years old. At this point, they have several things going for them. They still have all that drive and energy. They still are rebellious and scrappy. And they also have a big plus. They are more likely to be contemporary in life-style and au courant in language and speech patterns. Two very im- portant ingredients to fresh, modern creativity.

Still it takes patience and perseverance. They have to learn to sell their stuff. It's not enough to come up with something original. They have to convince their superiors that their ideas are worth trying. This means producing proof, if possible, that it will work. Some energetic kids will go out on the streets with their ads and ask pedestrians to give them a reading. Some of the art directors will shoot a whole commercial with their own home movie camera just to show how it will look. Many young people are not actually convinced themselves that advertising, even their own, will turn people on. It usually takes some firsthand experience to appreciate the power of advertising. For example, one young copywriter in a big midwestern ad agency got tabbed for what he thought was a crummy assignment. He was to prepare a calendar for a major oil company whose products were sold throughout half a dozen farm states. Each month's page on the calendar had to be designed with an appropriate picture for the month, plus an eight-line verse, also seasonal in content. "A crappy little job," he said. "I thought I could whip it out in a couple of days." As it turned out, it took him six weeks. The copy chief made him check out every tree, flower, and farm animal in each picture for absolute authenticity. The verses he rewrote a dozen times each before he got the right combination of schmaltz and cornball message. "I got to feeling like a regular John Greenleaf Whittier by the time I finally got that son of a bitch calendar approved," he said. Once done, he promptly forgot about it. Something like a year later, when he had been advanced to writing ads for the farm magazines, he was assigned to "riding a tank truck" throughout the farm belt for a week. This was supposed to be an educational junket to get him closer to the petroleum needs of the big farms in Iowa and Illinois. He rode with the driver salesman on the truck along miles of blacktop roads across the prairies. The farmhouses they stopped at were usually set back in groves of cottonwoods. Each stop was a friendly half-hour visit ending up in the farm kitchen, where the order for the various tank truck supplies was written up. He did this for a week. When he got back, the first thing he did was to race into the copy chief's office. "You know, in a week's time I must have been in a hundred different kitchens on those farms, and you know what? Every goddamn one of them had that calendar right on the wall, big as life, usually underneath the clock, and covered over with notes about birthdays, church suppers, and stuff like that. Made me feel pretty good."

When creative people can get this excited over a calendar, imagine how they feel when they see their first full-color TV commercials come out on a network show. It counts. It makes a lot of crap worthwhile. After all, there has to be a lot of ham in any good creative person. Why else would he work as hard as he does?

Ad making is easy to fake. There is no question that maybe as many as 50 percent of the creative people employed in ad agencies are creative hacks. They have drifted into the business on the strength of some personnel agent's recommendation. They inherited a creative position because the opening was there. Many, in fact, joined the agency with no intention whatsoever to become copy-writers or even artists. They were assistants in typing, traffic, or production and become "creative" as a result of a fortuitous opportunity. These people survive, and many of them do quite well, purely on their ability to adapt, imitate, and heist ideas. Any reasonably intelligent young man can read the trade papers, study competitive ads, watch what others around him do, and eventually call himself a creative man. This sort of impersonation is not that difficult to put over. The business-oriented account executives can't tell the difference between a really creative person and a mediocre one. Top management is concerned only that the ads get approved and run. Clients can be conned because no one on their side of the desk knows how to evaluate creativity either. Moreover, clients are often delighted to see that the advertising you suggest looks quite a bit like their biggest competitor's advertising. This assures them that you are on the right track. Who can quarrel with success?

Faking talent has become so institutionalized in ad agencies that a whole structure has developed to encourage and protect the fakers. It goes something like this: Beg, borrow, and steal. Specifically: An ad, of course, should start with a product difference. A promotable difference. This should be an important challenge to a self-respecting creative man. However, it is easily avoided. You beg your product difference. You put the responsibility on the account group within the agency. They, in turn, put it on the client. "You have to give us something to talk about, after all, you make the product, you're the experts. You have the labs, the research and development department, the new-product workshop. Tell us, and we'll be happy to write your ads." Astonishingly, many clients accept this responsibility without a grumble. They even test a variety of ideas and finally hand the "product concept" to the ad agency on a silver platter. This fakery is, however, catching up with many ad agencies. The ones that operate this way find themselves losing substantial billings to bright, young, hardworking creative agencies who are strong on developing not only new-product differences but whole new-product categories.

Assuming now the creative person has successfully conned this first stage out of his client, the next stage is making the ads or commercials. Obviously, this is a prime creative obligation, calling for imagination, innovation, ideation. You'd think so, but watch again. The crafty creative man need not bend his mind the slightest bit. He starts first by researching the problem. Agencies assist him here with an assortment of cribs and crutches. They buy a flock of services such as Starch reports, which tell the creative drone precisely which kind of ads will get the most readership, which the poorest. Similarly with TV commercials. There are reels after reels of previously scored commercials, so that any cabbagehead can decide upon an approach to guarantee high attention. For example, demonstrations, before-and-after, slice-of-life, and the like. Pick any one. All are safe. At this point, it is wise to take a look at what the competition is doing. Here again agencies are generous to their creative men. They'll let you call in a reel of fifty soap commercials if that's what you want. A hefty sheaf of magazines and newspapers with the latest auto ads if, again, this is your problem area. Browse through these for an afternoon, picking out those you like best, and check them against readership or sales figures just to be sure you are borrowing high-quality stuff. Clip out pieces of illustrations you will be revising later; copy down words and phrases that sound nice. Trace the whole page layout if you want to save the mental strain in designing one yourself. About the only brain power you may have to bring into play is in the recombining of elements. You'll have to take care not to reproduce an exact copy.

Cribbing, copying, and counterfeiting TV commercials is standard practice. In any given year, there are about five original new visual concepts. All the rest are knock-offs. The right way to start this kind of plagiarism is to latch onto a batch of award winners. Here at least, if you don't know good from bad, you can rely on some expert opinion. The judging committees may often be made up of political cronies, but their picks are probably better than your own. And, again, you'll be praised for a clever takeoff.

The next step is to pick a good TV production studio or hire a top-flight still photographer. Many an ad agency has built a lustrous reputation for creativity when in fact they were clever only in whom they hired to provide the creativity. Howard Zeiff,

174

Andy Warhol, Arthur Penn, Mel Sokolsky, Art Kane, and other well-known photographers have often been the secret weapons of many of the big-name agencies. Some of these high-priced outside stars are so independent that they take over entirely, don't even let the agency make a suggestion. Some of them also were responsible for the enormous costs of not a few of the spectacular commercials made during the late 1960s: $300,000 for one Braniff commercial; $150,000 for a Contac commercial; scores of commercials costing $100,000 for one minute of film. One client found that its agency had spent nearly $300,000 for three commercials. This used up nearly all his budget. He could only afford to run them a few times.

Another means of appearing creative without actually being creative is to hire moonlighters or independent creative teams. The agency creative department, with permission from management, can go outside for consulting creative help. Ogilvy & Mather, an agency that prides itself on creativity, was at one point using five outside teams. Most of the moonlighters are hired from the well-known creative agencies. Obviously, Doyle Dane Bernbach people have always been in demand for these assignments. There are problems with using these people. The moonlighter may accept the assignment because he is in a temporary bind: a down payment on a sports car, rent money for a chick he is keeping on the side, or an overdue bar bill. Creative people are notoriously bad managers of money. They are nearly always in hock. So they accept an outside assignment. They get halfway through it, and a big rush comes up on their regular job. To the outsider he says, "Tough, man, can't get with it for another week or two." Moonlighters are also used in helping an agency get new business. This surely is a confession of inadequacy. Here is the agency pitching an account, showing them how creative they are, using outside people to demonstrate the point. One moonlighter recently found himself working on a new-business pitch on his regular job, at the same time having accepted an outside job. He found that they were both pitching the same account!

Research is a great cop out for noncreative types. You can literally let research do all the creativity. It's like painting with numbers. Research can, from past banks of information, spell out for you every facet of an ad or commercial proven to be effective. No sweat whatsoever.

Creative people who believe in research strongly are usually cowards. Such belief sounds good to management and to clients. "Sensible man, no blue-sky stuff with him." The plain fact is, they are often gutless wonders who, like many top management people today, won't make a move without statistical support. In short, they don't dare risk original thinking. This might work in some industries; in advertising, it's disaster.

On the legitimate side of ad making, there is a minority group of truly creative people. Most of these are people who knew they wanted to do something creative way back in grade school, high school, and college, if they went to college. Good creative people generally come equipped with a restless curiosity; a specialized ability to see new relationships in mundane things; a contentious, suspicious, distrustful attitude toward accepted truths; an aptitude for insightful thinking (a whole new look at something); an appreciation for the form and shape of things; and an irresistible compulsion to change these to even better or more esthetically pleasing shapes and forms. The honest creative person also seeks out new experiences, new people, new geography. The impressions thus gained are his storehouse, food for his head, sparks to ignite ideas. Often as not, good creative people are subjective, introspective, inner-directed people. This may not be a native personality trait but simply one that has evolved as the creative man matures. It comes from selecting pursuits that help him with his craft, such as reading a great deal if he is to be a writer or spending time alone with pencil and paints if he is headed toward a career in art. The best creative people are obviously creatively occupied all their waking hours. The top artist is "framing" pictures wherever he goes: on the street, in the country, indoors, and outdoors. The good writer is watching for good writing in everything he reads. He is listening for the sound of words wherever he goes in crowds, in subways, in elevators, in all communications media. He compares, evaluates, stores up, and synthesizes words, phrases, conversations. How else can he learn the language of people, the mood of people; their needs, wants, desires? And—ah, yes—their vulnerability to his persuasion.

Advertising has been depicted as a jungle. It does have its own set of rules. Suppose, for example, that you are a reasonably hopeful young tyro hoping to make your mark in this much-touted business. Here, perhaps with some slight overplay of the hand, is what you might do to advance yourself onward and upward in an advertising agency.

First you get in. This is the easy part, provided you don't waste time knocking on doors or writing letters of application. Leave all this to a reliably recommended placement agent. These cats are experts. They'll provide all the cover you need to overcome a total lack of education, experience, references, or talent (especially the latter). Once in, go on the offensive immediately. Check out the uniform (protective coloring). If the top management mix is old suburban (Rye, New York, Princeton, New Jersey, or Evanston, Illinois), then you'll wear white buttoned-down shirts, narrow rep ties, muted gray suits, dark brown shoes with laces. A vest on client-meeting days. If the chiefs are new suburban (Westport or New Canaan, Connecticut, or Oak Bluffs, Illinois), then you'll take up colored shirts, wider ties, shaped suits, and strap shoes. Note: the former group carry boxy dispatch cases; the latter, thin black leather folios.

Now, right away, you have to learn the jungle language. A few good buzz words will get you through the first year: "relate," "dialogue," "interface," "parameters," "input," "playback." You'll need a few creative words, too: "soft focus," "hard line," "Art Deco," "shaved lettering," "*cinéma vérité*." If nothing else seems to fit, just toss in a phrase like "derivative of the Bauhaus school." And if you should stumble into a research meeting, watch for a chance to drop in one or two of these: "probability sample," "Latin square," "share of mind," "brand indices," or "Monte Carlo numbers." Of course, you won't know what these mean. Don't worry. Slip them in thusly, "I'm not so sure we have the right attribute matrix." Then sit back while the outflanked research man defends it.

Now comes the real testing of the fittest, physical superiority, important in the early years. You have to be in shape. Accomplish this with as much prestige as possible (indoor tennis, squash at an athletic club, skiing in season). On the job, remember: Running is good. Always trot or jog en route to anywhere, even the men's room. You look busy. Keep your reflexes sharp so you can leap up when brass enters the room, jump into a seat near the head of the conference table, force your way into an elevator containing a client, sprint to get in the same taxi with the boss on the way to a client meeting. Learn to carry heavy weights. As a promising tyro, you should never be seen empty-handed. Always carry something (rejected storyboards, old files, trade magazines). Another physical thing, join the office sport teams. You don't have to excel, but your name will appear in the house organ (self-publicity will be all-important on your way up). Better still, team play will give an opportunity to size up the weaknesses (short tempers, bad knees, poor sportsmanship, and so forth) of some of the peers you'll be zapping in the days ahead.

Speaking of this, learn some of the infighting tactics soon. Like on your second day. Some of these, of course, are ancient and classic rules: Never let a competitor get into the office before you do in the morning or leave later than you do at night. Always outdress him, even if you have to invest in a Bill Blass tie. Flirt with his secretary if he has one. If not, outflirt him with the boss's secretary. Always arrive at a meeting first and immediately ask, "Where's Joe?" Be the last to leave a meeting with top brass. Joe will never know what was said in his absence. Beat him to a first-names relationship with your mutual bosses. Make a mistake, leave something behind when you are visiting in Joe's office (an underground newspaper, a telephone message from an employment agent, an off-Broadway nudies playbill). Be patient. The word will get around. Other obvious outsurvival tactics: Question your rival's background in front of the right audience: "Did he graduate from college?" "How many times has he been married?" "Is it true he sees his shrink three times a week?" "Doesn't he ever get any sleep?" These are, of course, hypothetical questions, but they can hype-up management.

Now, more direct tactics. You'll have to do something about the competitors who are simply outworking you, the overachievers, the homework boys, the stay-late crowd. These you chop down adroitly with "harmless" observations: "Jim's overdoing it" (whatever it is). "Jack is headed for a crack-up." "Bob sure is a beaver."

"I'm worried about Al." (Don't elaborate.) If the overachiever is still scoring points, see that he really is busy. Slip him some extra dirty jobs. Put him in line for some field work. Volunteer his name for work on a wild-goose new-business presentation. Given enough, he really will crack up. If he is a creative man, you'll use different tactics. Make a big thing of the way he dresses—flattering, of course—but among old-suburban execs, where it will do him the least good. Drop hints: "He's a genius, I doubt if we can hold him." "Don't let him get too close to the client." Or suggest that the conference room may get a little "stuffy" with too many creative people at the meeting. You haven't actually said there is a deodorant problem. If all else fails, and the client does take a liking to him, see that he is uninvited to the next meeting under the pretext, "He's much too valuable to sit around meetings. He's back there now winging out great stuff for you." He's back there all right, way back. After a while the client will forget him, and he can be safely fired for "cause"—any cause will do.

As you move up into middle management, tactics change. Now brute force counts for less. Rather, progress is made over bodies broken in spirit, sensibilities crushed, egos hopelessly deflated. These bloodless victories are often verbal sullies: "Bob is playing with a nubile in the media department." "Joe is a plugger, too bad he isn't profit-oriented." "Did you smell pot on Al this morning?" Or power-bloc politics might be used. Like switching out of a bloc about to lose a big account. Or deft omissions. Like leaving a rival's name off a conference report or a client meeting announcement and putting it on a volunteer project (a new campaign needed for a nonprofit public-service outfit, such as Religion in America, Stop Forest Fires, or Save the Grand Canyon). But don't be a bully every day. Save up some of the unhealthiest observations and hang-ups of your rivals until profits are low, clients are edgy, a staff shuffle is in the wings, stock distribution is about to be made, or something of the sort. Timing is everything.

The godsent group system, which big agencies especially value, is a choice arena for survival operations. Get into as many as possible. When you are locked into about five, you can coast along for months (if not years) doing absolutely nothing, "Sorry, sir, they are clobbering me in Group 3." The group protects you in other ways. When it is doing great work, you can take credit. If it is running ragged, back off. If a full-blown debacle is shaping up, plant hints in the upper branches. "I'm not sure I agree with what Group 4 is trying to do." When doomsday finally dawns, you told them so. Also on groups: Attend all the meetings. You'll learn about people and accounts in trouble. A man in trouble is playing catch-up ball. Mark him down for early zapping off. An account is in trouble when it's unprofitable, is using outside services, when the third new campaign idea is flogged to death. Your move: quick disengagement, but leaving as much egg on rivals' faces as possible, of course. Meetings also afford you a chance to pick up good (and bad) ideas, plans, strategies. Good ones (with the blessings of top brass) are obviously "our idea," "our plan." Bad ones are "Joe's idea," "Bill's plan." Also, take voluminous notes at meetings. Someone is bound to say something he wished you hadn't put on the record.

The low profile is important during middle management years. Ambition can be your own worst enemy. Sooner or later it is bound to land you in a vulnerable position. Besides, you should play down the energy bit now. It's okay for tyros, but now it suggests you are running scared. Speed is absolutely fatal for senior vice-presidents. Naked panic. Actually, you should have plenty of time, provided you have deputized everything to eager overachievers (who can be blamed for anything). Use these golden hours for smoking out skunks, smelling out upcoming holocausts, and filing away unhealthy tidbits about your rivals. If you do get saddled with a trouble-prone account, there are several respectable maneuvers. One, swap it with one of your enemies. If he is ambitious, he will leap at the chance and go down with the ship. Or hire an outsider to take over when you are sure the account is beyond saving. He'll go down in flames. A third way is to pin something scurrilous on the client (he's getting kickbacks). Meanwhile, you hurriedly elbow yourself onto another, more secure, account in the house. Maybe one now handled by a marked man. Do these things early when the original account first gets on thin ice (who knows better than you?). When the ice finally gives way, you are high and dry. You've got a new account. The one you moved in on. You might even be a hero for putting up with that s.o.b. client as long as you did.

The bloodiest battles for survival are between rival account men because they are all inherently political animals; they know what their rivals are up to. Outwitting has become a way of life. However, some old ploys still work. Like getting increased responsibility without actually assuming it. You do this by sharing decisions, such as whether to hire so-and-so. If he works out, fine, you take the credit. If he is a cropper, you can always say, "Well, you all met him. I guess we were all taken." Or if the decision involves the client and it's tough, give it to the top boss. Flatter him: "This one is in your court." If he whiffs it, he whiffs it. You didn't. The account man has to chop down rivals every chance he gets. Like telling the creative department that "Joe is anticreative." That'll slow down his jobs. Or that Jim doesn't believe in research. That'll cut his tires with that department. Or Jack is "pretty generous" with his expense account. The treasurer won't overlook that one. Or watch for chances to slip in big typing jobs into the pool just ahead of the big ones you know Jack is about to unload. The girls who work late after a few of these will get Jack, but good. You can also show compassion by hinting that "Bill really has a plateful" or wonder whether "Poor Freddie is up to such-and-such an account." This will put you in line for the next assignment plum. Or try this oldie: "Saw Al lunching with a crowd that looked like they were from Y&R, couldn't be sure of course."

On the looking-good tactics; these usually work: a clean desk, a decent late arrival every morning, a big lunch date (never mind with whom) every day, a first-name basis with all clients and a nickname-dropping of all promising new-business leads, a *Harvard Business Review* under your arm, a high-styled haircut, and going out of your way to be buddy-buddy with the rising new creative star. It helps an account executive to get along well with creative types (to their faces, that is).

More could be written about survival in the uppermost branches, but it would be cruel. A sad choreography of nearly extinct species locked in a twilight battle over "early retirements."

9

How Agencies Mismanage People

THE HARPER AIR FORCE or, as Marion preferred to call it, the Starflight Airline, was unique, at least among advertising agency operations. Among the airline staff were two former air force generals, the former chief pilot of KLM Airlines, a world-famous maître d'hôtel, stewards, stewardesses, ground crews. There were five planes in the fleet; the largest, Marion's personal transportation, was a full-size, four-engine commercial airliner built to carry a hundred passengers. Sometimes it carried Marion alone, even across the Atlantic. The interior was furnished in French provincial style with curved lounges in all directions. In the rear was Marion's exclusive suite, which included bedroom with a king-size bed, a sunken bathtub, and a private library. The other planes in the fleet, smaller, executive commuter models, carried people to and from meetings or resorts such as the Montauk ranch. The base of operations was LaGuardia Airport, New York.

Many of the sorties of the Starflight Airline were mysterious. A group of top executives would be hastily informed that they were to report at the airfield for a trip to an unknown destination. They never knew what clothes to take. Never knew how long they would be gone. Aboard the plane, in the luxurious lounge, the executives sat drinking cocktails and eating tidbits far into the night. At some late hour, Marion would emerge from his private suite and begin a series of individual cross-examinations. After a half hour of this, he might again disappear, still having failed to mention the destination or expected hour of arrival. The executives would then try to sleep on the tortuous pieces of living room furniture. On one of these flights, after fourteen hours of circumnavigation all over continental United States (Marion's order to his flying generals was to avoid any conceivable confrontation with turbulence), the executives deplaned at Los Angeles. They made their way to awaiting limousines, humped over in sickle shapes after their night on the curved furniture. Arrival brought little further enlightenment about the nature of their trip, for Marion sent the executives to one hotel while he went to another. These trips apparently occurred frequently, always as mysteriously conducted, always to an unknown destination.

Marion loved to hire generals. At one point he had five on staff. Most of their duties were never clear. One had been head of army procurement, for whatever that was worth. Others had impressive combat records that covered their chests with medals. Marion never hired an admiral. There was something about the ring of a general's title that pleased Marion. He insisted that they use these in all company affairs. Actually, some of the generals and many of the dozens of top executives hired by Harper over the years were equally unclear about the nature of their positions. They were apparently not told very much at the hiring interview. And after that, it was always impossible to get an interview with Marion for further elucidation.

When asked once about these "unassigned" superexecutives, Marion replied, "It's true, they have no assignments, but my theory is a good man will rise to his responsibilities." This was a difficult and risky thing for any Interpublic executive during Marion's reign. If they rose too openly or conspicuously, they risked banishment. Marion, according to reports, handled this ostracism procedure in the identical fashion every time. The executive who had for one reason or another earned Marion's displeasure was called in. Take Mark Bolon, for example. Marion began, "Mark—a very *crucial* situation has arisen in one of our important offices." He would then outline some vague emergencies, delaying the actual destination for an excruciatingly long time. Mark Bolon ultimately learned that the "important" office was Johannesburg, South Africa. Many other key executives slated for banishment went through the same experiences. Bill McKeechie, a "crucial situation" in Brussels. Bob Cole, a "crucial situation" in Milan. Dick Bowman to Bavaria. A female executive to a "crucial situation" in Caracas, Venezuela. And Robert Healy (who later came back to replace Marion) was sent to handle a "crucial situation" in Geneva. The Johannesburg spot was Marion's most popular banishment. They say he considered this the ultimate "safe distance" for a dangerous executive. Actually, those who went there enjoyed the climate and conditions immensely, as Machiavelli might have predicted.

Ad agency management has never been very good at managing people. Maybe it is because there is no easy way, no simple operation. "It's the way the tree grows," says one ad agency president. "Responsibility and authority spread all over. Nobody knows who the hell is working for whom." Or as Betty Corwin, of Corwin Consultants, advisers to ad agencies for twenty-two years, puts it, "They do the goddamnedest things to their people! You wonder how they can be so stupid." No wonder labels crop up to describe the kind of management ad agencies have. One is a "meat grinder"; another is a "money machine." Or they may be described as run like a "Marine barracks," "a rip-off joint," or a "prep school."

Creative types have explicit descriptions for various kinds of agencies. "It was a great shop once, but now it's gone to shit." Or "squaresville," "disaster area," "smart-ass shop," "boutique," "rags goods agency," "Seventh Avenue shop" (fashion-product agencies), "ad factory," "boondock joint" (branch office), "production line," "sweatshop," "dreck place," "fat cats," "schlock shop," "country club," "Rotary club," "university club," "WASP office," "a place run by Yaleys," "one-man shop," and "he's a ball-breaker." The worst: "Never heard of the place."

Equally vivid are some of the descriptions of work they produce: "10 percent horseshit," "basic Bates," "formula crap," "boiler plate" or "buckeye" (both archaic), "standout stuff," "breakthrough stuff," "award-type stuff," "contemporary" (now out of date), "Doyle Dane look," "packaged-goods dreck," "weaselly ads," USP ads (for "Unique Selling Proposition," from Bates), "safe, conservative stuff," "ballsy ads." A good commercial is a "gas" or a "gasser."

The way agencies are run is sometimes described in terms like these: "They are all whores"; "a great place to work if you like to dance with someone shooting at your feet"; "the accountniks wipe the floor with the creative people"; "it's run by a slide rule"; "they are running scared"; "playing catch-up ball"; "shitty-looking place, paint peeling off the walls, but the pay is sensational"; "it's run like a hospital with bells and public-address system"; "has a sickroom smell"; "they hang 'em by the thumbs over there"; "the place is like a city under siege, they'll be eating the rats next week."

Oftentimes, fairly or unfairly, all the faults of management are heaped on one top person. Norman B. Norman, of Norman, Craig & Kummel; Al Seaman, of SSC and B; Mary Wells Lawrence, of Wells, Rich, Greene; and Robert Healy, of Interpublic, are frequently maligned with or without cause. Sometimes the motivation is simple jealousy. Other times it is the resentment of any strong power head. All the shops just mentioned are profitably, if not happily, managed.

Poor management is especially hard on ad agencies. They need to attract and hold good people far more than most companies. Excessive turnover of personnel is a serious and costly problem. It may very likely jeopardize relations with clients when a star creative man or an efficient account man resigns. An agency with a reputation for poor morale has a harder time soliciting business. These agencies also have to pay higher salaries to get new people, and they pay more fees to recruiters and placement agencies. For a major ad agency, such fees can total over $100,000 annually. A good head hunter (executive recruiter) can earn as much as 20 percent of a year's salary for finding an executive. That's $8,000 for the typical creative or account supervisor who is usually traded at the $40,000 tab. And lastly, the agency's product—its creative work and its services—suffer badly.

To an outsider, ad agencies give the appearance of easygoing permissiveness. This is part of the ad agency mystique, the pizzazz business, the often-deliberate effort to look and play the role of glamor, excitement, and creativity. "Hell, what we've got here is a freak show," says one ad agency president, "and the clients love it." The alleged permissiveness is supposed to be a part of the occult arts of advertising, the better-you-leave-it-to-us attitude agencies hope to foster with their clients. As a result, you can walk into many agencies and find creative vice-presidents wearing blue denim pants and shirts (open to the waist if he has hair on his chest), dirty sneakers, and handlebar mustaches. Girls will be braless, girdleless, and dressed in clothes that might be worn at a commune or a rock festival.

This is permissiveness on the outside, on the surface of ad agencies. It is for public and client consumption. Inside, it's a different matter. The limits of permissiveness are short and tight. Ad agencies are far from the swinging, carefree places they appear to be. Most of the big old shops have rigid rules and regulations. And some of them are small, mean, archaic. Compton, for example, recently released a policy statement on one-hour lunches. It took three pages to cover all the various executive types who were excepted from the rules. J. Walter Thompson has a rigid check-in, check-out system on every floor. Employees get a monthly report on exactly how many minutes late they were on every working day. Nearly all ad agencies have time sheets on which executives have to account for every fifteen-minute segment of the day. In fairness, this is supposed to make it easier for profitability control on accounts. It is an aggravation to everyone. Other agencies have chickenshit rules about coffee breaks at certain hours, what kind of decorations can go on the walls of offices, who qualifies for executive men's rooms, no use of phone for personal calls, charges for phone calls made to the executives' suburban homes (except to say "I'm working late again"), and stingy allowances for supper money, for taxi trips, or for hotel rooms on the road. Of course, efficiency is important, but so is morale. Here are some examples.

It was during the noon hour. A phone rang in the almost-empty typing pool. It rang a second and third time before one of the typists went to pick it up. The blast of insults and bad language that greeted her reddened her face. She kept her cool, however, and replied, "I don't care who you are, I will not listen to talk like that. I'm going to hang up now, and if you ring again and speak like a gentleman, I'll take your message."

She hung up.

The phone immediately rang again. The secretary answered

pleasantly, took the message, and rung off. A copywriter in a nearby office overheard this and was curious. "Who was that? You certainly straightened him out."

"It was the president," the girl answered calmly.

Norman B. Norman, president of one of the top fifteen ad agencies, who was making plans to retire, hired two key executives, both $100,000-a-year men. Norman had spent nearly a year working with management consulting firms to find and bring in these two important men. One was to be president, the other executive vice-president when Norman retired later in the year. No formal announcements were made when the two men joined the firm because it was understood that they would familiarize themselves with the operation of this large agency first. At the end of three weeks, however, the president decided that despite the long, careful search, these were not the men he wanted. How could he tell them? How could he handle it?

This is what the president did. On a Sunday morning, he called in an independent public relations expert, Bob Morgan, a man he had known and worked with on many previous occasions. "A very important assignment, Bob. Can you get in here the first thing tomorrow?" Bob agreed. When he arrived he found an executive office already fitted out for him with a secretary and a title: "Robert Morgan, Executive Assistant to the President." An office-wide memorandum was soon prepared and distributed. In it were directions to the entire staff that Robert Morgan would speak for the president on *any* matters pertaining to Norman, Craig & Kummel. This was the first of many memos signed by Morgan that were to issue from the top echelon during the next three weeks. On the fourth week, Norman called Bob in and said, "Well, I guess everything is set. I'm booked on a plane to Europe tonight. Will be gone for three weeks." Bob knew what was coming next. Norman then said, "Fire them."

Firing is always a difficult job for top management. Ed Stern, a recruiter, estimates that 50 percent of the assignments management consultants receive are for "executive reevaluation surveys," which result in executives being fired. This way the top executive does not do the hatchet job; it is "recommended" by the outside expert. David North, another consultant, has developed a special staff to handle "terminal separation assistance," a service to ease the blow and help relocation of the executive.

Another unfair practice involves deciding who goes and who survives after an account is lost. Agencies as a rule try to keep valuable talent despite the loss, but often politics take over, and the drones are kept on while the best people are let go. Too often, also, the people on the lost account stay on while others are displaced. Or the old rule "last one in, first one out" applies. This again assures the old retainers of their positions. After a decade of this, most of the fresh young talent is gone; the hacks with tenure stay on. Nearly every one of the top ten agencies is steeped in these old political pros.

When an ad agency is on a firing binge—it usually happens on Friday afternoons—the word runs through the agency business like the news of a great ship disaster at sea. If there were a Lloyd's of London bell to toll, it would toll. The descriptive terms are something like these: "There's a blood bath at BBDO"; "they're walking the plank at Doyle Dane"; "they are tearing them off at Thompson"; "Ogilvy's having a massacre"; "there's a big shoot-out at SSC and B"; "the guillotine is working day and night over at Lennen & Newell"; "Interpublic is having another purge"; "they are lopping 'em off at Wells, Rich." The British agencies are more polite. They are more likely to refer to dismissals as "cannings" or "sackings." For example, "Benson's Sacks Ten."

The way agencies fire are sometimes unique. Bill Casey got called out of a Sunday night hot tub by George Gribbin of Young & Rubicam to get fired. "You're too late," Bill replied, "I quit last Friday. I'm all packed up." J. Walter Thompson once fired a senior art director, Jerry Bulmer, by cable.

One firing that backfired, however, happened at McCann-Erickson a while back. Mary Hardin, who worked there at the time, tells about it. An old retainer in the mail room spent so much time drinking during the noon hour at a place called Hamburger Mary's that the company finally felt they had to dismiss him. He was given the word on Friday afternoon. On Monday morning he was back. There was an embarrassed buzzing of conversation around the mail room, but nobody knew what to say. Finally, the supervisor of the department took him upstairs to the treasurer's office. "Look Joe," they said, "we are sorry that it wasn't clear to you last Friday. But you were fired." Old Joe nodded. "Yep, I heard you. Then I thought it over during the weekend and made a decision. I decided that it would be financially inadvisable for me to stop work now. So I came back." The executives were so flummoxed that he stayed on until he was retired a few years later with full pension rights.

Agencies sometimes hire people, especially creative types, away from a good job only to help them make a new-business presentation. If the pitch fails, they fire the man. Another common and unfortunate practice is the dismissal of employees just before they reach profit-sharing benefits. This has been done by dozens of agencies. J. Walter Thompson, Chicago, fired a typist after four years and eleven months. She lost nearly $5,000. Unfortunately for JWT public relations, the girl's father is a taxi driver and may still be telling his passengers the story even now. Another agency, Kenyon & Eckhardt, dropped a $40,000 executive just weeks prior to his five-year benefit date. He was out nearly $20,000. Young & Rubicam reportedly forced one of its executives into early retirement for the same reason: to save pension benefits for those remaining.

When executives between the ages of forty-five and fifty are beached, the going is rough. They are too young to retire. Often their expenses are higher because many have children in college by this time. They seldom have enough capital to start a business, of their own. Creative men can do free-lance work, but account supervisors find the pickings slim. They are too old for positions on the client side. Their agency skills are not transferable to many other allied fields. As a result, many take jobs in smaller cities. "I moved to this shop in Elkhart, Indiana. Never been happier," so the executive says. "I'm now a representative for a printing company. It's a good deal. I call on many of my old friends in the agency field." Good deal? Or this one: an agency executive who once earned handsome salaries had moved down the scale to selling real estate in his commuting town. Recently, he received a phone call from an old friend who said he would be passing through on his way to a football game at New Haven. The conversation:

"Stop in by all means. Love to see you, Bill."

"Still at the same home address, aren't you?"

"Yep. Same address. But Bill, stop at the gatehouse first."

"Pretty fancy, heh?"

"No. We live there now."

Agency morale often suffers when people are asked to perform tasks beyond their regular duties. Sometimes these are shopping trips on their own time to check distribution of a new product in stores. Other times they are asked to go out on the street to interview people about their reaction to ads for a new analgesic, dessert topping, or a feminine douche. Rex Taylor, a publicist, tells this one about an agency called Lambert & Feasley. The staff at this shop got fed up with a weekly request from management to enter a jingle-writing contest for one of their radio clients. The winner would get all of $10. The losers, nothing. After many losing weeks, one secretary sat down on a glum Monday morning and wrote her entry.

> The girls at Lambert & Feasley
> Fornicate both often and easily
> In this pleasant way, they augment their pay
> Which at Lambert & Feasley is measly.

Agencies are often vague about which people are assigned to which accounts. This allows aggressive or highly competitive types to invade the turf of others to steal some of their choice assignments.

Agencies often keep on old retainers in jobs, which can cause many morale problems. Typical is the overaged or obsolete account executive who is made "business manager" of the creative department. He knows nothing about hiring and assigning creative people, but yet he does it and does it badly.

Agencies unfairly pirate employees from one group to another. Media and production are typical targets. The heads of these departments work for years to bring good men along to take over responsible positions but find themselves raided by their own management. Often this is done because management can get the man cheaper than they could on the outside. These two departments don't have enough clout to offer resistance.

Management often causes serious morale problems in the way

they distribute stock. This is often offered not to the most deserving or the best people but to young executives with private incomes. This is easier for management because it does not have to make bank-loan arrangements with such employees to finance the purchase. In the long run, the agency is owned by rich drones.

Agencies will often ask people shortly after they are hired to make a list of all the relatives they might have who work for various big corporations. This information will later be used in soliciting business. Is it necessary?

Some agencies will be more than generous with the help they may give an employee, such as financial help with a home mortgage, hospital bills, an emergency loan. Obviously the employee is grateful. He is also obligated to the hilt. He is reminded of this when he may think about moving for a better job or asking for a raise.

Another devious device of ad agencies is the payment to the placement agent when the person is hired. It is customary for ad agencies to pay this, but some will bill the employee. Or expect repayment if the man leaves.

Another morale crusher is the planted rumor that there is going to be a big bloodbath soon. There is talk that ten, twenty, maybe more people will be let go. Management does nothing to stop the rumor. It believes it will keep people on their toes.

And one more, management stands by quietly or ineffectually while department heads and others in supervisory positions behave like bullies and tyrants. Nearly every large agency has some key executive who is regarded as a "holy terror," "a mean son of a bitch," a "sadistic bastard." Everyone around this man is intimidated daily, yet managements in ad agencies seldom do anything about it.

Some of these thoroughly disliked men eventually got their just deserts. Three for example—one each at Ted Bates, D'Arcy and J. Walter Thompson—with reputations as hatchet men or back stabbers are all out of action today. Either "on the beach," eased into early retirement or in a back office limbo position.

These illustrations of mismanagement (and the list is by no means complete) could happen in many business organizations. No matter, they are inexcusable. But in the ad agency business, they are much more serious. For here, people must work closely together, must trust and confide in each other, must work long hours and under stress conditions in order that the ad agency can get out its difficult and intangible service. Moreover, mismanagement, with resulting poor morale, is unquestionably one of the major reasons ad agencies overall are losing respect from clients and posting lower and lower industry-average profits.

Many of the examples of mismanagement are the result of stupidity, carelessness, or negligence. It would be ridiculous to assume that ad agency executives are more malevolent than executives elsewhere in business. There is, however, an important contributing factor. Ad agencies, as companies, have poor training programs for management. Most, in fact, have none at all. Executives simply learn by example, learn from their immediate superiors, or use whatever native management skills they might have. There are very few methods or systems used universally by ad agencies. Moreover, as indicated in other parts of this book, opportunities for office politics, Machiavellian maneuvering, and outright power plays are indeed more prevalent in the loose, intransigent environment of an ad agency.

Basically, the problem is management's attitude toward people. In all too many cases, it does not understand them. And admittedly this is not easy to do in an ad agency made up of a dozen different kinds of specialists from many different backgrounds, educations, life-styles. Perhaps no management system would work without flaws in an ad agency. The attitude that hurts, however, is the one that is condescending, patronizing, sometimes thinly disguised snobbery. It is as if top management in many big agencies, and small, conservative shops as well, is slightly embarrassed that it must hire creative people who make them uncomfortable by their dress and talk; or media and production people who frequently have no more than a high school education; or sales promotion, public relations, and merchandising people who, although necessary, are not management's personal "types." "I wouldn't have him out to the house."

Few agency presidents or top management people would admit to such attitudes, and many may honestly not be aware of their feelings in this respect. Yet it is there, and it is devastating in many agencies. It not only makes for tensions; it contributes to poor craftsmanship, inefficiency, and must certainly affect the success and profitability of companies in the long run.

Agencies are not unaware of their personnel and management problems. Just recently, for example, J. Walter Thompson hired a psychiatrist to interview people *after* they have left the agency. They hope that maybe these now-free-to-speak people will give them some advice on what is wrong with their personnel and management systems. Other companies use staff psychologists and sometimes outside psychiatrists to delve into their management problems. Many use expensive management consultants to make studies and give recommendations. Many others, often with too much confidence, turn to placement agents and executive recruiters to help solve chronic personnel problems. Some of these veteran placement people can indeed tell management where they make mistakes. They certainly hear the bloody details as the applicants stream through their offices between ad agency jobs.

Things are perhaps no worse today than they have been in the past. The recent recession, however, put the squeeze on management and forced them to forego many of the niceties of personnel handling. Moreover, the ad agency executive today has learned something about modern management in his business courses and in his relationships with large business corporations. In some ways, however, there has been a decline. There is less, surely, of the personal proprietorship pride and behavior of the earlier generations of advertising. One of the last agencies of this type probably was the old John Falkner Arndt agency in Philadelphia a decade ago. This shop was the prototype not only of the one-man, one-rule operation but also embodied all the formal etiquette of an old-line Philadelphia business firm, unchanged in a century.

For example, every single day, promptly at 9:15 A.M., Mr. John Falkner Arndt would set out on his "Good morning" rounds. He would visit, on a regular prescribed route, every one of the ninety-five people he employed. He prided himself on the fact that he knew the full and first names of everyone in the office, especially the clerks and typists. Puffing his briar pipe, dressed in his Main Line tweed suit and shirt with high white detachable collar, old John would bound through the office, popping his head in just long enough to say, "Good morning, Charles"; "Good morning, Miss Smith"; "Good morning, Joseph." Everyone, that is everyone at his desk, beamed and returned the greeting. He wasn't checking up on arrival times. He was doing the time-honored job of greeting his loyal help each working day.

Art Montgomery, a copywriter there, now a supervisor in a big New York shop, recalls that John Falkner Arndt began to slip a bit in the years before his retirement. The copywriter Montgomery shared an office with was new. His name was Bernie. The previous one was named Eric. For something like a year and a half, Mr. Arndt never noticed this change. It was "Good morning, Eric," month in and month out. Bernie always returned the greeting without letting on.

In the big New York shops with from 500 to 2,000 people, there is little of this familiarity. Presidents and top executives know perhaps fewer than 20 percent of their people by name. Many employees have worked in an agency for several years without ever being introduced to or meeting the president. Stories based on this sort of anonymity are numerous. The president of Kenyon & Eckhardt recognized a well-known creative man in the elevator of his building one day and, after a quick introduction, said, "Stop around some day, we might have a place for you."

The man replied, "Thanks a lot I've been working here for a year."

A top executive at one agency, passing through the reception room on his way to lunch, noticed two people in conversation. One, a young woman wearing gladiator boots, a miniskirt, and a form-fitting, braless knit top, was passing photographs back and forth with a young man wearing a conservatively cut suit. The senior executive, presuming this was a job interview, mentioned quietly to his friend, "Well, I hope he doesn't hire that tart." The executive's younger companion made no comment. He knew that the "tart" was the agency's very capable art buyer. The man was a photographer's rep.

John Churchill, president of the old Donahue & Coe shop, had a reputation for going round at night turning out the lights. On one of these trips, Bill Heck of Best Foods, then a client, reports Churchill popped into the mail room. There he ran into a hippie youngster who was playing a transistor radio and dancing to the music. Churchill was furious. Even though it was after hours, he couldn't stand indolence. "Young man," he shouted, "how much do you make?" The youngster turned down his radio and said, "Fifty-five dollars a week." Churchill whipped out his billfold and counted out $110. "Here's two weeks' pay. Take your radio and get the hell out of here!" The young man did, quickly. He was a messenger boy from outside, waiting for a package.

Obviously, all agencies are not this far out of touch with their own people. Once, during a meeting in Shep Kurnit's office at Delehanty Kurnit and Geller, a young shirt-sleeved creative man burst into the room, glanced around, went to Shep's desk. Shep was sitting on a couch. The creative man literally rifled the desk, opening and slamming every drawer. Finally, he saw what he was looking for. Without a word, he marched over to Shep, the president, reached into his shirt pocket, withdrew a pack of cigarettes, helped himself, lit it, and left. The young man was the creative director Jerry Della Femina. Shep always ran an easy-going shop.

At a screening of a reel of commercials at a young agency, the creative director seated in the small screening room was explaining the strategy and production techniques of the commercials as they were projected from the small booth in back. Every once in a while, he would yell out, "Hey, rerun that one." Or shout, "Out of focus, out of focus, goddamnit!" There were other commands throughout the showing. At the end of the meeting, the projectionist was introduced. He was the president.

There are other ways in which management tries to be human. At Young & Rubicam, people get cards or a small gift such as a dictionary on their birthdays. Sometimes a copy supervisor will take his group of a half-dozen people out to a freebie lunch at an "in" bistro such as Maxwell's Plum or the Ginger Man or a new place such as the Great British Disaster. Some agencies, attempting to be more understanding and modern, relax the rules. Carl Ally Inc. has a four-day-week operation. Gilbert Advertising, DKG, and several others have initiated a full week off between the December holidays for all hands. The bosses, however, have to stick around to take care of emergencies. J. Walter Thompson's

Chicago office has had its annual golf day for many years. And its New York office has been experimenting with intimate luncheons in its quaint colonial dining room at which time some of the young new people are seated alternately at tables with senior executives. Many ad agencies have a top-level policy that encourages their senior account men to be more fraternal. It's called the take-a-creative-man-to-lunch-once-a-month policy.

Another kind of management-and-morale problem involves participation. It is true that although the ad agency business does indeed have a great deal of glamor and excitement, much of it passes by the people in the ranks. The Hollywood shooting locations are attended by account men and creative men. The posh media luncheons held at places like the Saint Regis roof, the Delmonico's Gold Room, or the Princeton Club are for the account and media executives only. Similarly, when a convention or a trade show is held in Miami in midwinter or at Greenbriar in the spring, it is the account people who make the week-long trip and come back with the rich tans. New business trips that might include a jet trip to Chicago or Houston are usually made only by a select group. This uneven distribution of the plums in ad agencies causes jealousies and bad feeling. Obviously, agencies must restrict free junkets to a limited number of people, but sometimes the hard-working creative person or research man who has contributed much to a new campaign or a new business presentation should be taken along, if only for morale's sake.

The most serious and difficult-to-solve management problems are innate to the business. These involve the high turnover of accounts, the dichotomy between the people who make the product (the creative staff) and the people who sell it (the account service people), and the more recent problem, the changing structure of the advertising agency business. Yet better management systems might well slow down the turnover of accounts. For example, top management could improve its communications with account groups. They should know more than they do about the day-to-day failures, the number of times creative work is rejected by the client, the personality conflicts and tensions that exist in the agency-client relationship. Often these problems are neatly and quietly kept away from top management by the overly protective account group. Another conspicuous failure on the part of management, usually the president, is inexcusable neglect of important clients. The American Dairy Association, which moved its $5-million account recently, stated that they had not seen anyone from the agency's top management for over a year before they decided to move. The Ford Motor switch of some $20 million was said to have been caused at least in part by the fact that the agency's president had not been present at a crucial meeting, the one at which an entire campaign was rejected for the third time. At still another agency, an $8-million client complains that it has not seen its agency president for eighteen months.

When Ron Holland, now a partner at Lois Holland Callaway, was young, he began writing ads for a major southern bank. Ron was good and lucky. Four ads in a row were approved. A tough chore in bank advertising. On the fifth one, the client changed *one* word in an ad of over a thousand words. When Ron heard this, he took it out on Mike Sloan, the account executive. "Why the hell do you let the client walk all over you like that!"

Creative men hate to be hurried on jobs. Especially by the same impatient account executive. Kenyon & Eckhardt decided it best to use three men for this task. They were called "check," "double check," and "follow-through."

The second problem—the eternal feud between account people and creative departments—is also endemic. They are different breeds of cats. They dress differently (the account men in their conservative suits, narrow ties, white shirts; the creative people in their peacock attire). They work differently. The account people arrive later, go home earlier, travel more, eat in better restaurants, are quartered in fancier offices, have prettier secretaries, drink their coffee at their desk in china cups, and spend most of their days either in meetings or pushing papers. For example, a creative man reporting on a trip to an account executive office said, "They didn't want to be interrupted. The lazy bastards were practicing golf chip shots on the carpet." "With clubs?" asked the creative man's partner. "No, that shadowboxing shit. Elbows tucked in. Asses waving, fanning the air with make-believe swings." Account people and creative people think differently. Separate vibes and wavelengths entirely. The account man is a graduate business

school man; a political conservative; an orthodox business management man; a stickler for detail, schedules, timetables, and carbon
copies; a believer in research, information systems, data proof, and
never trusting to judgment. This is opposed to the creative man,
who, if he is good, is an intuitive thinker, a hunch player, a person
who depends upon flashes of insight, bursts of imagination, and
fuck the research. The chemistry between these two types is
bound to be bad. It crackles in the air at almost every confrontation.

Management's problem is to equalize, neutralize, or somehow
find a way for these two essential functions to operate smoothly.
The perfect balance is almost never struck. At Ted Bates, Esty,
and Compton, the account men dominate. The result is undis-
tinguished creative work in general but smart marketing and businesslike operation of accounts. At the other extreme are Doyle
Dane Bernbach; Wells, Rich, Greene; DKG; Leo Burnett, and
possibly Young & Rubicam, where creativity generally has the
upper hand. Neither emphasis works well. At Doyle Dane Bernbach, for example, account men are so subordinate that they often
leave in frustration. Agencies such as Bates and Esty have generally
had to pay higher salaries to attract, if they can, good creative
people.

The confrontations, a daily occurrence in ad agencies, are
often bitter. They may go like this. The account man speaks: "I
don't like it. I know the client won't buy it. I don't think we, as
an agency, should show it. It makes us look superficial, dilettante,
wise-ass. Besides the research doesn't support it."

The creative reply: "What makes you think the client is so
stupid? He may go for this like shit through a tin horn. Look at
it, you son of a bitch! It's a gas! It's breakthrough stuff! Standout
advertising! Can't you see it! This will set the goddamn client on
his ear. He'll love it! It is contemporary as hell! Look at that Art
Deco touch, nice, heh? And in the TV commercials, we'll soft
focus the background and shove the goddamn product right up
front like titties. Can't you see it? Christ, man, you just don't
relate."

When differences like this can't be resolved among the two
parties, the problem goes higher. Management has to decide. Here

it is: the management supervisor on one side, the creative director on the other. The ultimate decision is certain to leave one of the original contestants miffed, discouraged. "We've been screwed again."

Management might correct some of this by doing a better edu cational job with both parties. They could make it easier for creative men to understand the marketing and selling problems of the account. They could make it a duty of the account men to know and appreciate the current trends and fashions in creative work. Neither job is done well in the typical ad agency. The account men generally couldn't care less about new foreign films, visiting exhibits at the museums, rock music, new literary styles, visiting a discotheque, or a trip through Greenwich Village. And the creative man, try as many of them do, cannot read a Nielsen (brand-share) report intelligently; hates to plough through massive market research data, even when provided to him; cannot get excited about trends in the marketplace, new merchandising tactics in shopping plazas, or food-store audits. No way. His head can't get it all together.

The third basic problem of management today is facing up to the ground-swell changes taking place in the advertising agency field: the breaking up of traditional functions and services, the new resourcefulness on the part of clients, the rapid rise of new independent services that are taking away or are eroding the value and usefulness of ad agencies. The logical approach would be to tighten up controls, make each function more efficient, and improve the quality of work rendered by each department. This is difficult to do in many cases because agencies have never been very smart about developing strong interdepartmental cooperation. Too often, frictions between departments are allowed to develop.

The solution to this would probably mean more training and educational programs within the agencies. But "training programs are for the birds," say college graduates. M.B.A.s, especially, react violently to additional training. Also many ad agencies have dropped huge investments into programs that simply trained young people so that they could go off to better jobs elsewhere. American ad agencies have been burned badly with training programs for their foreign executives. Foote, Cone & Belding brought a promising executive up from Brazil one time for a six-month indoctrination program. The man asked to bring his family—wife, five children, and a maid—with him. FC&B obliged with a nice suburban home, a company car, and many extras. Two weeks after the man returned to Rio de Janeiro, he left to take a better-paying job with a rival agency.

When David Ogilvy got the big Shell Oil account, he was concerned about rendering top service in all phases of this sprawling account. He was especially worried about Mike Sloan, his young West Coast representative. He called Mike to New York one time. The conversation, as Mike recalls it, went as follows: "These Shell people like golf, I understand. How's your game?" Mike replied, "Fair, ninety-five or so." Ogilvy was concerned. "Not good enough. Won't do. Go back and hire the best golf pro out there, join the best club, improve your game." Mike did. He hired Dutch Harris, a well-known pro, and joined the famous Olympic Golf Club. Six months later, on the very last day of his coaching, Mike played his first par round. The same day he quit to go to work with Papert, Koenig, Lois.

By way of indoctrination, a fair number of agencies publish house organs. BBDO, Ogilvy & Mather, NH&S, J. Walter Thompson, N. W. Ayer are typical. Doyle Dane Bernbach's publication, edited by their P.R. director, Doris Willens, formerly an ad columnist for the old *World Telegram,* is one of the best of this sort of thing. Many are pap, with softball scores, birthdays, want ads, and an annual "salute to our hardworking switchboard operators." Ad agencies are always embarrassed or tongue-tied when they talk about themselves, even for internal consumption. The feeling engendered by house organs is that they are whitewashing a lot of crummy practices.

Another effort made sporadically by agencies is the after-hours or noon-hour department pitch. The head of the media department, for example, might put on a one-hour show purportedly to educate the younger people about the mysteries and purpose of his department. Attendance, if voluntary, is dismal. Some agencies have truly dedicated after-hour classes for aspiring people in different lines. J. Walter Thompson's copy class will assure the top-ranking students a crack at a regular creative job. Benton & Bowles has a sharp training course for media men.

Borrowing from industry, agencies have also tried one- or two-day "retreats." The entire executive staff, from all departments, treks off to a country club, an executive's estate, or a large motel for a series of hair-down sessions. Presumably the country air, the freedom from phones, and the casual clothes will spark friendly new relationships and understandings. They often end up as drinking bouts. A president of one shop was tossed into a motel pool with his clothes on. Bozell & Jacobs took a crew of twenty executives on a trip in rubber rafts down the rapids of the Green River in Idaho.

Overall, the best-managed shops, as far as personnel relations go, are those managed by one man, the founder. Somehow the monarchical system works better than the perhaps more democratic corporate system. Everyone seems to work harder and put up with more inconveniences for the "old man." Maybe it is because the agency business is a personal service business, a people-to-people business. Employees in the one-man agency don't stop to ask, "Who wants this done?" "Who authorized that?" "Who the hell says so?" They know. Everything is done because the boss wants it done. That's sufficient. This may sound contrary to modern management thinking, but it seems to work, especially among creative people. They, particularly, respond better when working for a respected person than when working for an impersonal system.

Until its founder died recently, the Leo Burnett agency in Chicago was archetype of the one-man shop. This highly successful ad agency, which developed such campaigns as "Fly the friendly skies of United" and "You've come a long way, baby" (Virginia Slims), operated for three decades under the firm but benevolent hand of Leo Burnett. It was always a hard-muscle, hardworking shop. But people liked to work there. They put out more, worked later and longer than other places. And the shop grew from zero billings in the bottom of the depression to fifth-ranking in the world. Applicants came from everywhere to work at Burnett. They came from the Great Plains, the Mississippi River towns, from the Eastern seaboard, and some from England and

Australia. They didn't come to get high salaries, to build flashy proof books, or to meet congenial people. They came because there was a man running the place who seemed to know what he was doing. The place had a philosophy, a way of managing that held people together, got the most out of them for the shop and for themselves.

There was in the Leo Burnett agency, as there more often is with a sole-proprietor operation, a kind of old-fashioned paternalism. Modern management doesn't believe in this any more, but it worked here, and it has worked for many other ad agencies.

Leo once hired a young writer from a small town in the midwest (I'll use only his first name, call him Pete.) This man was a slim, wispy Irishman, son of a large ranching family, who wanted to become a good writer. Under Leo's supervision, Pete became a good writer. He was credited with some of the first great Marlboro campaigns, including the idea of putting tattoos on the backs of smokers' hands to register masculinity. In due time, Pete got offers from top agencies all over the country. He turned them down. This was home. Yet, eventually, one irresistible offer came from one of the top shops in New York City. Pete took it. He stayed on his new job for several years, turning out excellent work. He was soon known as one of the best writers in the city. Except for one problem Pete found himself getting inordinately tired, nervous, literally trembling much of the time. He didn't understand it and worked even harder. He changed his job but then lost it after a few months. He got another one and soon lost this one, too. Then began a long siege of job hunting. He had to send his family back home. Weeks went by. Two months. A close friend, who suspected that maybe Pete had a health problem as well as bad luck, suggested a physical examination. The diagnosis: Parkinson's disease. And dangerously advanced.

Somehow Leo Burnett in Chicago learned about this. He found means to communicate. The long-distance phone call reportedly went somewhat along these lines: "Pete, this is Leo."

A "humph."

"I hear things are not going so well."

Another "humph."

"Now you come on back home. Back to your old job. And don't

202

worry about a goddamn thing. Chicago's got the best ad agency and the best doctors in the world."

Pete took a bus that night. The brain surgery for Parkinson's disease costs a minimum of $10,000. Burnett paid for it. For a deserter, too. But a *midwestern* deserter.

One area where ad agency management fails conspicuously is in its inability, or perhaps incompetence, to eliminate the pervasive fear that is so rampant in the business. Admittedly, there is no simple way to cut down on the high turnover of accounts that is one of the basic reasons why it has become such an insecure, thin-ice, what-the-hell-next business. Actually, most ad agency people can learn to live with that fear. It becomes a fact of life. There is no excuse, however, for the other fears agency management either generates or allows to grow and spreads. The fear of failing, the fear of doing an inadequate job, the fear of being fired abruptly. After all, advertising people at work are weaving a flimsy skein. Nearly every job or function is nebulous, unmeasurable, imprecise, and intangible. Who knows what the perfect piece of copy is? Who knows whether the TV commercial will really deliver sales? Who knows whether the media schedule has the best-possible skew? Who knows whether the research is positively accurate, the marketing plan watertight? Was the presentation to the client as good as it could have been? The answers are always subjective. Maybe, maybe not. So an ad person, unlike a banker or lawyer or manufacturer, can never measure his productivity, value, or personal progress in any clearly defined manner. As a result, he worries, stews, builds up anxieties, grows ulcers, often gets clammy with fear.

Reports of this fear in the ad agency business are not exaggerated. Anyone who has been around an agency—especially a big, high-pressure shop—can see the shaky hands as a memo is read; the jolt forward as the senior vice-president answers a routine phone call; the furtive look on the young account executive as he scurries down the corridor; the hard, tense lines of the copywriter's face above the typewriter; the conference-room meetings where shoulders twitch, fingers tug at collars, perspiration shines on the back of the neck. Fear is pervasive in many ad agencies. And often it is ugly. The gulped Martinis at the bars near Grand Central before catching commuter trains, the divorces, the nervous break-downs, the pills, the constant catch-up ball game. Like the $30,000 executive dashing up eleven flights of stairs rather than wait for a slow elevator. He may shave a minute off his arrival time. He does. But the price he pays is a nosebleed spurting luridly down his shirt front. Or the less-fortunate forty-one-year-old ad executive hurrying into 666 Fifth Avenue one morning. He doesn't reach the elevator. Instead, he drops to the lobby floor with a fatal heart attack.

Managements can do more than they now do about removing anxieties and improving morale. How? By showing more apprecia-tion and consideration when something is done well. A comment to a creative man: "The client loved the stuff. Keep it coming!" By removing doubts when possible. A visit to the account man: "We checked out the rumors about trouble at Company X. There is nothing to them. Relax." Memo to the staff: "As you all know, business during the past quarter has not been good. But please be advised, there are *no* plans to reduce staff in any department at the present time."

Marion Harper, if not an ideal manager, was said to be a man of his word. Once on a blizzardy night at a house party of Mc-Cann-Erickson people in Westchester, after everyone had been partying for hours, Marion took the floor. He went around the room asking everyone what kind of a position each hoped to attain in the company. All the executives, half in jest, spelled out their individual aspirations. Marion listened carefully. He then stomped out of the house and promptly fell into a deep snow bank. His glasses weren't found until the following spring when the snow melted. Within two years, each executive who was in the room that night had the exact position he had requested.

10

The Enemies of Advertising

Chocolate bunnies have always been hollow.
Presidential candidates wear makeup on TV.
A house-for-sale ad never lists a leaky roof.
Mickey Mouse gets thousands of fan letters.
FTC commissioners wear black robes, but they aren't judges.
A capon is a chicken.
Gold domes of state buildings are usually gold paint.
Easter rabbits don't lay eggs.

LIFE is full of deceptions; and advertising, reflecting life, contains many. This fact, more than anything else, is the basis of most of the attacks on advertising. The critics both inside the government and outside level most of their charges against practices they consider to be misrepresentations.

Take Santa Claus, for example. The Fisher-Price toy company had to scrap more than $100,000 worth of TV commercials last year because the National Association of Broadcasters code authority said they used a Santa Claus in the action. It was an implied endorsement.

In another case, the FTC charged Du Pont and its advertising agency BBDO with deception in a TV commercial showing a can of Zerex stabbed with an ice pick to demonstrate how the fluid stopped radiator leaks. BBDO fought the case for a year and spent more than $100,000 to document the action. The FTC withdrew the charge. The only basis for the widely publicized attack was an article the FTC had read in a Michigan newspaper. There were no apologies.

Then there is the celebrated case of the marbles in the Campbell Soup commercial. They were put in by a TV director who used them to prop up the chunks of vegetables to get a better camera view. "Fraud," shouted a group of George Washington University law students who organized a whole team of activists to fight the case through the FTC for many months—and at who knows how much cost to taxpayers. They demanded a retraction or correction from Campbell Soup. It all washed down the drain eventually when the case was dismissed, but for a while the "Case of the Glass Marbles" was large-space news in the *New York Times*.

These cases of advertising deception may seem something short of earthshaking, but the critics are serious. And advertising men cannot afford to take them lightly. "But there is no Santa Claus." Never mind. He cannot endorse a product. "Well, how about Mickey Mouse?" Better not try. This is what confuses advertising people. Deception is a relative thing. Is the United States Treasury Department deceptive when it promotes savings with savings bonds although it knows people in most states can earn more money by putting their money in banks? Is the American Cancer Society deceptive when it says smoking causes cancer even though the cause of cancer is still unknown? Is a politician deceptive when he promises more jobs, lower taxes, and prosperity even though he knows he cannot deliver these things?

Advertising people obviously feel they are being judged too harshly on this deception charge. If they are, they have no one but themselves to blame. There is a large legacy of abuse of the truth, of deliberate lying in print, of transparent attempts to hoodwink the public. It may take years—if advertising survives that long—to correct the long-tarnished impression. And it will take diligent self-policing to keep the intransigent advertisers in line. Assuming that advertising will exist, and assuming that there are dedicated and interested people in advertising who hope to clean it up, what action should ad people take toward their critics?

Perhaps what is needed is a better understanding on both sides. Many ad people are stunned by the intensity of the most recent attacks. They fail to understand what is happening in our society today. The aggressive push for a better life, a better environment, a better-informed public. They tend to interpret all attacks against advertising as attacks against business itself—and as a growing demand for socialistic or stronger government control. Some old-timers still subscribe to the "Let the buyer beware" philosophy. And others are simply opportunists—they exist in all professions—hoping to get away with anything they can.

Astute advertising men realize that things must be done soon to save advertising. Some have joined together with the Better Business Bureau on a multimillion-dollar program of self-policing. There is hope, too, from the young new breed of advertising men who genuinely deplore the practices of their predecessors and who are trying to inject a new breath of candor into their advertising.

There is a need for understanding on the side of the critics, too. A typical misunderstanding on the part of many critics involves the role of advertising in the economy. Too many of these people believe, or have been taught to believe, that advertising is an economic waste, that it is an added cost to the price of goods, an unnecessary intrusion in our lives simply to boost profits for big corporations. They believe that business could get along very well without any advertising. Mr. Thoreau, in his musings at Walden Pond, started much of this trend of thought. It is called the "better mousetrap" theory, "Build a better product—and the world will beat a path to your door." Beautiful. But it doesn't work. Advertising—without getting into a long economic argument—is an indispensable tool in marketing. It is the most efficient way to introduce new or improved products to audiences of millions of people. It is the only way to keep a good product on the mass market. It is the best way to foster vigorous competition among brands to prevent monopolies and provide consumers with better products and services. The only substitute would be personal salesmanship. And the cost of armies of salesmen would be prohibitive.

Another common fallacy on the part of critics is the supposed enormous power of advertising to make people do things and buy things they don't need and want. This is flattering but highly improbable. Advertising must fight very hard for the attention of a jaded and apathetic audience. A recent study showed that some

207

75% of all advertising is largely ignored or leaves no memorable impression. Perhaps the cigarette ban on television last year is an example. After the first full year of commercial prohibition, cigarette sales rather than falling off drastically went up 3.4%. Tobacco makers were able to save an estimated $70 million dollars. Advertising does work however—if the product is good—if the message is right—if it reaches the interested prospects. It can't force anybody to do anything. At best it can expose ideas and products to people. As Tocqueville said so well in 1832: "In America, everyone is his own best judge of his needs."

There is also a misunderstanding over the value of brand name advertising. The "brand" or "mark" on merchandise is as old as commerce. Customers have always sought for and found assurance in something known and familiar in their purchase. In earlier days the guild mark or importer's stamp sufficed. But as commerce grew the names of makers had to be established in a larger marketplace, usually by advertising. Good companies, good products, along with the advertising to spread the word, have become an important guide to buying for consumers in all capitalistic societies. Yet to many critics, the concept of brand preference is anathema. The denial, however, is amusing to admen. They smile, for example, at the college professor who rails against advertising. There he stands, a complete example of the brand-conscious individual. In his hand, a well-known brand of Scotch. His suit has proper labels from J. Press or Brooks Brothers. His hi-fi, playing in the background, carries a distinguished name, seen regularly on the advertising pages of the *Saturday Review*. His pipe tobacco is a well-advertised Danish brand. Outside his window sits the inevitable Volkswagen, purchased, he will maintain, because of his individual, rational choice. The adman knows how carefully and adroitly those Volkswagen messages were written to appeal to just such in-group, Calvinistic morality. Now there are ten million individualistic Volkswagen owners.

Another misunderstanding is over the tone and style of advertising. The critics are wont to accuse the creative advertising man of crass and commercial language: esthetically degrading, grammatically incorrect, and appealing to "dim-witted louts." The criticism of this sort can get quite vivid: "Raucous ballyhoo," says Clifton Fadiman. "Extolling of massed drums," says John Kenneth

Galbraith. "The nadir of vulgarity," said Henry Steele Commager. "Temptations to tantalize the basest passions," says Alan Pryce-Jones of the London *Times*. And back farther (criticism of advertising has a long history), old Dr. Samuel Johnson, two hundred years ago, said "It plays wantonly on human frailties." Many of these expletives are apt. But advertising people today are more likely to be college-educated men and women who have a close, almost intimate, feel for their audiences. They regularly meet their readers face to face in consumer interviews. They know their needs, desires, and, yes, their weaknesses. But the attitude is essentially friendly, helpful; and advertising people talk to them in their own idiom.

There is another sort of criticism of advertising that perhaps needs more understanding on both sides. At least it is confusing to advertising people. Call it *class-action* criticism. As the consumer movement grows, there seem to be more and more "spokesmen" for the consumer rising up out of the law schools, the women's service groups, the campuses, and the suburban clubs. To advertising men, these advocates or critics seem to be self-appointed representatives of the masses. They designate themselves to speak for all the other mute members of the public. They seem to judge what "ordinary" people ought to like, ought to buy, ought to read or see in their advertising. Now unquestionably, many of these class-action activists are well-educated and well-intentioned people. But what confuses advertising people is that their choice of products, their choice of advertising, their choice of proper behavior in shopping and buying all reflect their own narrow view of life, not especially the broad view of society. For example, they do not object to advertising for stereo record players, no matter how deceptive it might sometimes get. Nor do they mind advertising for foreign cars, imported wines, fine cheeses, and book clubs. But these same people can get quite violent over advertising for candy bars, dry breakfast cereals, big Detroit cars, cigarettes they don't smoke, soaps and detergents, and TV dinners. Advertising people wonder: Are these class-action activists really trying to protect ordinary people from the products they don't happen to like? Advertising people suggest that perhaps there is a form of elitism at work here along with the good intentions. And they wonder, too, why these recommendations should not be coming instead from public educational channels and from our elected representatives.

Another criticism and another misunderstanding, perhaps, is the furor over advertising's contribution to materialism. This is tough because, yes, materialism is what advertising is all about. It sells products. There is no way around that. It also sells services, but critics have not yet come to complain about an excess of services, which in fact represent about 40 percent of expenditures and are growing fast. It is the excess of products that rankles most. Too many convenience goods. Too many cheap, disposable products. Too many artificially made products. Too many showy, show-off products. Too many loaves of white bread. Too many snacks, candy bars, individual-portion puddings, soft drinks, and dog foods. Advertising, critics believe, forces people to buy all these things they don't need or shouldn't need. It prevents them from buying worthwhile, nutritious, unstylish, durable, well-designed products. If an advertising man takes this criticism seriously, he really is on the horns of a dilemma. Suppose, for example, his client makes plastic dog collars. He knows that although Christmas is coming up, forty million American dogs are not waiting for the great day. Yet he knows that his client will sell perhaps 90 percent of his year's output as Christmas presents for dogs. Now this really is materialism. The adman knows it. What should he do? Suggest that his client close down his plant and instead make yogurt, which apparently is an acceptable, nonmaterialistic product? Or close down the plant entirely and send the workers home? He does neither. He says if people want to buy plastic dog collars or doggie donuts or doggie sweaters, let the client make them. He'll help him sell them.

Our economy is loaded with unnecessary, expendable, nonutilitarian, nonnutritious, useless gadgets, widgets, face creams, nostrums, gimcracks, and what have you. Who is to decide whether people should make them or whether people should buy them? After all, some 37 percent of the median-income family's earnings are discretionary, that is, money not needed for basic food, clothing, and shelter. What should people do with this money? Why shouldn't they do what they wish with it?

Criticism of programs shown on TV probably began on the

very first day of broadcasting. Obviously, nothing was going to be able to please everyone. Very early, the Federal Communications Commission, in issuing licenses, insisted that every station be obliged to broadcast a certain amount of news, public-affairs material, and local programing. Beyond such restriction, stations and networks tried to please the biggest-possible audiences. This meant programs with mass appeal. Mass appeal also suited advertisers, who, in general, want to reach as many people as possible. What the large audiences like and prefer is determined by the ratings. This is a sort of continuous voting process. High-rated shows stay on the air. Low-rated ones are dropped. TV audiences are fickle. They vote "no" much more often than they vote "yes." So there is a high turnover of shows. Providing new material within budgets is difficult. There are a lot of hours to fill up in a day. The sharpest criticism of programing usually comes from the intellectuals who would like to see more esthetically gratifying or educational programs. Many attempts have been made in all sincerity by groups such as the Ford Foundation and by the networks themselves. The result is always a pathetically small audience. Even the intellectuals themselves (as shown by research) elected to watch comedy or pro football rather than a Shakespeare play.

Commercial clutter is another problem. A typical hour of TV programing is interrupted as many as twenty-five times. The number of interruptions, but not the amount of commercial time (about eight minutes out of a network hour, more on local stations), has increased because the high cost of television has made thirty seconds, rather than one minute, the standard commercial unit. Critics suggest that all commercials be eliminated, especially during prime time (6 P.M. to 11 P.M.). The recommendation is naïve. There would be no prime time, no commercial programing at all, without advertiser support. There would be only educational and pay TV. The alternate suggestion critics make is to cut down the number of commercials. Say in half. The result would be cutting program quality in half. Obviously, somebody has to pay the fiddler. Clutter, alas, is common to all commercial media.

On this same subject, there are moves afoot to eliminate all toy advertising from children's TV programs. The ACT group of children's protectionists feels that no amount of restrictions will make the commercials acceptable in their eyes. Hence, they are asking that they all be removed. Fine. Then what happens? All children's TV programs will be removed, too. For who will support them without advertising? Perhaps this would not be serious for the families of the suburban women backers of ACT, who have alternative entertainments, but for ghetto children the loss would be great. Critics can't understand why networks can't afford to do anything they ask. But the major network channels are commercial operations. They must pay their way. They lost some $300 million in cigarette investments last year. When the "fairness" doctrine spreads beyond autos to a wide range of other "controversial" products such as beer, fattening foods, toys, drugs, and others asking "equal time" rebuttals, the losses will be staggering. Few advertisers will spend money to go on the air knowing that their commercials will be followed directly by counterattack commercials. They'll take their advertising budgets elsewhere.

Another frequent charge is that advertising forces expensive style changes upon a gullible public. Seductive ads, they say, manipulate people into buying new cars, new rugs, new-model refrigerators, new apparel styles every year. They call this fictitious obsolescence, a grotesque misuse of power. And again the ad people are guilty. Yes, they are. Although they don't set the styles and the designs, they certainly do their best to promote them. They are guilty. But guilty of what, actually? The demand for newness, freshness, uniqueness has always motivated human behavior. Fashion is the timeliness of today versus the mundaneness of last year. Of course money could be saved if styles were not popular. But they are. And they were in Victorian England, in the Renaissance, probably in the Stone Age, when hunters brought in a new bear's claw necklace or a new berry juice. Style is novelty, the thrill of being different, perhaps bold and adventuresome. Is this wrong? Isn't there enough grimness in the world already?

In practice, however, advertising has mixed results in its efforts to promote style and fashion. Did women obey the ads featuring midi skirts? Do they buy every new fashionable cosmetic that is offered on the market? (Only three out of ten new cosmetic products survive.) With men, the record is worse. Hosiery manufacturers have advertised new styles and colors in men's socks for years. Black is still the choice of 90 percent of the males. For many years, Volkswagen ads, appealing to their select group of ever-so-sensible puritans, promoted the advantages of no style changes. But, alas, fashion conquers all. Volkswagens can now be bought in five styles, six colors, and new changes every year.

The important point is that advertising, in promoting style, is simply offering alternatives, choices, new recommendations. Consumers can very easily stay with their favorites as long as they wish. A women's fashion expert says that basically some 65 percent of all women's styles are the same year in and year out. Brooks Brothers clothing store can go that somewhat further. Recently, when a movie producer asked the store for its recommendations on the clothing styles worn by an American in England in the 1920s, the management replied, "Walk out on the floor and pick anything you see." Advertising doesn't force styles, it makes styles and choice possible.

There is one final area of criticism that seems of keen concern among the critics. This is the use of emotional appeals in advertising. The use of sex appeal, appeal to pride and vanity, to social approval, to athletic prowess, to any promise of psychological or social gratifications is wrong, say the critics. Instead, all products and services should be sold strictly on the basis of cold logic. The only criteria of value should be those that involve weight per penny, grade, size, nutriment content, and so forth. The implication that the product produces a psychic gratification or an emotional pleasure is false and misleading, according to the charge. The adman cannot agree with this. The selling, promoting, and marketing of nearly any kind of product, including a candidate for public office or an opera performance, requires emotional appeals. The total value of a product is seldom determined by its physical properties alone. The purchase nearly always evokes a matrix of emotional responses, some slight, some important. The purchase reflects the purchaser. In a normal, mobile society, people are judged every day by the kind of products they own and use. It is the prime means of establishing personal identity, individuality. Their selection of products and the advertising that helps them select are necessarily emotional as well as logical. The critics say this is wrong. People aren't supposed to buy in this manner.

They should be protected against themselves. Little children, yes, but admen have more faith and respect for American adults.

Overall, the critics who worry admen most are the ones who seem to have the influence with congressmen, the ear of the FTC and the FDA, and access to the pages of important newspapers and magazines. These critics mean business, and they are getting results like never before. Suddenly their combined strengths are being translated into action. Serious, damaging-to-advertising action like the forcing of products off TV, which in turn makes the programing correspondingly poorer because the income is reduced. Like scaring advertisers so much that they dare not say anything in their ads. The trend is toward vapid, toothless, meaningless advertising, which is bad for the companies and little help to consumers. And like discouraging advertising expenditures in total, which can only depress the sale of many products and perhaps close the factories where some of them are made. These are not hysterical reactions. They are as real as the new court judgment that says from now on all "big car advertising" on TV will have to allow a corresponding number of opposition commercials to run against them. This, when it takes effect, will drive most car advertising off the air. If TV programing is poor now, wait to see how bad it can get when $500 million worth of car advertising is withdrawn.

Because advertising is an essential tool of business, advertising people are concerned, too, with the stepped-up attacks on all business in recent years. Especially, against big corporations. Here, too, the effects have been telling. A recent study showed that negative attitudes toward business have increased from 44 percent to 62 percent in this period. Where is all this leading? Do our critics wish business to go away? Is there any conceivable substitute in American society? There surely aren't enough additional jobs in government, the educational system, or other nonbusiness functions to keep eighty million people employed, plus the two to three million young adults entering the labor market annually. Our standard of living is based upon an economic machine that must gross a national product of $1 trillion a year, pay the cost of running the government (which is now at the rate of nearly $250 billion a year), and support state and city expenses (which are

214

mounting alarmingly). Taxes on corporate profits (50 percent plus) pay many of these bills and obviously provide many of the jobs that enable individuals to pay their income taxes. It seems hackneyed to mention the goose that laid the golden egg, but no other simile seems appropriate.

Advertising as a business is ill equipped to fight back against all its critics, Although it is often thought of as some monolithic power with an army of deviously clever experts, actually the ad agency business that creates nearly all national advertising is a pygmy operation. There are fewer than sixty thousand people in the ad agency business. More than half of these are clerical workers. Moreover, it is a very loose group of small businesses. Some 75 percent of all ad agencies have fewer than twelve people on staff. Hundreds are mom-and-pop affairs. There are only a few associations, and these are embarrassingly underfinanced. There are no lobbying funds, so the business has less clout in Washington than the avocado lobby. Actually, the whole industry has not more than three paid men in Washington and none in the state capitals. Only one trade paper can afford a correspondent in Washington. When legislatures, FTC committees, and state and city councils get together to make new laws against advertising, admen are seldom present to defend their cases. They are too busy running the store.

In an economically pluralistic society such as ours, individual industries must have organized support in both people and dollars to present their side of laws and regulations. The big industries (automobiles, textiles, petroleum, and the like) have huge staffs and large treasuries. Advertising as an industry literally ranks in size along with the pickle and condiment industry and the women's blouse business. In fact, the total dollars spent on national advertising in magazines, newspapers, and broadcasting represent something close to 1 percent of our nation's gross national income. And this percentage has grown proportionally smaller every year since 1958. It could be stated properly that advertising is a dying industry. These statistics are presented only to show that as an industry, advertising is in a weak position (and is growing weaker) to fight its enemies. There is no war chest of funds, and there are too few warriors.

Obviously, there will be few mourners if advertising withers away. Admen can expect little sympathy. Yet, perhaps the critics should examine the traditional role advertising has always played in the growth and expansion not only of our economy but in another important area: mass communications. Since the birth of public newspapers (the "penny dreadfuls" of eighteenth-century England), advertising messages have carried the major cost in dispensing news and information. It has been estimated that 75 percent of all public information in democracies is "written on the backs of ads." Oddly enough, the marriage has always been compatible. The editorial pages brought news of events and issues. The advertising pages brought news of products and services. Neither party felt compromised. Advertising has long been the traditional financial support of all newspapers, magazines, commercial radio and TV and in dozens of other ways has paid for theater programs, college yearbooks, student newspapers, neighborhood directories, and the like. Thus advertising has helped mass communications. And mass communications are vital to a democracy. As a University of Chicago Roundtable Seminar summarized the role: "It is the obligation of a free and democratic society to expose as many ideas as possible to the public to reject or accept as it sees fit." If advertising is controlled and restricted into a smaller and smaller role, the advertising man can say with justification: "There will be fewer ideas to expose."

Any student of mass communications can see what has happened to the progress of mass media in recent years. The great era of mass publishing passed its crest more than two decades ago. Ever since then, the number of daily newspapers has declined at the rate of some twenty per year. The famous mass magazines such as *Saturday Evening Post, Liberty, Colliers, Woman's Home Companion,* and more recently *Look* have failed. *Life* magazine is tottering. The "fairness" doctrine spells the eventual demise of commercial television. The cost of mass media has risen far faster than the inflation curve. The newsstand price of magazines on the average has gone up 600 percent in a decade. Newspapers, at least 500 percent. The cost of home delivery of the *New York Times* in New York City is now $114 per year. Is this a mass medium? Can the welfare or ghetto people afford even a daily newspaper?

Why has this happened? The answer is always the same: declining advertising revenues. Mass communication coverage declines in direct relationship to the decline of advertising investments in the media. Simple arithmetic. It is debatable whether mass communications in a free society should "be written on the backs of ads." But it has always been that way. The cost of paper, ink, and production, plus editorial staffs and distribution, have always resulted in a unit cost far too high for the mass public to pay. There are books of course, but $7.95 for a typical hardcover book today is hardly a mass communication product. It is acutely ironic that this generation—the most literate and best educated—faces a future of declining accessibility to informational materials, that the more equipped the people are to appreciate and use mass communication materials, the less available these materials are to them.

The question then is: Can advertising survive its critics? And if it doesn't, can mass communications survive?

11

What Advertisers Know About You

SOME PEOPLE are afraid of advertising. They suspect that the ad makers are clever rascals who have a vast arsenal of high-powered techniques that are capable of unmasking your innermost secrets, weaknesses, and frailties so that they can then exploit you. They've heard about the vast armies of interviewers roaming the country, invading homes, buttonholing people on streets, in bus and airline terminals, to ask probing and often very personal questions. Or enticing people into conference rooms for long discussions on products while creative people eavesdrop behind one-way mirrors. Or bribing people to spend hours in darkened movie theaters to review reels of TV commercials. Or they know about whole towns used as hamster colonies to test new products, ideas, or ads. All these efforts to find things out about you: your behavior patterns, habits, likes and dislikes, and other things that should be none of their damn business.

Is this true?

Yes, advertising people do want to know what makes you tick. They have to know or else waste millions of dollars on new products that fail. Or lose thousands of dollars on ads or commercials that you won't look at or won't respond to. Or they can waste both time and money putting their advertising messages on television shows you, as a prospect, don't see, or in magazines you don't read, or on outdoor billboards when you don't drive a car. Advertising is expensive. A TV commercial costs $65,000 a minute. A national magazine color page ad costs $50,000. This is too much money to gamble if you aren't going to be there to see it or, if you do see it, either don't pay any attention to, don't like, or forget two minutes after it is gone.

That's why advertising people need research. To cut the risks.

Are they successful? Only part of the time. And many times, despite the most highly refined and very expensive research, they fail disastrously. For example, a big food company set out to make a better chocolate cake mix. They put home economists to work for a year creating every conceivable kind of chocolate cake: German chocolate, Swiss chocolate, sweet chocolate, semisweet chocolate, dark chocolate, light chocolate, chocolate mint, chocolate fudge, chocolate malt, chocolate of forty-five different varieties. Then they went through all the cake textures: light, heavy, moist, and so forth. More variations. Finally, after more than a year of testing among small panels of typical consumers, they came up with the perfect chocolate cake. Now they went to hundreds of people for further tests. Not ordinary people. But "heavy users." People who eat cake three or more times a week. The real, serious cake eaters. They asked them to compare it with other chocolate cakes in blindfold tests. This took months because they had to sample different parts of the country to be sure the new chocolate cake would be popular everywhere. And hurrah! The cake was a winner. The cake eaters ate it up.

So then the company, congratulating itself on its diligence and hard work and confident of their scientific research, launched the product on the market. Several millions of dollars had been spent up to this point. And out it went into the stores. Where it bombed.

Many months later they discovered their error. They had researched the chocolate cake among cake eaters in general. They should have researched it among chocolate-cake eaters. There is a difference. People who like chocolate cake, the heavy chocolate-cake eaters, have much different preferences. They like a darker, richer, moister chocolate cake than ordinary cake eaters, who eat an occasional piece of chocolate cake.

This is what marketers are up against all the time. It is called *market segmentation*. That is, there is no such thing today as a mass market. America is split up into thousands of small groups of customers. Segments of people who need a shampoo that helps with dry split ends. People who want a fine-ground, dark-roasted, medium-rich coffee. People who want a breakfast cereal that both adults and children like but that is not too low in nutrition or too sweet and that does not get soggy too fast in milk. Or people who insist on specific colors, tastes, textures, and qualities of products. How are companies going to know these things if they don't go out and ask the people?

The trouble is when you ask people, they often don't know themselves or they give you the wrong answers, not purposely, but maybe because of the way you asked the question. If you asked someone if he would like to read *The New Yorker* or buy a high-priced brand of Scotch, he might say "yes." But left to himself he buys *Playboy* and an average-priced Scotch. This is the prestige error or bias. There are a multitude of errors that can be made in research. Asking the right questions of the wrong people. Asking the wrong questions of the right people. Interpreting the answers incorrectly. Not asking enough people. Having the wrong people asking the questions. If the interviewer is a smart-looking young woman, the answers she gets will be different from those given if the questions are asked by a not-so-good-looking middle-aged woman. If the questionnaire is too long, fatigue sets in and the answers at the end are useless. Then there are interviewers who are not honest. They fake the questionnaires rather than make the calls. There are techniques that are wrong. For example, if only demographic studies are made (age, income, education, and so forth) as a basis, the answers might come out wrong. Psychographic studies should have been used, too. These classify people by their life-style habits (do they play golf? take foreign trips?) and by their behavior patterns (how many books do they read? which magazines? which brands of liquor do they buy? which programs do they watch on TV? what records do they listen to?). For example, people who drink Scotch are more likely to own hi-fi sets. Or if a man owns a small foreign car, doesn't smoke, and likes a glass of wine with his meals, he is a bad prospect for a Hawaiian vacation, for an outboard motorboat, or a subscription to *Reader's Digest*. Similarly, if a woman sews some of her own clothes, sees a play three times a year, and belongs to a civic group,

220

she is a poor prospect for canned spaghetti sauce or Bisquick. These are called *cluster patterns*. People who like one set of things will subconsciously prefer another set of things. So says research.

Americans today pride themselves on their individuality and independence of thought. Researchers know different. They know that some of the most fiercely independent people are slavishly addicted to faddism. The fads, however, are in-group, "our crowd" imitations. College professors and their Volkswagens, their organic-food eating habits, their concern for pure streams and the preservation of imperiled species. Young metropolitan liberals have their cluster of beliefs, behavior patterns, and consumption habits. Blue-collar workers also follow a long list of predictable actions. For example, a construction worker on vacation is more likely to buy first-class tickets than a business executive is. He will spend more money on a brand of liquor than a doctor will spend. People who belong to book clubs are good prospects for records, seeds, and bulbs by mail and are more likely to be in the thirty-five-to-forty-five-year-old bracket. This mysterious kind of information is extremely important to companies. It helps them locate those tiny slots in the marketplace where their particular kind of product will sell.

This segmentation aspect of research and marketing is the prime reason for the high standard of living in America. It makes choice and diversity both possible and profitable. It is the reason why a large supermarket will carry from 6,000 to 8,000 different items. Why there are approximately 45 different brands of breakfast cereal, 138 different kinds of snacks, 150 brands of coffee, 35 varieties of bread, and at least 30 flavors of ice cream, despite the fact that more than 50 percent of the people will buy vanilla. It would seem incredible that a manufacturer would make a product that he knew beforehand would appeal to less than 1 percent of the people. Yet they do it every day. More than 25 brands of cigarettes hold less than 1 percent of the market. Popular Virginia Slims is considered by Philip Morris to be a very successful brand. Only 1.2 percent of smokers buy it.

Drug products are segmented into even finer slices. A typical drugstore carries 40,000 items. There are dozens of products for a simple headache. But to each sufferer, only one is exactly right for him. In fact, to show how research works, medical scientists know that no headache remedy, including aspirin, can actually bring relief from a headache in less than twelve minutes. It takes that long for the ingredients to get into the bloodstream. Yet most people will swear that they feel relief from a product like Alka-Seltzer, Bufferin, or regular aspirin within a few minutes. And, in truth, they do. Once the product is ingested and given a few moments to get into the stomach, the sufferer's mental attitude changes. He knows that he has done something concrete about relief. And amazingly, this mental attitude releases tensions and nerves. He does, indeed, begin to feel better. This is called the *placebo effect,* named after a simple sugar pill that, when given to people who cannot take any other kind of medicine at a particular time, brings immediate relief.

These facts are important to researchers because it reveals how products are segmented into even finer and more subtle groupings. That is, by psychological as well as physical differences. A cough remedy for a hypochondriac, for example, is different from one for a normal person. The product might be similar, but the package, the taste, and the name should reflect an understanding of the attitudes peculiar to the hypochondriacal cold sufferer. Maybe the pill is larger, the taste is bitter, and the package is old-fashioned looking, with much small type. These embellishments instill confidence in the user. He feels he is getting the really powerful stuff. As a result, he gets relief faster. Again, the psychological response.

How do researchers find these things out?

As already mentioned, the heavy user is the key person. The success of the brand will depend ultimately on whether this customer is pleased. Also as noted before, the heavy-user group can be very small and still provide a sizable business for the company. A food or a drug brand can usually make a profit if total sales reach at least $5 million per year. Nationwide, this is not a great many people. For example, what percentage of the population are regular purchasers of Tabasco sauce, a devilishly pungent red sauce that comes in a tiny bottle not much larger than a lipstick? Yet this family-owned company in the bayou section of Louisiana has been operating profitably for more than a hundred years. There is a steady market also for fresh French bread flown in daily from Paris.

222

And for whale steaks, fresh baby octopuses flown in from Sicily, and imported honey made by bees who feed only on roses or alfalfa.

Finding the special audiences and then determining how heavy their usage is involves some strange kinds of research. Some of it is Orwellian. For example, households are induced to save their trash in plastic bags so that researchers can pick it over. Others permit researchers to come into their houses periodically to count the contents of their bathroom medicine cabinets. Others are checked by researchers in supermarkets who politely stop people and ask, "I noticed you just picked up Maxim freeze-dried coffee. Why did you prefer that over Brand X freeze-dried coffee?" The researcher may get a brusque reply for an answer, or she may find the customer willing to talk. The answer may seem ridiculously vague such as "Oh, I don't know, I tried the other kind for a while, it didn't seem to satisfy my husband." The word *satisfy* is significant. Enough replies such as this could mean that Brand X is milder, blander, not dark enough, not strong enough in aroma, or too something else. The point is: People can seldom articulate the precise reasons why they like or dislike a product. Their actions speak louder than their words. Here are some actions that marketers have discovered about women.

Three out of five women don't make breakfasts for their families.

Forty percent of housewives do not put the spread on the bed in the morning when they make it.

A large percentage of women will not buy eggs without peeking into the box. (So, coming soon is a clear plastic egg box.)

Women will buy a round package faster than a square package.

Women prefer reds, blues, and yellows to browns, greens and grays.

Women often prefer to do a little preparation work in cooking rather than simply dumping the package into a pan. A sauce sells better if she can add something. A cake mix sells better if an egg or milk has to be added.

Women will pick up a package faster if it has a picture on it than if it simply has a design.

Women who own pets consider the animal a member of the

223

family and often buy things like snacks, Christmas presents, and clothing, knowing full well the animal doesn't need or want these things.

Women who have children are hostile to women who don't, although it may never be outwardly visible.

Women will look at a picture of a nude woman longer than a man will. The explanation: She seeks comparison.

Women, when overhearing a conversation about hair, will automatically reach and touch their own hair. Similarly with a conversation about fingernails. It is impossible to stop a woman from looking at her own. Moreover, she will look at them outstretched with the backs toward her face; a man looks at his palms forward.

Women will watch a commercial more closely if it has people in it than if it has only objects.

These are just a small handful of the thousands of items of information advertising people have cataloged about people and human nature. It is not that they are nosy or trying to invade people's privacy, but these often tiny observations can make or break expensive marketing projects. And for ad agency men, it can mean the difference between holding a big account or losing it.

We shouldn't let the men off so easily. Here are some things researchers know about them.

Men TV viewers, perhaps as expected, like professional sports programs, news, action movies, Westerns, and foreign locales.

Men respond faster to illustrations or ads with action, violence, conflict, adventure. They are left cold by romance, emotional problems between sexes, babies, and children.

Men are attracted to symbols and objects that are squared off, dark in color (browns, dark reds, and the like). They are fascinated by tools, gadgets, cars, modes of transportation, guns, and military equipment.

Men are haphazard shoppers. They throw all kinds of extravagant things in shopping carts. They hate to shop for their own clothes. They seldom compare prices for routine purchases.

Men often worry more about inadequacies than women (sexual prowess, masculinity, health, progress in careers, retirement, and so forth).

Men's interest in products is obviously selective. Automobiles, airlines, beer and liquor products, machine tools, boats, and sports and recreational equipment stop them first.

Men are less sympathetic, compassionate, or charitable about social issues than women.

Men's reading habits are somewhat different from women's. Men prefer crime and detective, history, war and military, sports themes, and biography. Women's high interests are personal appearance, family and children, romantic fiction, travel, cooking, health, and interior decorating.

Men today are less action-oriented and bellicose than previous generations. In fact, recent inkblot tests show fewer differences between college-age men and women today than a generation ago.

Again, it is obvious why ad people must study consumers closely. It is all part of the new accountability companies are demanding of their advertising agencies. "Okay, but why?" "Prove that this will work." Or, "If this commercial turns out to be a cropper, you know whose nuts will be in the wringer."

Testing TV commercials is a special complication. If you find a lot of commercials on the air that annoy, irritate, or drive you up the wall, don't be too hard on the advertising people who created them. You, or people like you, were the judges. Hardly any frequently seen commercial on the air appears there without testing. Some panel of people, supposedly a statistically valid sample of potential consumers, has seen this commercial, compared it with others, and made their choice. For example, those thousands of apparently silly little episodes involving two women talking over the virtues and faults of a laundry product are on the air because more women respond to this technique than they do to other ways of presenting the story. Creative people would love to see other more creative and exciting things on the air. They fight, shout, squabble, and often quit their jobs because they can't get fresher, newer ideas on the air. But who can fight the "voice of the people"? If the audience of housewives sitting in a small test theater doesn't like the new idea, it's thumbs down.

Some of these tests of commercials are weird. The women seated in the theater allow instruments to be attached to their wrists or palms. This will register minute differences in the rate of perspiration during a commercial. Others will be tested by the movement of their eye pupils. If the pupils widen, they like what they are looking at. If they narrow to catlike slits, they don't like what they see. Other tests measure the rate of breathing, the movement of feet or arms; and in some rare cases, brain waves will be recorded. The most accepted final test of a commercial's value as a selling tool is taken when the women leave the theater. They are invited to take one free sample of the various branded products they have just seen in the commercials. This is the moment of truth. The commercial might have been noisy, in bad taste, and irritating; but if it made the woman pick the product over other brands, you can be sure the client will put his money on that one.

The spooky thing about research is that it often reveals things about people they didn't know themselves or would never openly admit. This is why there are so many apparent paradoxes in making and selling products. A furniture company, for example, was certain that young people would prefer smart, modern furniture for their new homes. Yet research said no. Although everything else about these young people's life-styles is youthful, swinging, and contemporary, something subconscious happens when they buy furniture. They seek stability, instant heirlooms, a feeling and look of tradition in their new homes. They would buy antiques if they could afford them. Or another company, a maker of sports cars, was certain that his best prospects would be performance-minded, speed-conscious, style-conscious young men. But no, older men, over forty, turned out to be the best customers. They were apparently seeking a youthful image.

Other paradoxes often upset companies and ad agencies. You'd think, for example, that food products rich in nutrition and low in price would appeal primarily to lower-income groups for whom the cost of food is a large part of their budgets. No, again. The heavy users of high-nutrition health foods are among well-educated and, often, youth-culture consumers. The poorer people buy the more expensive, more convenient, less nutritious foods. And they do this even when the differences are clearly pointed out to them. Marketing is full of such contradictions. The fashion industry was certain that it had a winner with the new long-length skirts and dresses. They had read their research, which told them that people were in the mood for a return to the thirties and forties in styles

226

and fashions. The revival trend was evident everywhere—in movies, in art, posters, theater. Yet when they came out with the long skirts, women turned them down. Detroit auto makers, hurting from the inroads of foreign car sales, have done everything possible to capture some of the foreign magic. They copy the styles, put European-sounding names on the cars, try to match them in economy and performance. Yet month after month for the past five years, the foreign cars have increased their share of the market.

The methods of testing such subconscious responses are often freakish. Dr. Ernest Dichter, the famous motivationalist, sometimes uses role playing. He will gather a group of people together and ask them to act out the role of products. "Make believe you are a stick of celery. How do you show your feelings?" Or he may purposely get a group of people into an intense and hostile argument, during which time they will reveal things about subjects that would not otherwise come to the surface. Another researcher, Dr. Emanuel Denby, is a specialist on psychographics. His researchers will study a community in great depth for a long period of time. He will observe how they socialize with each other. How they will purchase one brand of liquor for themselves, another when they entertain. They will be observed on vacations, on trips, in backyard barbecues. All this provides a pattern that marketers can then follow successfully in deciding what products to sell to which people. Dr. Burleigh Gardner, a noted sociologist, has discovered important new facts about the upwardly mobile blue-collar worker. Dr. Daniel Yankelovich has made many revealing contributions about how social issues can affect people's attitudes toward buying products. For example, how serious is the anti-Establishment attitude of young people in the purchase of products from large corporations? How does the increased interest in conservation and ecology affect the use of products made with artificial ingredients? There are many other specialists, including anthropologists, psychiatrists, and behavioral scientists, who are used by ad makers to learn about their markets and shape their messages to reach the targets.

There is also a great deal of follow-up research to tell companies what you actually do when you go shopping. The speed of movement of products are tracked almost every inch of the way from factory to warehouses to stores. Companies use a research firm such as Arthur Nielsen to tell them how fast certain brands sell in supermarkets. Another company, such as Sales Area Markets Index, will track the movement of goods out of warehouses into stores. They are able to tell how much faster one brand sells in St. Louis than in San Diego. Another, such as the Lloyd Hall Company, will tell marketers whether the brand is out of stock, whether it is in the wrong location in the store, whether promotion signs are on display. Another company, such as Simmons, will compare the ranking of brand popularity among different cities. It is surprising, often, to see how wide the difference is. Kellogg's corn flakes might be number one in Boston, number three in Philadelphia, number five in Houston. Still another kind of research organization will tell companies that you are switching your shopping from downtown department stores to suburban stores, that you are eating more meals out of the house, that you are doing more buying by mail and telephone.

Then there is the whole area of research that reports the kind of response you give to advertising. The difference between a one-minute commercial and a thirty-second commercial. The difference between humor and a straight pitch. The difference between commercials that tell a story and commercials that demonstrate the product. The same kind of research measures your likes and dislikes about magazine ads, about TV program preferences, about newspaper reading habits. There are ratings, ratings, ratings on everything. And they often drive advertising people, especially creative people, out of their minds because (as pointed out before) research can be wrong. If Doyle Dane Bernbach followed research findings, it would never have run its many famous campaigns over the years for Volkswagen, Avis, Polaroid, and others. If companies had listened only to research, many products such as frozen foods, instant coffee, and even Coca-Cola would never have appeared.

Some of the things advertisers know about you may be surprising. Here are some random bits of information.

Two out of every five garments worn by women and children are home-sewn.

Two-thirds of all china is bought by brides. And more than ever, this is coming from Japan. The most popular design is white with gold trim.

Thin women pay more attention to ads about diet foods. Fat women apparently try to ignore them. Sixty million Americans are on diets.

Imported foods are getting more popular. The increase in travel is one of the main reasons. The most popular imported products are wines, cheeses, jams, jellies, spices, snacks, teas, and cookies.

Wine has one of the fastest-growing sales pictures of all alcoholic beverages. Light table wines are most popular, especially among young marrieds. Champagne sales are also increasing rapidly. So are soft drink and wine combinations.

Desserts are in trouble in America. Fewer people eat them daily. Fewer housewives care about cooking or preparing them. Pies and cake mixes are on the decline. Frozen desserts and baked goods are increasing.

Hair conditioners, many with protein for body and control of hair, are hot products among women these days. Hair "thickeners" are selling well to older men. The "dry" look for young men is popular. Also, for young men with long hair, sprays are popular.

Cigars are losing out. Even with the boost after the cigarette warnings, the old-fashioned, smelly image hurts sales to new users, except for some of the thin, stylish, small cigars (about 20 percent of the market).

Cheese consumption is rising. Its use increases with income, education, age, and suburban living. This is said to be a result of increased travel. Cheddar is still the most popular form, but new imports, especially Italian cheeses, are widening tastes.

Beef and then chicken are still the favored meats. Lamb and pork are declining. Cold cuts and sandwich meats are increasing in popularity and variety.

Fish is consumed mostly on both coasts. Consumption in the middle states is much lower. Most housewives know very few kinds of fish and how to cook them.

Twenty-five percent of all food consumed by Americans is eaten between meals. These snack products are getting more popular every year. The favorites: potato chips, corn chips, and pretzels. Cheese and ham flavors are popular. The new dry-roasted nuts are helping increase the consumption of nuts

The fastest change in eating habits by Americans is the switch to highway eateries. There are now 40,000 of the places and the number is growing by about 25 percent every year. Hamburger and chicken joints are the most popular.

Fashion styles are upsetting manufacturers greatly these days. This is because the styles, instead of filtering down from the famous designers of Paris and New York, are filtering "up" from young people (communes, high school students and hippies). Also, the everyone-is-wearing-it faddism may be gone forever. More women dress entirely to please themselves today, and the stores are accommodating them.

Advertising people accumulate thousands of bits of information like these before preparing ads. As one adman said, "A lot of it is crap, but it's like a racing form. A nice thing to have when you are at the track betting on unknown horses."

Advertising research, for all its flubs and failures and its occasional success, serves the American consumer very well. After all, its primary aim is to find out what you want and the best way to get it to you. All the research on products, either improved ones or new ones, ultimately benefits consumers. All the research on communications (which commercials are most effective? which programs most popular?) in theory results in constantly improved communications. Obviously, the selfish aim of the manufacturers is to make more profit. But that's the way the competitive system works. If you make a better product, you will make more money. Better advertising creates less waste. Nobody profits from waste.

The area of new-product research has expanded enormously in the past decade. As companies have come to realize that perhaps half the products they make today will be outmoded or unwanted in five years, they have been forced to develop systems for creating a steady stream of new products. It has been a traumatic experience. New products within a company are hot potatoes. Nobody wants to be associated with a costly disaster, and the percentage of failures is very high.

Oddly enough, companies are not the best sources of new

product ideas. The new products developed by companies are often created simply because of certain production facilities, previous experience, or the whims of certain executives. None of these reasons are likely to produce an outstanding new product idea. Astute corporations get help from outside. They retain new-product experts and new-product workshops, or they buy new product ideas outright

Every new-product idea has to be researched in great depth. Is there a need for it? Who wants it? Why? What form should it take? What price? For what age group? Income group? For what psychological group?

A new system used by the Marplan division of Interpublic checks out more than 100 different product characteristics (color, taste, texture, convenience, weight, shape, mildness, harshness, softness, flexibility, smell, safety, ease of use, type of package, length of storage life, and so forth, and so on), and all these have to be tested against all other existing products of a similar nature in the marketplace. For example, Cool Whip, a new whipped-cream substitute by General Foods, went through thirty-four different versions. They even tested different shades of whiteness. Detroit works three to four years ahead on new car models. One of the important things tested is whether the product has what is known as *perceived* value or *dramatizable* newness. The first electric shaver had this, the first ball-point pen, and instant coffee. Then it is very important that it have a good name, a name that tells what the product is, what it does. Head & Shoulders for a dandruff product had this. So did Popsicle, Campbell's Chunky Soups, and a new product called Rain Barrel (a water softener).

Will Rogers once said that research is like a weather report: "It tells us what kind of weather we are having." And so it does. But doesn't everyone like to hear a weather report before going out in the cold?

12
Advertising's Sex Life

THE ADVERTISING BUSINESS has always been edgy about its women. J. Walter Thompson, Young & Rubicam, and other shops had rules for years that males and females could not share the same office. Other agencies set off separate wings or sections where all women sit together. This only leads to names like "women's detention ward," "the nunnery," or "the cave of the man-eaters." Other rules still in existence in this women's lib era include no out-of-town travel, no after 7:00 P.M. working hours, no staying on the job after the fifth month of pregnancy. And if an affair is discovered in an office, it is always the female who is asked to resign.

Everybody knows it's not fair. And, in fact, it is getting better. Executives think twice before asking secretaries to fetch them coffee or do noontime shopping for them. They listen a bit more carefully to women in meetings, take them along with them to meet with clients more often, and gradually are paying them better, if not yet fair, salaries. One major agency, without explanation, canceled its annual touch football game between its junior executive team and the Bunny team from the Playboy Club.

Women are important to advertising. In order to create the right kind of ads, agencies need the "woman's touch," the "feminine mystique," and, yes, the proper "sex angle." After all, 85 percent of all advertising is directed to women. Women control the largest share by far of the household budgets. Women also outnumber men in ad agencies. The typical staff is 65 to 70 percent female.

232

Many of the top specialists' jobs are dominated by women: casting, fashion coordinating, librarians, media buyers, and many big jobs in television production. About 35 percent of the typical creative department is female.

It's never easy for women. The successful ones often take on the man's-world characteristics. They play the political games. They use their rank and titles for all they are worth. They build up reputations for being "tough," "demanding," "hard-driving," "just like a man." And who can say that this is perhaps the only way to success? For all that men complain about women in business who "lose their femininity," the records prove that the soft-spoken, quiet-mannered girl is not likely to advance rapidly in the aggressive atmosphere of today's ad agencies. Sometimes the women can combine the two qualities successfully. "Think like a man; act like a woman." Some who do are: Solita Arbib, of Norman, Craig & Kummel; Nadeen Peterson, of D'Arcy-MacManus; Jacqueline Brandwynne, head of her own agency; Shirley Polykoff (Foote, Cone & Belding), multiple award winner for Clairol; Margot Sherman, top woman at McCann for many years; Mary O'Meara, number-one female at Young & Rubicam for a long period; Franchelle Cadwell, head of Cadwell Compton; Reva Korda, vice-president at Ogilvy & Mather; Jean Rindlaub, BBDO's top woman for years; Janet Wolfe, executive vice-president, creative, at William Esty; Mary Ayers, member of the board of directors at SSC and B; Harriet Rex, copy supervisor at J. Walter Thompson; Virginia Miles, the only senior vice-president at Young & Rubicam; and Phyllis Robinson, creative vice-president, and Dorothy Parisi, V.P. & general manager of Doyle Dane Bernbach.

Male creative people are guilty of baiting the women. They dub them with names such as "the iron butterfly," "the velvet claw," "the dragon lady," and "Baby Jane." The resentments go both ways. One genuine gripe women have is that for years many of the top creative people on women's products (detergents, food, even cosmetics) have been men. Another is the lack of respect they get from many clients. Nadeen Peterson, a top creative director now at D'Arcy-MacManus, got this treatment from a client one time. In the middle of an important meeting, the client turned to Nadeen and said, "Hey, little girl, how about running down and getting

233

some Cokes." Nadeen could have been earning twice the salary of the client.

Another woman lost this battle. She had attended an important trade show and just happened to fall in behind a group of executives from the agency's major competitor. The conversation, as she reported it back at the agency, was all about a new product they were putting into a test market. As she told the story, all the agency execs leaned forward saying, "Yeah, yeah, yeah, then what happened?" The end was, alas, anticlimactic. "Well," the lady reported wistfully, "they were just at the point of saying what the product was—and they disappeared into the men's room."

Women creative people are often caught writing headlines with double entendres that they fail to see until the last, and often embarrassing, minute. A copywriter at J. Walter Thompson writing on the Libby tomato account uncorked this one at a meeting. "All our tomatoes come blushing from the can." When the laughs quieted, she asked innocently, "Is 'blushing' a bad word?" Shirley Polykoff had a long siege getting her famous headline for Clairol approved: "Does she, or doesn't she?" It wasn't until a survey among women, who found it guileless, that *Life* magazine would accept it.

In Canada a while back, a headline got away before the double-entendre critics got a chance to stop it. It was an outdoor poster showing a pretty housewife with a bottle of catsup on a tray. The catsup, long used in restaurants, was now being introduced to homes. The line: "He gets it downtown, now give it to him at home!" In this same bag is the bread campaign that uses the slogan: "You had it at Grossinger's, now have it at home." (Grossinger's is a resort specializing in "singles" weekends.)

BBDO girl copywriters must lead a cloistered life. One top female writer working on the Dupont nylon hose account, back when stockings went only to the knees, pleaded with a conference room full of men to accept a headline she insisted was perfect: "Now, 14 inches of sheer delight!" Also at BBDO another mixed up the Dupont slogan "Better things for better living" with this version: "Better things for better loving."

Woman copywriters in England apparently have the same problem many American women have when it comes to writing headlines with double meanings. For example, there was a woman at Young & Rubicam in London who wrote this classic. (First, an explanatory note: In England a man gets a "rise" in salary, not a "raise.") So here is the headline: "How to help your husband get a rise. Give him Grape Nuts every morning." And another written for a round-shaped chocolate malt candy called Malt-teasers. The girl's headline, written in all innocence, was: "Reach for the best balls in Britain."

Some of the women get back at the men, one way or another. At Compton, the unmarried female executives always made a point of working on any holiday that came in the middle of the week. The following day, they sprung scads of terrific work on the inactive men. Another woman, one of the smartest in the business, Paula Green, who is now a partner at Green Dolmatch, wears her hair in a long pony tail. When she gets in an elevator full of agency men, she talks animatedly all the way down and emphasizes every word with a sharp snap of her head. On one occasion, three men got stinging slaps of her tail across their faces during the elevator trip. Then there are other women who win over their rivals the best way of all. They marry them.

Still there is the uneasiness. And sooner or later it comes to that *vive-la-différence* business. The conflicts, the confrontations, the competition between sexes. No matter how careful or strict an ad agency is, the female as sex object messes up the smooth running of an agency's affairs. Eyes and hands begin to roam. Clandestine dates are made. Affairs develop. Romances flourish. And so, inevitably, a certain amount of off-premises intercourse takes place. It happens in every business. It happens more in advertising because of the way the agency business is put together. Unlike most business offices, which are populated largely by an executive corps and a staff of high school graduates, female clerks, and secretaries, ad agencies have a very high percentage of professional women. Smart, good-looking, college-educated, and many of them single.

Besides, there is that reputation the ad business rightly or wrongly has. A swinging, hang-loose, morally permissive occupation. Novels and movies have exaggerated this, but then there are quite a number of admen and women who feel obliged, or at least

235

willing, to live up to the fiction. The atmosphere and climate of a typical ad agency can often get sex-charged. There is indeed much close working together, much give-and-take, fun-and-anger, much necessary intimacy. There are the common pressures, the tension, the winning and losing of accounts, the breakneck deadlines, which demand close personal relationships. If sparks develop between men and women, they are quite likely to ignite into something bigger, sooner or later. However, the senior vice-president and the branch manager of a major agency should not have been caught taking a shower together in his private office bathroom. He was fired.

The president of a highly respected major ad agency on Madison Avenue had an office-wide reputation for paying too much attention to the women. The chairman had heard these comments but failed to act. The president was a very competent executive. One noon hour, however, he chanced into a little-used conference room in a remote corner of the office and found his president on the top of the conference table with one of the young lady employees. This was it. The president was gracefully retired. The agency, however, has never regained the momentum it had at the time of the dismissal.

Another president, also with a reputation for high living, had been dodging his chairman for days because he anticipated a stern lecture. One day, however, he got an especially good piece of news from one of the ad agency's major accounts. He decided that this was the ideal time to get the confrontation over with. He hurried to the chairman's office, only to find the man headed into the executive bathroom. He followed him in and, as the episode was reported by the president, "I joined him at the urinals." Sure enough, the chairman began his lecture right there and then. The president, however, was prepared. Again in his own words, "With my free hand, I whipped out the telegram and held it up against the wall where he could read it. It said, "Thanks to your efforts, we are awarding your agency an additional $5 million in billings." The chairman, as the president reported, "sputtered and turned blue."

So the business is perhaps freer and morally less inhibited than many others. Sexual compliance, however, is not expected of women, or demanded. There are no casting couches, no females hired because an executive wants a personal office concubine. This is because advertising is a tough, exacting business, depending upon skilled performers. There is no room on payrolls for those whose talents are demonstrable only in bed.

Let's be realistic. Of course, there is a certain amount of "entertaining" that is expected in the agency business. If a client wants to see an off-Broadway nude revue, he'll be accommodated. If a printing supplier should decide it appropriate to bring a couple of female exhibitionists to a catered luncheon in a hotel suite, it won't be considered scandalous. Or if an out-of-town client wants a call girl, and he doesn't make too big a deal out of it, he'll generally get cooperation from his agency. This is usually handled with a black book of phone numbers. Although one agency exec handled such requests by passing out a nicely engraved business card with a phone number on it. The card tactfully said, "Acme Car Rental," with no street address. This just in case the client's wife found it in his suit later. Also listed: "Hourly, evening, and *weekly* rates."

The need to entertain varies with the type of clients. Most of today's major packaged-goods advertisers are staffed by generally well-behaved executives. They enjoy being taken to fine restaurants such as Le Pavillon, Le Madrigal, Lutèce, Café Chauveron, Brussels, or La Grenouille. They may be happy to know that you have made theater reservations for them. If they play squash or handball, an after-work session at an athletic club is appreciated. In general, most top executives don't expect a wild time. There is still a class of clients, however, many from the major oil companies, tire companies, and Detroit car makers who do expect an old-fashioned night on the town when they come to New York. Amazingly, some of these men are *Fortune* 500 names. And conversely, many New York ad agency men on business trips to Chicago, New Orleans, San Francisco, and Los Angeles let the traces down.

Getting home from extracurricular activities seems to be a special frustration of philandering admen. The last commuting train is missed; the illegally parked car is towed away. The taxi trip to the suburbs is prohibitive, maybe $45 in cash. One executive lived in Princeton, New Jersey, an exclusive ad and publishing habitat. The train he stumbled onto from Penn Station at 3:00 A.M. made a scheduled stop at Princeton Junction, and theoretically he could have been in his own bed by 4:30 A.M. However, he slept soundly to the end of the line, Philadelphia's main station. It was now 6:00 A.M. A fuzzy look at a train schedule told him that the next train back would get him into New York City at 8:50. He caught the train and headed immediately for the dining car where he ordered a pot of hot coffee. He decided he would pull himself together first with some nourishment before trying to wash up in the tiny men's room of the train. He was mildly congratulating himself on his clever plan to arrive in the office with no one the wiser. At about this moment the train slowed down to the single stop it made between Philadelphia and New York, Princeton Junction. He looked at his watch. "Christ! I'm on my regular commuting train!"

In the next harrowing five minutes, everyone he knew in Princeton and in advertising swarmed aboard the train, most of them passing through the diner en route to coach seats. Not one of these clean-shaven, well-dressed commuters, including several executives from his office, failed to miss him. The most distinguished of the lot sat down in the diner as was their usual custom and ordered breakfast. He claims that those at his table included Hank McGraw, of McGraw-Hill; Atherton Hobler, chairman of Benton & Bowles; and George Gallup.

On this same train route, there is another relevant incident involving a late-returning adman. This one climbed aboard a 10:00 P.M. Friday night train out of Penn Station after a round of roistering in West Fifty-sixth Street bars. He promptly went to sleep. A half hour later he was awakened as his legs got tangled with those of a pair of young college girls who had squeezed into the double seat facing his. He came to life quickly and was shortly engaged in an animated conversation. The girls, he learned hazily, were en route to a college weekend. Somehow he got the impression that this was at Rutgers, which meant they would be detraining at New Brunswick. At any rate, the conversation lagged; the adman popped off to sleep again. When he awoke the next time, the seat opposite was empty. The train was stopped at New Brunswick

Then he suddenly noticed that the girls' suitcases were in the rack above their seat. Still groggy, but with a chance to be a hero, he leaped up, wrestled the two heavy cases down from the racks, struggled up to the vestibule. Quick now, the train was already moving out. He looked up and down the dark platform and shouted to anyone, "Hey, the two gals who just got out here forgot their suitcases!" The train was picking up speed. He did what he thought best. Out they went into the night. Now feeling proud of himself, he reentered the car. Back at his seat, sitting opposite from him again, were the two girls, looking prettier than ever after their trip to the rest room. Obviously, they hadn't missed their luggage yet, for one of them asked sweetly, "Is Princeton the next stop?"

Ad agencies often have a mystery woman on staff. One they still talk about at McCann-Erickson was a woman we'll call Marge. She was a single lady in her early thirties, trim, nice-looking, but not a beauty; and her job in the office was relatively unimportant. Her private life, however, must have been fabulous. On one occasion when the agency was having deep problems on a major packaged-goods account, Marge came in one morning and told the account group exactly what they had to do to save the business. They thanked her politely but disregarded her advice. The account left.

The next time when a crisis came up on the Callaway Mills account, Marge was more direct. She arrived late one night at a cocktail party held by a group of McCann people with Pete Callaway of Callaway Mills on her arm. That account was saved. There were other occasions when Marge modestly dropped important names into conversations. One day someone in the office reading an annual report of the United States Steel account came across a picture of Marge's friend Pete Callaway beside the chairman of the board of United States Steel at the time, Benjamin Fairless. She rushed out to find Marge. "Look, your friend Pete is a director of United States Steel. Did you know that?"

Marge looked at the picture and said pleasantly, "Yes, I knew, and there's dear Benjie, too."

Male-female meetings in ad agencies are sometimes lively affairs. Discussions can get fairly heated over personal feminine products, over Freudian implications in ad appeals, or arguments

239

over whether too much of a woman's anatomy is showing in an illustration. One somewhat embarrassing episode occurred when a TV director, trying to demonstrate intuition and imagination, introduced a film he had shot on his own time and with the cooperation of attractive models who were hoping to get into TV commercial work. The product was Celanese tricot lingerie. The setting: woodland and hilltop scenes in Westchester. The action: wood nymphs dancing and demonstrating the garments. The TV director had not seen the film himself before it was shown to the mixed group. He wished he had. For the bright sunlight pierced the transparent lingerie completely. None of the models had worn anything beneath their garments.

On another occasion the half-dozen men had arrived at a conference before the women and were inspecting a neat cylindrical package, about fourteen inches long, which contained a rolled-up girdle, the subject of the advertising they were all to discuss. "This package is a gas," said one of the art directors. "It must be a wow with the gals, a great phallic symbol." The other execs disputed him. "Get off it, Paul," they said. "You sound like a dirty old man." Then the women joined the meeting. Four of them. For the next hour, the men did their best to keep straight faces while the four girls literally fought over the tube-shaped package. They snatched it from each other's hands. Stroked it fondly. Tapped it on their cheeks. Manipulated it in almost every way possible. The men finally broke up.

There are other compromising situations. Some of these occur in the quiet hours of evening work sessions, during the empty office lunch hours, and not infrequently when certain people come to work on weekends. One agency, Trahey/Wolf, thought it would be a sensational idea to redo their offices with a complete living room decor rather than desks and the conventional, dull office furnishings. The shop was a fashion-oriented agency, very savvy with the latest modern furniture and decorations. The results were fantastic. Exotic as a harem. And that's just about what happened to the place. Jane Trahey, the president, reported, "I can't keep these kids out of here on weekends. I don't know whether it's terrific or terrible."

Not unexpectedly, many of these agency relationships develop

240

into marriages or divorces. The divorce rate is fantastic among agency people. We could name a dozen executives who have been married three times; a half dozen, four times; and at least two, five times. Alimony becomes such a burden that some of these ad executives actually flee the country. Several live and work in Canada, a half dozen in England. One successful ad agency owner who is a three-time loser finds it more comfortable to live in Paris. Some have taken jobs in Texas, where male chauvinism is such that alimony courts supposedly never prosecute. One executive married all his wives from one ad agency. The third one, sitting at home for the first year, got smart. Before it happened again, she made him quit his job. Still some of these marriages have been very successful. Especially for some of the women. At one count, some six presidents of agencies met their wives in their offices. This includes the presidents of BBDO, K&E, D'Arcy, Case and Krone, and several other important agencies.

There are some unusual marriages as well. Like the top executive who married his daughter's college roommate. Or the one who married his psychiatrist. And others who married their clients. Mary Wells Lawrence, who married Harding Lawrence, president of Braniff, when he was her client, is the most illustrious of these. Others have married important people they have met in the course of business. A LaRoche executive, Tom Lewis, married Loretta Young. Arlene Dahl, working for Kenyon & Eckhardt, recently married her lawyer. Agency president Bill Casey married a well-known cover girl. Many have married TV actresses, models, and starlets.

When agencies sponsor their own social-business events, they usually do it with a flair. Press parties to announce an agency merger, an important new campaign, an anniversary, or perhaps the succession of a new top command in management will usually be held outside of the offices. Private suites at the Plaza, the Saint Regis, and the Regency are often used. The Four Seasons, the Twenty One Club, the Sign of the Dove, the Stratosphere Club, the Board Room, and the fine private clubs are all popular. Sometimes an effort will be made to be original or imaginative. Press parties have been held in exotic restaurants such as Maxwell's Plum, discotheques such as the Hippopotamus or Yellowfingers, and supper clubs such as the Plaza 9 or the Royal Box. Continental breakfasts are the rage recently. Bloody Marys at 9:30 A.M. Or croissants and coffee for the sissies.

The business-social party is not likely to be a swinging event. Cooler heads are in control here. Clients are present. The press is invited. Reputations are on the line. Hence, the catering will usually be good and well served. The agency will invite only its top, dependable executives. A few pretty girls will be on hand to pin name badges on the guests. The impression should be one of restrained elegance, hardheaded business men relaxing a bit. And some sort of a new announcement that never comes as a surprise to the press, since in this business the managed news announcement is rare. Still, to be charitable, due credit should be given to the eagerness and élan of the hospitality. There is always the pervasive fear that no one will show, that the party will be a bust. Even the greenest trade reporter is greeted as one might welcome a survivor from a lifeboat. The booze is first-class stuff, urged upon you by uniformed waiters bearing glittering trays. The hors d'oeuvres are exotic (at the Four Seasons, for example, such tidbits as sautéed duck's liver with raisins, mussels in pink sauce, soused shrimp with mustard fruit, smoked eel, deviled crabs, and pronged bay scallops). Everyone is grinning with graciousness, but all are tight-lipped about any facts, specifics, or speculations concerning the news announcement. "It's all in the press kit."

A very important part of an adman's life, in New York or other cities, is his favorite restaurant or bar. Most admen sooner or later settle on two or three regular places where they lunch, entertain clients, have drinks after work. The relationships are often astonishingly strong and enduring. It is not unusual for a senior adman to have standing friendships among proprietors or head waiters that cover a span of twenty to thirty years. The Ratazzis, senior and junior, have hosted admen and ad columnists at their Forty-eighth Street address for nearly three decades. Tim Costello's, favorite for years of Thurber, E. B. White, and other *New Yorker* staffers, has also long been a favorite of admen. So have Christ Cella, where Vice-President Agnew eats when he is in town, and the Bull & Bear in the Waldorf, where Lou the head bartender has served admen for twenty-eight years. Upstairs, for the senior executives, is the Marco Polo Club where BBDO, SSC and B, and McCann-Erickson people can be found. Manny Wolf's, the Brasserie, Le Cheval Blanc and Danny's Hide-A-Way are other popular spots for admen on the East Side. Gallagher's, Mercurio, the Ground Floor, and Manuche are all typical of West Side eateries admen like.

For more than twenty years, Marie and her chef-husband, who cooks exquisite North Italian food, have been confidantes and intimate friends of admen, especially from Compton, SSC and B, Benton & Bowles, and other shops at their Marie Cin Cin bistro. Publication people are also frequent patrons. It has been said reliably that *Sports Illustrated* was born on the premises. The favorite drink for years has been the Marie-invented Purple Martini.

Top men have been hired here. Young people have become engaged. A priest once held a confessional behind a screen for a Broadway star. A South American monsignor used to play a guitar until three in the morning. Late one night, two admen sneaked a "friend" in and placed him in the darkest booth in the place. They asked Marie to take him a drink. The "friend" was a trained bear brought over from a troupe playing at the Radio City Music Hall across the street. One morning when Marie and her husband, Brag, opened the front door, they found a customer calmly sitting at the bar drinking a Bloody Mary. He had been overlooked when they locked up the night before.

P.J. Moriarty typifies the restaurateur who understood admen, especially young ones. Years ago, he ran a saloon on West Fifty-first Street, where he also served a generous ham and egg platter. Pat took care of his boys. If you were out of work, he understood; you ran a tab until you landed again. Pat also cashed checks, a risky business. For example, once a week, usually on Monday at about 12:30, when all the regulars were on hand, Pat would ring a schoolteacher bell next to his cash register to get attention. Then in a clear voice, he would read off a list of admen's names: Bill Casey, Andy Sayles, Pat Clark, Ed Buxton, and others. All would file up to the cash register to settle up their bounced checks. Pat's hospitality paid off. He has since expanded to four Manhattan restaurants and is frequently seen riding to work in the springtime in his personal one-horse surrey, often with a pretty advertising model on the seat beside him.

Now that there are more women in advertising and more successful women ad executives and owners of agencies, the business will become more social and more fun. The new female executives will have their problems, too. Here is an example, told by the woman involved:

The Gotham Hotel is a favorite place for young ad agencies to launch themselves. A half-dozen successful shops started there. The old hotel, also, at one time, had a reputation for catering to very high-class call girls. The most recent agency to start here was Helene Mahoney & Company. Helene, a stunning-looking woman, came down the steps wearily late one night during her first week in business and practically fell into a taxi cab. The old-time driver said sympathetically, "Long day?"

"I've been at it since seven thirty this morning," Helene replied.

The old taxi driver put down his flag, and as he started off, he said, "I don't know how you girls can keep it up."

13
The Superstars of Advertising

THERE ARE several similarities between Hollywood and the modern advertising business. The star system is one. Nearly all the brightest, fastest-growing, most successful ad agencies that burst onto the scene during the late sixties and early seventies were founded by big name creative people: Mary Wells Lawrence, Bill Free, Ron Rosenfeld, Len Sirowitz, Gene Case, Helmut Krone, George Lois, Jack Byrne, Ed McCabe, Jacqui Brandwynne, Ben Colarossi, Jerry Della Femina, Steve Frankfurt, on and on. All were stars, superstars, award-winning, news-making, talked-about personalities. Of course they had talent. Of course they had enterprise. They also had to have good sound business sense to make out successfully. In advertising today, success comes faster and bigger with a name.

Is this stupid, phony, unfair? No it is not. Not if you back off, take a look at the inherent nature of the business. As has been mentioned here before, advertising is a nobody-knows-for-sure business. It's that old intangible bit again. The nebulous, arbitrary, is-the-king-wearing-any-clothes thing. It can't be pinned down. It can't be neatly added up and measured precisely. So what is the next-best thing you can do? You run with the winners. You trust only the pros. You bet your money and your client's money on a known quantity. That means a name, a figure, a personality, a reputation. These are the only credentials you can go by, the only assurance, if assurance is ever possible, that the job will be done well. The name is the union badge.

The hardest words in advertising are, "Sorry, I've never heard of you." These words, in effect, close the door. They say, "Don't call us, we'll call you." Or they say, "Come back when you have earned a reputation."

It is the same all the way through the business. Who is going to direct the TV commercial? Shoot the color photograph? Write the jingle or design the package? Somebody known, somebody with a name, a star, a superstar, a winner. To pick anyone else, a person nobody has ever heard of, is a gamble few executives in advertising are willing to take. It is hard enough to succeed with any ad or commercial. To fail despite the fact that a star was used may be excusable. To fail with an unknown puts all the blame on you.

This is not cowardice, lack of guts. It is common sense. The agency is a custodian of client's money. It has to spend it as wisely as it knows how. It can't eliminate all the risks, but it can at least reduce them by sticking with the pros, with the best pros. Clients, too, have the same decision to make. Middle management executives are responsible to top management. "We did the best we knew how." And top management is responsible to the company's stockholders. "We are managing your investment to the best of our ability. We use only the very best suppliers and talents in conducting the company's business."

So enough. The name, the reputation, the star stuff is important. Alright, already, but how do you get it?

Ad people are promoters by profession. Mostly they promote the products or services of their clients. But they are no mean shakes at promoting themselves either.

The phone rings on the bedside table at 6:00 A.M. Barbara Sullivan, a publicist, can guess which client it is. She listens to an exuberant woman's voice: "Just came in from a big night at Elaine's. My date was an important feature-film director from London. I think we ought to be able to get some mileage out of this." She suggests the name of several society and gossip columnists, tells what she had been wearing that evening, the name of the most recent film the director had produced, who sat at their table—and don't forget, a romance is in prospect. Barbara, a good public relations girl, writes all this down on her bedside pad. When she gets to the office, she'll make a good try at getting her client's name in the papers. Her client? The head of a new creative boutique. It is silly? What does it have to do with advertising? Well, after all, didn't Mary Wells Lawrence parlay a sexy, jet-set image into a hot, successful shop?

Most of the current generation of creative superstars didn't have publicists or professionals to help them win their reputations. They did it on their own. And often with an amazing sense and feel for news-making and public relations. It amazes because it is unexpected, atypical of creative people, who are not by nature outgoing people. But they learn, and they learn fast.

Bob Wilvers—originally a modest, actually shy, art director from Milwaukee—proved his talent first and then began on his personality and his public image. He let his hair grow, but not too long, wore long, loose, expensive cashmere sweaters, threw press parties at Jack Tinker (where he had become senior creative partner) that were noted for their wild amiability. He dared to create a film, which was shown at a luncheon for five hundred people in the Plaza Hotel ballroom, that predicted the end of Jack Tinker a full year and a half before the ultimate demise. He never missed an award festival, where he was often a winner. And he always arrived in a mod variation of the required formal wear. If invited to make a speech or be a member of a panel, Bob never failed to introduce some startling, controversial subject into the meeting. Today, one of the city's top creative directors at Leber Katz Partners, he has a secure niche in the business.

Or take the trio at Lois Holland Callaway. They are all showmen. Bright, articulate, always smiling, always on their feet, in practically balletic motion, when making a pitch. They all talk at the same time, wave their arms, pass the repartee neatly among themselves, each keeping a close eye on the audience, as close as a nightclub entertainer does. This is show business in advertising, the star system in action.

Or take Charlie Moss at Wells, Rich, Greene. An accomplished advertising talent, he is also a consummate stand-up presenter. He can entertain an audience with the professionalism of a celebrity.

He can cajole, persuade, guide, and direct his listeners into buying any campaign he holds up. Maybe Charlie has a slight advantage. He was indeed a performer for many years as a child on the original "Quiz Kids" show.

Then there is Gene Case, handsome as a movie star, with long blond hair, high cheekbones, and an almost Prussian diffidence. Gene might have been just another good creative man except that he used his talent for showmanship wisely and with flair. He always dresses in Edwardian elegance, carries on unsettling, often acerbic dialogue, and when on a platform, dazzles audiences with sharp, satirical wit and very sound advertising insight. He is a superstar, self-made.

There are many others. Some of the women are fascinating public personalities. Franchelle ("Frankie") Cadwell, very tall, very glamorous, literally lashes out at audiences on everything from women's lib in advertising to put-downs on all hard-sell ads. Yet in person-to-person conversation she is as demure and gentle as a kitten. Or Jane Trahey, a star in a half-dozen specialties including retail, fashion, book-author, playwright, feature-film writer, syndicated newspaper columnist, lecturer, besides running her successful ad agency, Trahey Wolfe. Or Arlene Dahl, now a consultant at Kenyon & Eckhardt, who is every bit as stunning as she ever was on screen.

The stars are important to the advertising agency business. They put the yeasty, intriguing excitement into it. They get advertising talked about. They impress clients who not only like it but expect it. They bring criticism, sure; but criticism and controversy are better than being ignored, passed over. And the stars and the star system do something else that is vital and significant. They force creative standards up. If you are going to act the role of a creative star, you'd better be able to prove it. Many a lazy talent has been forced into being more productive to keep up to his reputation. They force salaries up, too. Although management frowns on this, it is good for the business. When the word got around that thirty-year-old men were earning $30,000, it attracted a lot of bright people into the field. The competition for these high-paying jobs is tougher now, which is also good for the business. The star system is also a constant reminder to ad people—and they often need reminding—that advertising is a communications business, a close relative to show business, a vehicle that turns big audiences on, a kind of news-making, excitement-generating, listen-to-me tool of marketing. When these things are forgotten, when the cucumberheads and bookkeepers take over, advertising suffers. It then becomes a coldly logical, statistically programmed, dull, and dreary business function. And this doesn't work. Advertising, the creative aspects of it anyway, deals with mass emotions, with subconscious motivations, with the same sensual, heart-and-gut-touching appeal that makes mass entertainment successful. So a sense of showmanship, a sense of drama, and a bit of ham are parts of the professional equipment of the successful adman.

Take the serious award winners as an illustration. This is a class of creative men who owe everything they are and every dollar in the bank to their success (and luck) in piling up awards. Winning awards has literally been their number-one preoccupation, the single driving force in their careers, the uppermost motivation in going to work. These people might be called, quite properly, professional award seekers. Currently, there are perhaps no more than 300 to 500 of these people in the entire creative end of the business, which might roughly include a population of 8,000 to 10,000 people. This small group wins practically *all* the awards. And breaking it down further, a group of about 100 people have won 85 percent of all the awards in the past few years.

Are these people so clearly superior to all other creative people in the business? Is this a charmed circle? Or is it an organized circle? It does seem a little strange that the same names keep appearing on the panels of juries, the same agencies dominate the lion's share of the annual winners, and the same individuals crop up again and again and again with the Gold Keys, the Gold Medals, the Andys, and the Clios. It is a fact that an ad agency like Doyle Dane Bernbach has spent as much as $10,000 per year in entry fees, has more members (hence more chance at juries and votes) in the professional societies, and as an agency, has stoutly defended award contests as company policy. There are other agencies that have also dominated the festivals. DKG, Inc.; Young & Rubicam; Jack Tinker & Partners, when they were active; Gilbert Advertising; Daniel & Charles; Carl Ally Inc.; Solow/Wexton;

Papert, Koenig, Lois, Inc.; Leber Katz; Della Femina, Travisano; and perhaps a half-dozen others who for a decade have supported the festivals to the hilt, have had more members on the juries, and have walked off with nearly all the marbles. So be it. There are useful awards in other fields, too, including publishing, movies, architecture, and journalism. For all their faults, they serve a purpose; and one of the purposes is that they help raise standards of excellence

How does the professional award seeker usually capitalize on the award routine? First, if he is a copywriter, he probably joins the Copywriter's Club. This gives him one vote right off for his own entry. Next, he makes friends in the club. He goes to all the boat rides, cocktail parties, and social shindigs they hold, however dull and dreary. He has to be a fixture, a power. After several years of this, he will be rewarded with a position on a jury. Obviously, close friendships and political alliances will help. If he is an art director, he typically joins their club. Same ground rules. Next, of course, come his entries. He will come to realize that only certain types of products can win awards. Soaps, detergents, household cleaners, analgesics, cough remedies, and so forth have no chance whatsoever. Few of these ever have won or ever will win an awards contest. So if the man is a dedicated professional award seeker, he will obviously shun work on these products. He also must shun work in all but about a dozen ad agencies, the ones who make awards an important part of their business policy and who invariably win most of them. So he must get a job in one of these shops. Once in the agency, he will find agreeable company. They are all award seekers, all pulling together. The bosses give them the leeway they need to pay the fees, attend the meetings, join the clubs.

Given a few breaks, now, he should be on his way. He will soon learn what is expected of an award-type ad. It has to be pretty, simple, funny, and very contemporary. The sales power of the ad is immaterial at this point because the awards are made usually before any sales figures are added up. He will also learn that certain accounts in the shop are automatic winners year in and year out, such as Volkswagen at Doyle Dane; Talon Zippers at DKG, Inc.; and Volvo at Scali, McCabe, Sloves. These are shoo-

250

ins. They have been winners almost without fail since 1965. So, obviously, if the award seeker has managed to be assigned to one of these accounts, he can practically be sure of an award before he does a lick of work. However, if he is eager, he will work because he is in a competitive environment. There is much back-biting and credit snitching in this type of shop. He'll have to win a lot of closely contested battles to get his name on the entry blank. Next comes the judging. If he is on the jury (or if members of his agency are on it), he (or they) will, of course, vote for his entries over anything else. They will, if the judging doesn't come out right, ask for rejudging. Many a lost cause has become a winner in the second, or contested, judging.

Assuming that the award seeker has played all these cards right up to this point, it is all over but the applause. In most cases, the following steps remain: He'll pay his $50 to $60 for two tickets. He will dress up for the big night in a tuxedo and a pink shirt with a ruffled front, buy his wife a spectacular evening dress (hot pants if they are stylish, a pants suit if they are "in," otherwise something backless, bare midriff, or diaphanous). They will arrive early because this is a mutual admiration society, and all members must be on hand to pump hands and beat on backs. The locations are usually stylish: the grand ballroom of the Plaza, the Hilton, the Americana, the Waldorf. The Clios are traditionally held in Philharmonic Hall at Lincoln Center. The ground rules must be observed if you are an award seeker who wants to hold on to his membership in the charmed circle. For example, abject modesty must prevail. "Christ, was I ever surprised!" "Man, it was pure luck. I just stepped in it." Other ground rules: Be sure to seek out and congratulate all judges, jury members, and other VIPs. And by all means check in with every one of the head hunters who will be there in force. Possibly they will set you up immediately with your next job and a quantum jump in salary.

A good award seeker, provided that he is willing to work hard (and has talent, because for all the fakery, the guy has to be good), can expect to win something like ten to twenty awards a year. At least a score of regular award winners have piled up well over a hundred awards of various kinds in a few short years. Some of these might come from a considerable distance, say, Australia, Cannes, Venice, or Cork, Ireland. But they are awards: tangible, displayable, framable.

Here are the names of some of these consistent winners: Steve Frankfurt (more than two hundred awards), Onofrio Paccione (more than one hundred), Ron Rosenfeld (more than one hundred), Ed McCabe, Jerry Della Femina, Neil Calet, Peter Hirsh, Dick Rayboy, Gene Case, Bob Wilvers, Bob Levenson, Bob Gage, David Reider, William Taubin, John Noble, Jack Dillon, Leon Meadows, Judy Protas, Phyllis Robinson, Charles Kollowe, Don Trevor, Bert Steinhauser, Phil Worcester, Carl Ally, Jim Durfee, Amil Gargano, Ralph Ammirati, Martin Puris, David Altschiller (from Ally, Inc.), Helen Nolan, Faith Popcorn, Mary Wells Lawrence, Charlie Moss, Larry Plapler, Ed Hanft, Alan Glass, Marty Solow, Autin Hamel, Alvin Hampel, Francine Wexler, Ron Travisano, Ned Tolmach, Steve Gordon, Alex Kroll, Tony Isadore, Barry Beiderman, Stan Ragoti, Marvin Leftkowitz, Neil Tardio, Robert Elgort, Eli Kramer, Bernard Zlotnick, Shirley Polykoff, Phil Parker, Jack Avrett, Ed Vellenti, Lois Geraci, Carol Anntine, Mike Chappell, Bill White, Sal Auditore, Jim Symon, Warren Pfaff, Ned Viseltear, Bruno Brugnatelli, Joel Wayne, Manning Rubin, Gordon Webber, Ron Hoff, Charles Ewell, Stu Greene, Herb Green, George D'Mato, Len Sirowitz, Dick Jackson, Dick Calderhead, Joe LaRosa, Walter Kaprielian, Larry Dunst, Gerry Andreozzi, Jack Byrne, Steven Baker, Larry Muller, Phil Peppis, Jerry Schoenfeld, Art Hawkins, Stan Kovics, Peter Palazzo, Rea Brown, Ken Duskin, Bob Sturtevent, Steve Herzbrun, Ron Holland, Jack Roberts, Dean Lierle, Don Dickens, Jim Nelson, Peter Hersh, Paula Green, Lois Korey, Lew Sherwood, Dave Wiseltier, Jay Chiat, Guy Day, Jay Blumenthal, Janet Carlson, . Alan Glass and at least a dozen others.

Credited for encouraging, if not actually inventing the star system, are the placement agents. Some of these have indeed discovered talents, promoted them, moved them from place to place into jobs of increasingly higher salaries and increasing fame. In the creative areas, Jerry Fields, Judy Wald, Betty Corwin, Mitzi Morris, Barbara Dana, and Gene Judd especially have worked with young creative stars. Their positions have often been so strong

252

in the creative community that Judy Wald and Jerry Fields have sat on award contest juries. Others have taken over careers so completely that they are managers not only of job placement but contracts, stock deals, and even holding and investing money for some of the young people. Judy Wald is credited with extending the New York City star system to Chicago, Los Angeles, London, Paris, and Milan. Management has not always been happy about this emphasis on stars, but when a crisis arises on a big account, they are quick to call one of these experts, "Send us over a couple of top-name people. They must be superdupers. Never mind the cost, this is an emergency." The willingness of hard-pressed agencies to grab talent fast is demonstrated in this example. A $27,000-a-year youngster arrived for an interview. It went swiftly and successfully. When he mumbled the $27,000 price tag, the agency interviewer mistook it for $47,000. Not a word of dissent. He was hired at the higher figure.

The creative route has been the most successful route to stardom in the past decade. Although there was some cooling off of enthusiasm for creativity, notably the excessive and costly television commercials, in the past year or so, the top-rated creative man is more likely to have the best crack at stardom than any other specialist in advertising. The creative superstar is more likely also to start a successful ad agency, more likely to command a large salary at an early age, more likely to pick and choose his place of employment. This is unlikely to change because advertisers still regard the big idea as the most important contribution advertising agencies can make to their success. And the creative aspect of advertising is the one function they, as companies, are not equipped to do for themselves.

There are creative men other than award winners who achieve stardom. Some of them accomplish it by gaining a wide reputation for being tough-minded, independent problem solvers. Bill Free, president of Marschalk for several years, gained that shop a massive increase in billings and an outstanding reputation for smart, brilliant advertising. Today, as head of his own agency, Bill has built up billings for himself at an impressive rate. His star qualities are based on his unorthodox approach to advertising, his sound marketing concepts, and his reputation for telling clients that this is the way it is going to be, take it or leave it. Bill Free keeps his reputation fresh by appearing often on panels and speaking at seminars and conferences.

There is another group of colorful and publicity-conscious ad agency presidents who qualify as public stars. Shep Kurnit, brash, honest, and creatively oriented, president of DKG, Inc., is one of these. Dick Gilbert, also a head of an agency with a sharp creative image, is also a name figure in the business. Dick, too, is shrewd about publicity. He will call editors with the slightest bit of news, attend all 4As sessions and meetings, make speeches throughout the country. He is an innovator, too, in public relations for his agency. Recently he ran a series of intellectual-cultural conferences for his office staff and guests that included such eminent speakers as Margaret Mead and other well-known social commentators. Ron Rosenfeld, copy, and Len Sirowitz, art, are two of the brightest superstars of the past five years. Together, this pair has unquestionably won more awards than any other two people in advertising. They are also basically smart admen, and with their third partner, account man Tom Lawson, they have won much new business for their shop. Another star, Jim Jordan, not yet president of BBDO but expected to be some day soon, is a colorful, dynamic advocate of strong-selling creative work and equally strong marketing concepts.

Among the other young presidents and executives of ad agencies of star caliber are Milt Gossett of Compton; Peter Greer of Greer, DuBois; Alex Kroll, executive vice-president, creative of Young & Rubicam; Ed Meyer of Grey Advertising; Alvin Hampel, executive vice-president, creative of Benton & Bowles; Don Tennent, chairman of Clinton E. Frank; John O'Toole of Foote, Cone & Belding, New York; Leo Greenland of Smith/Greenland, long associated with good creative work; Marty Solow of Solow/Wexton, who continues to write award-winning copy as well as manage his agency. Then there are Richard Ney, handsome head of Young & Rubicam, and Fred Lemont, formerly of Wells, Rich, Greene and Ted Bates, a newsmaker recently with his new concept creative service called the Project Group. Less than a year old, it is already serving nine major corporations.

Stardom doesn't come easy. Nor does it come without a willingness to invest some sizable chunks of cash. The typical creative man on his way up must start early improving such things as his personal appearance, his language (being glib with the right game talk is very important), his friendships, his public appearances (eating in the right restaurants, drinking at the right bars); and at an early stage, he must begin to develop a gimmick, an individual mnemonic device, a trademark of some sort. Preferably something that is transportable, like a beard, distinctive velvet Edwardian suits, Ben Franklin glasses, or canvas knapsacks, which are fashionable right now. One copywriter somehow managed to own a $25,000 custom Ferrari racer. He got a lot of publicity mileage out of this for a while. Another flies a World War I biplane. A third reportedly commutes to work in a hydroplane that he docks on the East River.

These gimmicks can get a lot of talk started, a lot of legends on their way. David Ogilvy, who has more gimmicks than anyone in the business, has made much out of automobiles. Aside from writing famous automotive ads for Rolls-Royce ("at 60 miles per hour the loudest noise in the new Rolls-Royce comes from the electric clock") and the long, excellent copy ads for Mercedes, he has always somehow managed to make chauffeured cars a gimmick. For example, for years his chauffeured Rolls could be seen waiting for him at his office building at 2 East Forty-eighth Street. It is reported that when David was to be honored as a Member of the British Empire in London, he drove to the palace in a white Rolls-Royce driven by a black chauffeur. On another occasion, so the story goes, David was visiting a client when neither his own nor a rented Rolls was available. The story states that he arrived in a Volkswagen, chauffeur-driven.

There are other gimmicks, some corny, some imaginative. Like Jack Byrne, who has all his female employees wear sweat shirts with his name on them. Or Steve Frankfurt's London-made suits with three-button jackets that flare at the hips. Or Jack Avrett, who wears loud plaid, waist-hugging suits. Or Burt Pense, with enormous granny glasses, sandals, and shoulder-length hair.

Then there are in-office gimmicks that sometimes build reputations for stardom seekers. Gene Taylor, once a creative director at PKG in Chicago and now in London, installed a large neon "panic" sign over his doorway. When it was blinking red, creative people were advised to stay away. Gene also held evening champagne parties in his office and occasionally, when the muses beckoned, marched his whole department of a dozen people out of their offices for a picnic on the nearby shore of Lake Michigan. Others use plants and foliage to establish a certain élan in office furnishings. Marty Lipsitt, a top art director at DKG, Inc., is so surrounded by trees and shrubbery in his Time and Life Building office that it is difficult to determine whether he is in or out. Milt Gossett at Compton has converted his corner office into what looks like a country store. Young & Rubicam, home of many stars, employs a different decor for every reception room.

Then there are the antics ad people use especially to build up a reputation for being a creative nut, a mad genius, or a wildly creative character. Joe Tonna, a TV producer at Dancer-Fitzgerald-Sample stood on his head outside an account executive's office for what was reported as one hour and twelve minutes one day. The account exec, in a meeting when Joe arrived with some storyboards, had told him to go stand on his head for a while. Joe saw the publicity value of taking this literally. After the first half hour some four hundred office workers were buzzing. "Is he still up?" There is also the one about the DDB art director who always threw every idea he didn't like out the window. On a bad day the air above Forty-third Street would be spotted with drifting layouts.

David Ogilvy, holding an afternoon meeting with some visiting admen (he called these sessions "teas") suddenly broke up the meeting with a shout: "Stop! Stand still." He rushed to the window overlooking Fifth Avenue, where he froze at attention. "My Queen is passing by" (Queen Elizabeth on her American tour).

San Francisco has always been a good ad agency town. Many top writers developed there, including Fairfax Cone and his mentor Jack Reynolds, both of the Foote, Cone & Belding agency. Reynolds wrote many great ads for the Southern Pacific railroad including the line, "Next time, take the train." Another well-known creative man was the late Howard Gossage, who wrote for Rover car, Irish Whiskey, Paul Masson wines, and Qantas Airways. Howard was not only literate but witty. His former partner, Joe Weiner, tells this story about Howard's sense of humor, matched, as it were, in top competition. The Weiner & Gossage agency had established a monthly series of luncheons to which they would invite well-known people who happened to be visiting San Francisco at that time. The occasion, Joe remembers, was a luncheon held in a famous restaurant to which were invited Mort Sahl, John Steinbeck, Herb Caen, a local newspaper columnist, and several other notables. Steinbeck, however, dominated the long, pleasant luncheon, which drifted late into the afternoon over wines and fruit. Steinbeck at the time was writing *Travels with Charlie*. He was regaling his audience with one last story about Charlie, the famous black poodle. The two had by this time traveled from New England to California.

"My friend Charlie," Steinbeck boasted, "can now lay claim to the world's pissing championship. I challenge any dog to beat this record. Before starting this present trip, he had already pissed on dozens of the most famous monuments in Europe. And now on this trip alone he has pissed on the Bunker Hill monument, the marble lions at the Art Institute in Chicago, the Black Hills of South Dakota, and just last week he pissed on the General Sherman redwood, the largest and oldest tree in the world."

Steinbeck now paused dramatically, then said, "Now the only problem is, what else can he do?"

The witty audience was stumped. Mort Sahl passed. Herb Caen passed. The eyes turned to Howard Gossage. Howard thought a minute, then said, "What else? Well, he can always teach."

The superstar system also sprung up in Great Britain during the sixties. Staid London broke out with a fever of new creativity that spawned stars, and it saw the inauguration of a group of creative emphasis ad agencies similar to those in New York City. Papert, Koenig, Lois and Doyle Dane Bernbach, both branch offices from New York, were bright on the scene for a while; but today PKL has sold into BBDO, and Doyle Dane Bernbach's luster has dimmed. The homegrown shops, however, have fared better. Collett, Dickenson, & Pearce; Saatchi & Saatchi; Kingsley Manton & Palmer; Ron Kirkwood & Associates; and Boase Massimi (an American) & Pollit are the brightest smaller shops. J. Walter Thompson, Ogilvy & Mather, Young & Rubicam, and Compton Partners all have creative luster as well. The individuals who have maintained stardom over the past few years would include Barry Day, of McCann-Erickson; David Bernstein, now with his own agency; Jerry Bullmore, of J. Walter Thompson; Peter Mayle, first with PKL, now BBDO; John Salmon, of Collett, Dickenson, & Pearce; and George Plante, creative director of Lintas. London also developed a quick reputation for TV commercial production quality and economy. Jim Garrett of the James Garrett Organization, Ltd., has been the dean in this area. New York star maker Judy Wald, the placement specialist, must be credited with boosting the star system in London when she opened an office there.

The quickest way to gain a reputation that can be parlayed into a stardom of sorts is to let the word get around that you are a tough son of a bitch, a hot-tempered, brass-balls bastard. This comes easily to many ad executives, especially on the client side. John Toigo was a terror when he directed the advertising for Schlitz; American Home has had a series of tough S.O.B.s; RJR Foods recently had an executive who had the reputation of being a "people eater"; and from time to time, Colgate has had some product managers who could qualify as cossack cavalrymen. Ad agencies have had, and still have, some presidents who gained notoriety on the basis of their authoritarian, tough-guy personalities. Rosser Reeves, at Bates; Norman B. Norman, at Norman, Craig & Kummel; Danny Seymour, at times at J. Walter Thompson; Bill Free; Ed McCabe, at Scali, McCabe, Sloves; and Carl Ally, a former air force pilot and reportedly a no-nonsense guy. Leo Kelmanson, president of Kenyon & Eckhardt, along with his old friend and buddy, Lee Iaccoca, president of Ford, are regarded as a couple of tough cookies, especially when the two socialize together after hours.

Some creative directors have tough-guy star status. One of the toughest was an old-time copy chief named Lou Thomas, a former newspaper city editor, who worked for Esty, The Biow Company, and other shops. One story they tell of Lou's temper happened at the old J. Sterling Getchell agency. Getch, the president, was a dynamic character himself; but Lou was more than a match for him on this occasion. Lou had brought in a new campaign idea to Getchell's office. They talked it over a few minutes, and Getch said, "Sorry Lou, it's no good. It's horseshit." Lou, who made his own layouts, happened to be carrying a yard-long steel T square in his hand at the time. The T square swished. Once, twice. It caught Getchell on the shins both times. Limping and yelping, he dashed out of the office and down the corridor. Lou Thomas was right behind, swinging his T square. At the end of the corridor, Getch ducked into a men's room, fled into a stall, where he bolted the door. Whack, whack! Lou was now slashing his legs under the door of the stall. Getch, they say, had to stand on the top of the john for ten minutes until Lou wore himself out whiffing the empty air space below him.

Toughness, swagger, a braggadocio attitude have helped carry many people up the ladder. At one time the whole crew at Papert, Koenig, Lois were known as battlers and big talkers, as well as big talents. Bob Fiore reportedly would leap across desks at opponents. Fred Papert, a lightweight physically, could nonetheless throw his voice down a hallway or burn up a telephone line. Bill Casey was there for a time, too. Bill's reputation as a scrapper was wide. He once knocked a copywriter, nearly twice his size, off a bar stool because the guy had asked him "How's it going?" Casey is a case in point. How to capitalize on a tough, independent, cocky point of view. When Bill was out of work, which happened often (always to move up to a higher-paying job), he had a perfect game plan. Here's how it went. Casey would move all his things out of his previous office in A&P shopping bags to a favorite Third Avenue saloon. He never took his sample book or his belongings home. "What the hell for? I'm going to be stepping into another job before the week's out." Which was likely to be true. In any case, Bill, once established in his noisy, hard-hat bar, would order a stein of beer, grab a handful of coins, and make his calls.

Casey: Put the president on.
Secretary: Sorry, Mr. Casey, he is in a meeting. Can I take a message?
Casey: You sure can, baby, tell him Bill Casey is available. And if he wants to reach me, he can call Moriarty's bar. Yeah, Moriarty's, here's the number. Tell him he'd better call before twelve. I might be out playing golf this afternoon. Otherwise, leave the message with Charlie, the head bartender.

Did this work? It did. George Gribbon, then president of Young & Rubicam, called Moriarty's, invited Bill in, gave him a job for $25,000. Two years later, after a shoutdown at a major client's office, he was out again, but to a bigger job at Ogilvy & Mather.

The opposite can also be true. Many top reputations have been built on the basis of the person being a good guy, an honest, beautiful person. Advertising has as many or more of these than of the tough guys. Bill Bernbach has been one such person to many hundreds of creative people who have worked for the Doyle Dane Bernbach agency and to those who have left to start their own shops or become creative directors of other agencies. Jack Tinker, who built the Jack Tinker & Partners shop into a top agency, was well loved by all who worked for him. Vic Bloede, chairman of Benton & Bowles, and Alvin Hampel, his creative director, have great rapport with their people. Sometimes this is shown in small, unpublicized gestures. For example, Carl Nichols, chairman of Cunningham & Walsh, whenever it was necessary for him to let a group of people go because of the loss of substantial billings, would spend many hours on the phone calling other agency presidents trying to find places for his ex-employees. Another gesture might be expressed in a salary negotiation. Gerry Carson, one-time creative director of Kenyon & Eckhardt, used this one. When the final salary figure was settled upon, he would ask, "Are you sure you will be happy at that figure?" When the new man replied "yes," Gerry would say, "Well then, we'll add $2,000 more, and you'll be more than happy. Right?"

John Peace, chairman of William Esty, often used a similar monetary good-will gesture. Peace was well aware that when a new man came onto a job, he was short of cash. At the handshaking point, John would say, "Oh, one more thing. You didn't start working today. You started two weeks ago. Go pick up your back pay now." Other nice-guy reputations are built upon the sincere and often hardworking efforts some men make in helping young talents on the way up. Joe Burton, a former senior vice-president in the Chicago office of J. Walter Thompson, has such a reputation. So do Ed Vellenti, now at Needham, Harper & Steers; Ab White, who has worked with several top shops; Holly Smith, of

Dancer-Fitzgerald-Sample; and Joe Stone, of Berger Stone. There are others of this type in advertising: Bruno Brugnatelli, of Gardner; Walter Kaprielian, of Ketchum, MacLeod & Grove; Joe LaRosa, of Waring & LaRosa; Paul Bauer, of Kenyon & Eckhardt; Francis X. Houghton, of Ogilvy & Mather; and many others. These men spent many a lunch hour or after-work time guiding, counseling, and making appointments for young people. These helpful people are often some of the most successful. They are in their own way "giving something back to the business" by helping newcomers get over their first hurdles. Maybe their memories are longer. They can recall their own early days, when they were told so many times to "come back when you get some experience." Oftentimes they may even help financially. One well-known creative supervisor told a young kid from out of town, whose clothes were hopelessly outclassed for interviews, to go over to Brooks Brothers and charge up a wardrobe on him. George Erickson, now chairman of Doremus & Company will read this episode about himself for the first time here. He had interviewed a young copywriter and was impressed, but it was during a tight period in the business, so he could not offer him a job. Some weeks later on a cold winter day during Thanksgiving week, he ran into the copywriter on the street. "How's it going?" asked George. The copywriter's answer was confident but negative. "Pretty soon though, I'm sure." George reached in his pocket, fumbled for a few seconds, then said, "Here, take my card, keep me posted." The copywriter took the card, said goodbye, then noticed that there was $50 folded together with it. Thanksgiving money. By December the copywriter had a good job with Doyle Dane Bernbach. He gave the $50 to another unemployed copywriter. Christmas money. That copywriter later reported that a short while later, he, in turn, had given the $50 to still another unemployed copywriter. Maybe—who knows—George Erickson's $50 is still making the rounds.

Amazingly enough, many such young people who have been aided by older and considerate people have short memories. One such beginning copywriter who needed a break got help twice from the same supervisor. When the man was out of work a third time, he called back again. "By the way," the supervisor asked, "how did you get the last two jobs you've had?" The applicant replied, "Oh, lucky breaks, hard work, you know." The creative supervisor said, "Yes, I *do* know, you ungrateful son of a bitch, I got you both those jobs, and you never had the courtesy to even call and thank me." The applicant paused, then said, "Oh, so you did. It slipped my mind." He hung up. He might have recalled how much he would have paid if a placement agent had gotten him the jobs. Well over $1,000. Another made a habit of borrowing money all over town whenever he was out of work. He never paid any of it back. After a while, he wondered why he couldn't find a job anywhere.

Other routes to fame in the ad business often are roundabout. Jerry Della Femina's best-selling book brought him instant popularity. Judy Wald, a top ad placement specialist and a superb publicist herself, gets much press coverage. David North, an executive recruiter who has a sharp sense for news about himself, gets into print often in top business magazines. Some write plays, music, children's books. Arthur Nielsen, a top researcher, and his son consistently win the national father-and-son tennis championship. Then there are the old-fashioned admen who send in pictures of tarpons they have caught off Florida, lions they have shot in Africa, or a moose shot in Canada. Former brand manager Peter Revson made star billings recently by taking second place in the Indianapolis 500. And Jeno Paolucci, of Chun-King fame, and Andy Granitelli, the STP promoter, are a pair of entrepreneurs who keep themselves in the news as they fly in private planes from one publicity stunt to another.

Generally, most ad agency presidents take the conventional route to name and fame building. They work diligently over the years to move up through the ranks of the industry associations: the 4As, the ANA, the American Marketing Association, and various industry councils and committees. This is hard, thankless work. The associations in advertising are always plagued with crises (like consumerism, fresh attacks from Washington, code regulations, minority employment, women's lib, and what's happening to profits).

Public relations can get tricky. Norman, Craig & Kummel, stung from rumors that they were to lose a large piece of Colgate-Palmolive, had its P.R. man hire a detective. He traced this damaging rumor right back into Colgate itself, where one of the marketing men had hopes of seeing NC&K agency fired so an agency friendly to him could get a chance at the account. There are many other cases of public relations people working to repair images, remove the effects of bad news, or to convert a bad press relationship into something more favorable. The usual ploy is to take the editor to lunch. Editors usually go. Why not? It might be a chance for more news, more bad news possibly. Even though the ad trade press is not very well paid, most buttering up of this kind is futile. The more the P.R. man pushes, the more resistance he meets.

Most agency presidents are sensitive about their press relationships. They nearly always come to the phone when an editor calls, or they call back if they are busy. The press in a small business such as advertising can carry a great deal of weight. A half-dozen ad agency presidents, however, are astonishingly naïve in their press relationships. Some grab the phone and shout at editors at the slightest bit of news that is unfavorable. Others threaten lawsuits, knowing full well the story they are denying is completely true.

Another mistake the big personalities in advertising make is taking their press relations for granted. When these people were on their way up—people like, say, Mary Wells Lawrence, Carl Ally, David Ogilvy, Marion Harper, Bill Bernbach, and many others—they were terribly polite and gracious to the press. But once arrived, they became less interested, less available, and inclined to leave it all to a P.R. girl or to a secretary. In the early days, when the road up was rugged, there were gifts of cuff links, Scotch, flowers, gourmet foods, and invitations to lunch and small press parties. Many others, however, such as Ed Meyer, Shep Kurnit, George Lois, Paul Harper, Edward H. Weiss, Jack Cantwell, Milt Gossett, the J. Walter Thompson people, Vic Bloede, Andy Kershaw of Ogilvy & Mather, and Maxwell Dane, of Doyle Dane, now retiring, are always fair and polite to the press. A few agencies, such as William Esty, Lennen & Newell, and Dancer-Fitzgerald-Sample, operate as if the press did not exist.

The agency business has a small, amiable corps of P.R. people who publicize the ad agencies either from on-staff positions or as P.R. firms. Several came from jobs as advertising columnists for

New York newspapers. Walter Carlson, *New York Times* columnist, worked first for Ted Bates and now with partner George Whipple with their own firm. Joe Kaselow, well-liked and well-known columnist for the old *Herald Tribune*, became P.R. director of Cunningham & Walsh. Bob Morgan, once a columnist for the old *World Telegram*, has done work for Norman, Craig & Kummel. Doris Willens, also a former columnist for the *Telegram*, handles Doyle Dane Bernbach press relations. Another ad columnist, Carl Spielvogel, parlayed his job from the *Herald Tribune* into an executive vice-presidency of Interpublic. A list of the better-known agency P.R. directors would include Jean Boutyette, Foote, Cone & Belding; Lou Tripodi, Needham, Harper & Steers; Tim Conner, BBDO; Al Dann, McCann-Erickson; Dick Detwiler, BBDO; Frank Kennesson, N. W. Ayer; Hal Gully, Leo Burnett; Betsy Levitt of Kenyon & Eckhardt; Wally Clayton, J. Walter Thompson, Neil Armadee, HD&B; and Hal Hoffman, the Bloom Agency.

The most image-conscious or name-seeking ad agencies often hire outside P.R. firms to write speeches for presidents, to promote the agency, or to handle special events. Among the best-known in this group are Lida Livingson, Annette Green, Jane Pinkerton, Nolen & Thompson, Larry Lowenstein, Betty Vaughn, Richard Weiner Inc., Ray Wood, Whipple & Carlson, Barbara Sullivan, Jo Yanow, Guy Shea, The Softness Group, and Wolcott Carlson. These individuals and firms are often people who have worked at some time or other with the advertising or business press. Most work hard for the modest fees the ad agencies are willing to pay. They often make mistakes, however, such as putting the press table at the back of the room, showing favoritism among various publications, wasting editors' time with stupid calls. "Did you get my release?" "Are you going to use it?" And, "Please send me five copies."

Advertising people often send gifts to editors. Like these: a set of silver-plated cuff links by Georg Jensen from Mary Wells; a silver-plated yo-yo from Stephen Baker Advertising; a musical Christmas tree ornament made in Sweden from Shep Kurnit; a solid chocolate cake (five pounds of Swiss chocolate) from a George Lois client when he was at PKL; two tickets to the National Tennis

Tournament at Forest Hills from Philip Morris; a boxed picnic luncheon with cold wine from Jane Trahey; a crate of Florida grapefruit from Tinker Pritchard Wood; a crate of peaches from Hoefer, Dieterich & Brown; a $36 bottle of Rothschild wine from Bob Wilvers of LKP, Inc.; six crystal wine glasses from Ruder & Finn (public relations); a six-pack of Johnny Walker Scotch from Smith/Greenland; a shopping-bag full of their client's products from Doyle Dane Bernbach, including Alka-Seltzer, Lever soap, Chivas Regal Scotch, a Buxton Key-Tainer, and ten other products; a two-month supply of colored toilet paper from Kurtz Kambanis Symon; a Nikon movie camera from Dentsu; a Panasonic cartridge tape player from Chirurg & Cairns; a magnum of champagne from Ketchum, MacLeod & Grove; and a luggage set from Burtow-Sohigian (Detroit).

In a typical year, an editor will receive several hundred gifts of this sort, including dozens of new products, from detergents to disposable diapers. He may also receive several offers of paid vacation trips. He will also get an average of eight to ten invitations per week to press parties, including breakfast, lunch, cocktails, and dinner. All, of course, "under absolutely no obligation."

14

It's a People Business

An EXCERPT from an article in the *New York Times*, September 19, 1971, headlined "Americans Lording It in European Castles."

> France was the choice of David Ogilvy, chairman of the advertising firm of Ogilvy and Mather. He became chatelain of Touffou, a 12th century ivy-covered chateau overlooking the Vienne River in central France six years ago.
>
> Mr. Ogilvy set up criteria to help him decide where to buy; climate, taxes, opportunity for gardening and servants. Britain lost because of the weather and taxes ("death duties there are horrible").
>
> At Touffou, Mr. Ogilvy says with pride, he is awakened each morning by "a groom who stands in the courtyard and plays three jaunty tunes on his hunting horn." The groom has a repertoire of more than 300 tunes.

Taking an ad agency public has been almost the only way admen have become millionaires in the present generation. Among the prominent executives who have taken out more than a million dollars or who own it on paper are: Ned Doyle, Maxwell Dane, and William Bernbach, of Doyle Dane Bernbach; Mary Wells Lawrence, Stewart Greene, Richard Rich, and Fred Lemont, from Wells, Rich, Greene; Dan Seymour, Henry Schachte, John Devine, and possibly others, at J. Walter Thompson; David Ogilvy, at Ogilvy & Mather; Arthur Fatt, Herbert Strauss, and Lawrence

266

Valenstein, of Grey; Robert Healy, Paul Foley, at Interpublic; David McCall and Jim McCaffrey, at LaRoche, McCaffrey and McCall; Fairfax Cone and others, at Foote, Cone & Belding; and Fred Papert, Julian Koenig, and George Lois, of Papert, Koenig, Lois.

Do ad people marry into accounts? They do indeed. And often just like in the movies. Here are only a few of the major accounts that have involved sons, daughters, in-laws, and other married connections. Prudential Life, S. C. Johnson, Bank of America, American President's Line, Anheuser-Busch, Jackson Brewing, Braniff International, Philip Morris, and Ralston Purina. Agencies, too, are sometimes connected by marriage. Recently the president of Altman, Stoller, Max Stoller, gave his daughter's hand to Don Kurtz, young president of Kurtz Kambanis Symon.

When Walter Weir, then president of West Weir & Bartel, decided to sell his agency to MacManus John & Adams, he had one serious hang-up. He had taken a lease for a large block of space in the new Penn Center Building, where he had planned to move his agency. Now he was stuck. Just moments before making a call to the Penn Center developers, he got a call from them. "Would you consider a sublease?" they asked. Weir calmly said he would think it over. He did, for a week. By this time, the offer was raised. He sold out for more than $100,000 profit.

Hal James, a former agency TV executive trying his first venture in an off-Broadway production, took an ad in an advertising trade journal offering shares at $100 each. There was not a single taker. The show was *Man of La Mancha*. Each $100 share was eventually worth $5,000. Hal, himself, realized more than $5 million.

Jesse Ellington, president of the Ellington Company, was a collector. His hobby was stamps. When his estate was appraised, the stamp collection was estimated to be worth nearly $400,000.

When Kenyon & Eckhardt moved into impressive new offices in the Pan Am Building, the conference room was a showplace of electronic devices, sliding walls, remote controls. The first meeting held in the room was with National Biscuit Co. After the agency had presented its part of the session, showing off all the modern gadgetry on hand, the client said, "Fine, but let's take a look at what our competitor is doing." He pulled a wrinkled ad out of his pocket. "Anyone got a thumbtack?" Nobody did. None could be found in any office on the floor. Only after a trip to a stationery store could the client see the ad tacked up on the board.

When Shep Kurnit, now president of his own $35-million agency, started in business, he had three small offices. In one sat his wife as secretary-receptionist. In another sat Shep. In the third they kept the playpen for their preschool children.

General Robert Johnson, president of Johnson & Johnson, was known to be a terror when he inspected his plants. On one such unannounced visit to the Personal Products division on the outskirts of New Brunswick, New Jersey, the advertising department had a fortunate thirty-minute tip on his arrival. Hastily they slicked up their department by transporting half a dozen cartons of promotional material to the roof of the building. When the general arrived, he was furious. "What in the hell is all that crap on the roof?" were his first words. How were they to know that he would arrive in his personal plane?

The cost of new-business presentations is critical to a fledgling ad agency. A new shop in Miami, Bogorad, Klein, Schulwolf and Masciovecchi, in business only a month, made an expensive presentation to a restaurant chain, Longchamps of Florida. They lost out in the competition. Sitting in their new office, looking at their expensive full-page layouts and beautiful copy, they arrived at a sensible decision. "Let's just change the name at the bottom of the page to another restaurant chain, like the Steak Thing, owned by Lum's Company." They did and, one by one, sent the ads to this chain's president. By the time the prospect got the fourth ad, his mouth was watering. They got a phone call. "You've got our business. Come on over and sign the contract."

268

When the J. Walter Thompson agency went public two years ago, there was an uproar from many employees who had previously been asked to surrender their stock and who claimed that they had not known the company's plans to go public. At the time the company went public the stock was in the hands of a limited number of key executives. Lawsuits by some of the employees were unsuccessful. The overnight millionaires, however, irked many. Especially when one of these recently turned out to be a minor executive whose job was at best peripheral. He took out over a million dollars, say insiders.

When Ted Bates was the official advertising agency for the Eisenhower campaign, Rosser Reeves was in charge of preparing the commercials. These were the famous "cost of living" episodes that hammered the general into the White House. One day Reeves needed six new commercials for a sudden TV buy. He was a writer himself, but time was short. He rushed to his creative director Gerry Gury and demanded help. Gury confessed, "I can't, I have to get out a batch of commercials for Stevenson." Undaunted, Reeves shouted back: "Help me out of this jam, write me some commercials for Eisenhower, and tomorrow I'll write you some for Stevenson."

A remark made about a "political" adman in a top agency: "He would rather see his friends fail than succeed himself."

Marcella Free, a top woman executive at Interpublic, was once attending a client meeting in which the agency was demonstrating the use of their complicated and expensive eye-camera device. After preliminary explanation, the director in charge of the meeting pulled Marcella out of the group and put her through the whole rigmarole of testing. Afterward, exhausted, she asked why she had been chosen. "We thought you were the client."

Henry Ford III only once visited the J. Walter Thompson Company, his agency for more than twenty years. This visit, on short notice, was obviously a special occasion, more so because the

269

agency had only recently lost a large portion of the Ford account. The itinerary planned for Mr. Ford would not cover all six floors of the large J. Walter Thompson offices. Hence these special arrangements were made. On the ground floor, a uniformed elevator operator was assigned to a specially designated elevator. All the elevators are automatic, but no chances were to be taken when Mr. Ford arrived. All offices, especially along the inspection route, were rigorously cleaned and spruced up. Floors were polished. And all the corridor walls along the inspection route—and only these—were quickly given a fresh coat of paint. One final detail: It was hinted that one of the Schrafft's coffee-wagon attendants was inclined to break into laughter frequently. She was asked to stay home.

Dolf Toigo, a recent chairman of Lennen & Newell, was once account supervisor on the Colgate-Palmolive business. One day, after a hurried last-minute collection of campaign materials, he and his staff rushed off to the Hudson tubes for Jersey City to make their presentation to the client. Arriving at the station, they found two trains flanking the same platform. They were late, hurried, confused. Dick Kelly, one of the group, remembers Dolf stepping in one and shouting out to the conductor, "Is this the Colgate train?"

Ted Bates & Company, started by a cadre of executives from Benton & Bowles, was always especially chagrined when the mother agency bested them in competition. At one time Benton & Bowles came out with a successful campaign for a new dog food from General Foods called Gravy Train. It was outselling a dog food handled by Ted Bates. Rosser Reeves, Bates's president, perturbed, called an emergency meeting. The account supervisor on the dog food business dismissed the competition with the exclamation "Gravy Train is supposed to make its own gravy, which is a lie. It's just water."

Reeves was enthusiastic. "Ah, we'll expose them! Get a box of Gravy Train in here right now." Orders flew around. The conference room was scheduled. All concerned gathered around as Rosser rolled up his sleeves and poured out the dry meal into a bowl.

Then carefully following directions, he added the water. The executive jury moved in close for a good look. They all waited, tense and eager. The water merged with the meal. It bubbled. It gushed. And it turned brown and soupy, like gravy.

Rosser, studying the operation with intense care, finally stood up and said in a loud voice: "I'll be a son of a bitch, it does make gravy." Then to the account executive who had built up his hopes: "You're fired."

The agency name Batten, Barton, Durstine & Osborn has always been the butt of jokes. The comedian Fred Allen said it sounded like a trunk falling down a flight of stairs. Former President Harry Truman had another comment. This happened when Mr. Truman, on an early morning walk from the Carlyle Hotel in New York, was asked by reporters what he thought of the BBDO ad agency, which at that time was handling the Eisenhower campaign.

"What do I think of BBDO?" snapped Truman, with no hesitation. "I think it stands for Bull, Baloney, Deceit, and Obfuscation."

Anything can happen at an advertising meeting. The Lintas agency in London was putting on a big dealer meeting for the Wesson biscuit account. On the stage were all important agency and client people including a guest of honor, Viscount Montgomery, the famous war hero, who was scheduled to give a brief pep talk to the thousand or so Wesson salesmen. Behind the dignitaries was a movie screen that took up the entire background of the stage. The meeting had just started when a workman behind the screen nudged it. The audience gasped as the huge screen toppled slowly forward and came to rest completely covering the whole entourage on the stage. The biscuit salesmen leaped to their feet to watch the spectacle. Muffled groans and voices could be heard. The shapes of biscuit-executive heads, elbows, feet could be made out as they scrambled to free themselves. All noticed, however, that one distinct shape stood ramrod still beneath the canopy. Never budged an inch until the screen was righted. It was the viscount, standing magnificently erect and unruffled

271

throughout. No wonder Churchill said of Montgomery: 'Indomitable in defeat, insufferable in victory."

Paul Foley, chairman of Interpublic, once came out of a particularly tough new business presentation. He remarked, "I felt like I was addressing Mount Rushmore."

Foley, once a Chicago police reporter, advanced, as they say, "via the creative route." He has a flair for words. Once commenting on a stubborn creative man, he said, "That man has a whim of iron."

Marion Harper kept an English visitor, Jonathan Abbott, waiting for an hour outside his office. When Marion finally rushed out, in shirtsleeves and his famous wide red suspenders, he asked, "Can you run a slide projector?" When Abbott admitted he could, Marion grabbed his arm and pushed him into the office, where he spent the next hour putting on a client presentation.

One former creative director of the Earle Ludgin agency in Chicago practiced a unique salute of recognition to clients. Whenever he met one, anywhere in the office, he would drop everything and stand on his head.

George Lois, one of the most renowned art directors in advertising in recent years, has obviously been a model to young aspiring art directors. Stewart Greene, of Wells, Rich, Greene, and a friend of Lois's, says that George's reputation has unfortunately had a bad influence on young art directors. He explains it this way. Lois's success formula was built on four basic premises: (1) Hard work. George would work seventy hours a week. (2) Genuine talent. Over a hundred awards. (3) A flair for showmanship. "Flaunt it!" (4) Abundant use of four-letter words. In Lois's case, the four basics were practiced in order from (1) to (4). All the imitators, according to Greene, practiced only (3) and (4).

An unemployed adman was having discouraging luck with his letters of application until he came upon a brilliant idea. He would make several thousand offset copies of his résumé and plant them in the railroad stations along the New Haven Railroad line, where hundreds of ad executive commuters could pick them up. The printer made the delivery late. The copywriter got to the railroad stations in his car long after they had been closed for the night. Undaunted, he placed several neat piles on baggage carts along the platforms all the way from New Rochelle to Greenwich. He went home tired but pleased with himself. Late at night, he awoke to the sound of a howling wind storm. He guessed what would happen to his résumés. He was right. They decorated the railroad right of way for thirty miles. Every tree seemed to be festooned with his life history.

Grey Advertising, originally a Jewish ad agency, hired a chap by the name of Jim Flanagan. Jim was good but temperamental. They called him the "golden goy." One day there was a meeting with a difficult Jewish client who had refused to approve anything shown for weeks. Jim sat back for a long while, then got up and walked around the table strewn with campaign ideas. He stopped in front of the client and said in a loud voice, which terrorized the agency staff in the room, "Come on, you son of a bitch, you know they are good ads, pick one for Christ's sake!"
The client roared with laughter. And picked one.

Admen are always trying to get as much exposure for their clients as possible. Gib Dannehower, then at J. Walter Thompson, saw this opportunity. For only $6,000, he bought season rights to a Listerine sign on the roof of the New York Mets bullpen. This was the Mets' first year, and Gib figured the bullpen would be a busy spot as new pitchers warmed up. He was right. In their first game, the Mets used twenty-seven pitchers, and each time the TV cameras picked up Gib's sign on national TV. Gib says he got the idea from watching the Phillies play when he was a kid in Philadelphia. He remembered a sign that said "The Phillies use Lifebuoy." One night someone painted a large postscript to this. It read, "They ought to, they stink!"

Every week Betty Crocker, the General Mills symbolic authority on cooking, gets hundreds of personal letters. The fiction of advertising is often interwoven with the truth. Elsie, the Cow, the famous Borden symbol, traveled the state fairs and public exhibits for more than thirty years. A new Elsie will now be on hand at Disney World in Florida. These myths are so pervasive that at one time when the famous "Showboat" radio program was "traveling" from city to city, this happened. The "Showboat" was scheduled for Cincinnati, Ohio, the famous riverboat's hometown. By the afternoon of the performance, tens of thousands of people lined both banks of the Ohio River waiting for the fictional "Showboat" to round the bend and dock at the city wharf.

The Interpublic Buffalo Preservation program, a pet project of Marion Harper, eventually became one of the thorniest problems left behind when Harper was asked to resign. After an unsuccessful attempt to give the remaining beasts to the Department of the Interior's Bureau of Indian Affairs, other solutions were sought. A legal hitch prevented their sale to private owners or zoos. The bison, an endangered species, could not be marketed for money. The final solution was made when the Honolulu Municipal Zoo agreed to take them, provided Interpublic paid all costs of air transportation to the Hawaiian Islands. The eventual cost, which included crating, attendants, food, and insurance, totaled $2,207.95.

15

Can Advertising Survive?

AT 8:15 A.M., Ed Meyer, forty-three-year-old president of big Grey Advertising, has a breakfast meeting with a young executive from SSC and B whom he wishes to hire. As they meet each other at the doorway of the Brasserie restaurant, the encounter is momentarily awkward. Ed Meyer is carrying three briefcases, so the handshake is dispensed with. The young executive is sharp enough to realize that he will not joke about Ed's luggage. He should not find it unusual for the president of a $250-million agency that has just recently added $20 million in Ford billings to be working that hard.

In other midtown restaurants at this early hour, there will be other pre-office-hour meetings. Joe Foran, general manager of Carl Ally, Inc., is meeting someone in the Biltmore Hotel dining room. Joe, who has five children, nonetheless spends four nights a week in an apartment in the city. The Ally agency has just picked up the Pan Am account, which doubled their billings in the past year. Over at the King's Inn at the Berkeley Hotel, Jack Cantwell, Dick Gilbert, and other agency presidents are breakfasting with important people. Still other groups are meeting in the already-crowded Tulip Room of the Plaza, perhaps Bill Free, Marty Solow, and Jim McGrath, all presidents, will be there talking, negotiating, planning. Down at the Ground Floor in the CBS Building, there is another aggregation of admen and media men, such as Mat Mattimore of SAMI (a Time Inc. subsidiary that produces a vital new kind of store auditing). Elsewhere throughout the midtown area, from the Avenue of Americas on the west boundary to Third Avenue on the east, young ad executives are meeting, perhaps at Schrafft's, Horn & Hardart, or Chock Full O'Nuts. They'll be talking over new jobs, possible mergers, new agency formations, new account solicitations. Some of these men left their suburban homes at 6:30 A.M.

The day starts early in advertising.

There must be some strong motivations at work here. If advertising is such a kooky, much-maligned, questionable kind of business, why do admen work so hard at it? Why do they give so much of themselves, ask so much of their families, fight, scrap, struggle, scramble to get ahead? Is there, after all, truth in the slogan, "What good is happiness, if it doesn't bring you money?"

Money is important, but more as the badge of success than for the material values it brings. Of course, a young high school dropout who two years ago was working as a waiter at the Proof of the Pudding and is now earning $30,000 at age twenty-eight is proud of his salary. So is Ned Tolmac, an ambitious young man who at thirty-three is highly respected by such hard-nosed M.B.A. types as Procter & Gamble and General Foods. So, too, of course, are the young millionaires scattered throughout the business. Mary Wells Lawrence, from an Ohio department store; Jane Trahey, from suburban Chicago; Danny Seymour, an ex-sports announcer; Bill Bernbach, from Brooklyn; Norman B. Norman, from a typical New York City kid to head of an international network of ad agencies and a $300,000 gentleman's farm in upper New York State.

The crux is the opportunity: the kind that is open to all with talent and determination. It's a kind of wildcatter philosophy. If you are not afraid of hard work and long odds, and if you are confident in your talent, you may strike it rich. Really rich. Pat Geyer, former president of D'Arcy, owns a grove of 120,000 citrus trees in Florida. Ned Doyle (ex-Doyle Dane Bernbach) owns a string of race horses and a professional basketball team. Multimillionaire Norman Strouse, ex-president of J. Walter Thompson, owns one of the finest and most expensive collections of thirteenth-century illuminated engravings in the world. Rosser Reeves, former president of Ted Bates, has extensive holdings in real estate in Jamaica, plus his vineyard in California.

These are the realities. But there is more. Admen are hams. Like a nightclub comic, an editorial writer of a small city paper, an off-Broadway director, a struggling artist in Paris, or a novelist in Rome, admen, too, are trying to communicate with audiences with what they hopefully believe is an art of dialogue. The need to be heard, seen, paid attention to is deep in the viscera of a good advertising man. He wants to see something visible and tangible happen as a result of his personal, subjective handiwork. Watch George Lois, Jerry Della Femina, Al Hampel, Ron Rosenfeld, or any of the other bright creative lights as they show you a reel of their own commercials. They'll laugh, whoop, cheer their own things, even though they've seen them dozens of times. It is the same kind of fierce pride and unabashed ham of a Dali, a Leonard Bernstein, an Yves St. Laurent, or a Fellini. All artists, all mass communicators, are well known for their appetites for approval.

These are the attractions, the lures, and promises that bring people into advertising. People from all backgrounds, all parts of the country, and all temperaments and personalities. The money, the promise of opportunities to be realized on the basis of personal talent alone, the artist's gratification derived from communicating with big audiences, and a sense of personal (rather than group) accomplishment. But there is something more that has to be part of the equipment of a successful advertising man. Call it the entrepreneurial spirit, the profit motive, the satisfaction gained from selling products or services. The good adman has a merchant's head. He enjoys selling, gets pleasure from the process of persuasion, gets satisfaction in serving customers well and seeing them come back. Not all people have this merchant's instinct. And it is especially rare among artistic and talented people. Yet the artistic talents and the skills of salesmanship are equally important to the good adman. It is not a common combination.

Will advertising survive? If the people in it can save it, they will. Not only because they enjoy it but because they know it works. For example, an adman or woman can write an ad this afternoon, see it set in type this evening, go into the newspaper

277

by midnight, and tomorrow morning walk onto the selling floor of Macy's and watch it work. The housewives all the way from northern New Jersey to mid-Long Island are there buying the item he or she described. Or his commercial appears on network TV tonight, and by tomorrow afternoon, a dealer in Spokane, Washington, wires his company headquarters for more merchandise. Or he can write an ad, as thousands of agency people do, for a social issue cause—contributions for Bangladesh relief, the passage of a rat control bill in Congress, or a plea to help hemophilia victims—and he can see the concrete results in the physical form of bales of letters to congressmen, checks to relief organizations, contributions to colleges. Whatever else might be said against advertising, it cannot be called ineffective.

But advertising is in danger. Or at least advertising as you have known it in your lifetime. The opposition toward all forms of advertising grows every year. Many forces in American society are working to control advertising far more rigidly than it has been, perhaps to the point that it will become impractical for companies to use it. Others are working for total abolition either through punitive taxes or through making advertising illegal. In any event, the voices of opposition are much louder than those in defense.

Would it make any difference to you if advertising actually did go out of business? If there were no commercials on TV, no ads in newspapers and magazines, no billboards, no brochures and coupons in the mail, no posters in buses, no commercials on radio? It is not impossible to contemplate. Communist countries have no commercial advertising. Many nations in Africa, Asia, and South America have very little. TV commercials are stringently limited in many countries of Europe. In France there is less than an hour a day for commercials. In Italy and Germany commercials are bunched together and run off only at certain hours. Great Britain has only recently agreed to commercial radio. It will begin in 1972.

What would happen to your life if advertising were outlawed? Immediately you would be relieved to find highways completely free of billboards. This would open up wide vistas of scenery, to be sure. Yet you might miss them occasionally, say late at night when

278

you are searching for a motel, a place to eat. Or if you have lost your way to a country fair, an antique exhibit, or a summer theater. Minor inconveniences. Newspapers, however, would be a different matter. Immediately there would be far fewer choices. Small-town weeklies would disappear for certain. Middle-sized cities could afford no more than one, either morning or night. Large cities might have two or three. The big differences would be in the size and cost. They would have to be priced at fifty cents or more. They would be no larger than eight to twelve pages in the bigger cities, four to six pages elsewhere.

Magazines? A reasonable guess would say that 75 percent of all magazines would cease publication. There would be no viable way to support them. The revenue publications now get from subscriptions would not even cover the cost of paper. Some magazines might emerge as paperbacks. The price then would be $1.50 to $3.00 for a pocket-sized magazine. Radio would retreat into the hands of municipal broadcast stations, college and university stations, and perhaps a few religious networks.

The absence of commercial television would make the greatest sociological change in America. Obviously, without commercials, the big networks and their eighteen hours of daily broadcasting would go dark. Their support comes entirely from advertising. Hence, no news broadcasts, no movies (old or new), no variety shows, specials, sports broadcasts—no free television whatsoever. There would then be pay television, as there is to a limited and discouraging extent now. Pay TV is not new. It has been offered in cities such as Hartford, Connecticut, for a decade. It has never paid its way. Without competition from commercial television, pay TV would unquestionably grow, but its audience would be limited to upper-income people. The costs of between $10 and $20 per week would rule out the mass audience.

There undoubtedly would be a federal television channel that would broadcast the type of material approved by Congress. Great Britain's BBC, for example, was the only television in England for some years. A special set surtax supports the cost of broadcasting and the programs. After years of public protest, however, Great Britain now has several commercial television channels. The gov-

ernment-owned stations in France, Germany, and Italy—all originally opposed to commercials—loosen the bonds a little more each
year, allowing more and more minutes of commercial time to be
sold.

The cost of TV broadcasting and eighteen hours of programing
is a fantastic financial investment. Just one evening of prime time
on all three networks costs about $4 million. This does not count
the hundreds of nonnetwork stations broadcasting at the same
time. In short, television as we know it now, unsatisfactory as it
may seem to some, would, without advertising revenues, cost
American taxpayers more than $10 billion per year. It could only
be paid for via taxes.

This is all supposition. It is unlikely that advertising will be
forced off the scene in the foreseeable future. For aside from the
effects it would make on media, it would have profound effects
upon the economy. Americans are simply too accustomed to the
free and alternate choice in the marketplace that advertising makes
possible. Our national temperament also requires a constantly improved economic environment. We do want newer, better, improved products year in and year out. We do expect progress. Not
many Americans would opt for a status quo life-style, a stagnant
economy, no matter how morally reasonable it might sound. Moreover, the typical American family income includes a larger and
larger portion of what is known as discretionary income. That is,
money above the basic necessities of food, clothing, and shelter.
Currently this is about 37 percent of all income. It is an important
figure, for it means that this much out of every dollar of income
is available for nonessential spending. These are the dollars that
go mostly for advertised products: the second car, the new carpet-
ing, the cosmetics and toiletries, the vacations and travel, the extra
things in life. Without advertising, many of these luxuries would
be difficult to be sold. Also anyone's job in these nonessential fields
would be in jeopardy. There is another crucial function of advertising. In a country of more than 200 million people, with tens of
thousands of manufacturers making hundreds of thousands of
products, there is simply no other way to get information about
products and services to all these people, except advertising. It
would literally be impossible to introduce new products, and new

products provide the only way companies can grow or new companies can be born.

Advertising, however, will see many changes. Some of these are already in motion, as indicated in previous chapters. The consumerists, the intellectuals, and the Washington regulatory agencies, with support from Congress, will continue to police and restructure advertising. The immediate effects on ad makers will be that the task of creating interesting, exciting, and efficient advertising will be much harder. The attempts to satisfy all critics will result in duller, less exciting, safer ads and commercials. The new, straightforward, explicit, unemotional advertising may get fairly hard to take commercial after commercial in your living room, ad after ad in other media. Advertising may lose some of its drama and excitement, its fun and laughs, but it will survive.

There is a question, however, whether the advertising business as presently structured can survive. It is in the midst of some fairly fundamental changes. Changes that could alter the traditional relationship of advertising agencies and their clients. Changes that could upset the whole big-agency concentration of power that is generally known as the "Madison Avenue crowd." And changes that could make the profitability of ad agencies extremely risky.

What will happen will be determined by a comparatively small group of top executives in the major corporations and in the major advertising agencies. The companies to watch are the twenty-five largest and most important corporations. This would include such names as Procter & Gamble, General Motors, General Foods, Monsanto, Firestone, Hunt Wesson, Gillette, Ralston Purina, TWA, Uniroyal, RCA, Colgate-Palmolive, Bristol Myers, General Mills, and an equal number of other giants. The ad agencies to watch include J. Walter Thompson, Doyle Dane Bernbach, BBDO, Benton & Bowles, Young & Rubicam, Grey Advertising, Leo Burnett, Ogilvy & Mather, Ted Bates, and Interpublic, among the big shops; and Wells, Rich, Greene; Carl Ally, Inc.; Scali, McCabe, Sloves; DKG, Inc.; Rosenfeld, Sirowitz & Lawson; Lois Holland Callaway; Della Femina, Travisano; William Free Company, among the middle-sized shops; and a group of important regional ad agencies including W. B. Doner (Detroit); Clinton E. Frank, Inc. (Chicago); Bloom Advertising (Dallas); Campbell-

Mithun (Minneapolis); Honig-Cooper & Harrington; Hoefer, Dieterich & Brown; Chiat/Day; and the branch offices of N. W. Ayer
and BBDO (all on the West Coast)

These are not necessarily the smartest companies and wisest
ad agencies. But they are the bellwethers, the mainstream companies, the pacesetters, both for better and worse. What they do,
how they grow, what policies they set, what kind of people they
hire and use will be copied and emulated by their counterparts
on the company side and the ad agency side. In advertising, as in
general business, the game of follow-the-leader is standard practice.
And there is a reason for it. Where else can executives turn to
find precedents, to find justifications for their own decisions?

Look at General Foods, for example, as an advertiser. What
are their marketing plans, their advertising policies? In a nutshell:
GF will continue to diversify into new food fields (soft drinks,
dessert products, cereals, and nutrition-emphasis products). In
other fields, they are open to any profitable field (home sewing,
plants and seeds, packaging materials, and so forth). Overseas,
they will continue to expand in a wide variety of packaged-food
products. More and more of their profits will come from overseas
investments. They will continue to innovate in new-product areas,
in new venture-group operations, and in strengthening internal
operational efficiencies such as computerized information systems,
market research capability, and research and development.

What will General Foods do about its advertising? On the
basis of current activities and the way they have operated in the
past year or two, it would seem reasonable to suppose that they
will do the following: They will continue to use a group of
large, established ad agencies for the bulk of their advertising
assignments. They will, however, explore the capabilities of independent services such as small creative-only firms and new-product
workshops; and they will keep their eyes open to the new media
services and outside research specialists. It does not seem likely that
they will set up an in-house advertising agency operation.

However, look at another large advertiser: Ralston Purina.
This is also an old, established firm in packaged-goods marketing.
They, too, will continue to explore new diversification routes, in-
cluding such areas as leisure products, fast-food franchising, new

products for human and animal consumption, new agricultural products, and perhaps wholly unique fields. They are not a conglomerate, but they will market a conglomeration of products. They, too, look for increased expansion overseas. And what about their advertising? To a much larger degree than General Foods, they will experiment with more new methods and sources of advertising expertise. They have already set up a quasi house agency arrangement. They have used outside media services, independent creative teams, new-product workshops. They will unquestionably move further in all these directions, which in essence means more advertising and marketing self-sufficiency, less dependency upon the typical full-service ad agencies.

Among the other major corporations, the ones who will be watched and the significant trends that will be followed are: Hunt Wesson, Alberto Culver, Monsanto, and Firestone have already set up strong internal operations to handle their own advertising, at least in part. The Monsanto system, still in an experimental stage, uses no major ad agency. It coordinates the activities of a long list of small, specialized ad agencies, creative teams, and media services. Hunt Wesson has begun to handle some of its own creative work, leaving the major portion still in the hands of large ad agencies. Firestone is also handling the direction and placement of its advertising on its own. These are all big companies spending $10 million or more a year on advertising. Their successes and failures will be watched closely.

Now look at some of the major ad agencies to see what directions they will go. J. Walter Thompson, Doyle Dane Bernbach, and Interpublic, all with billings above $250 million, and all public companies, are particularly significant. First, how has their going public affected them as ad agencies? These changes are obvious. They have become more efficient, more profitable, and considerably leaner in personnel. All three have shown steady growth, faster in fact than the average of all ad agencies (with the exception of J. Walter Thompson's sudden set of reverses during mid-1971 when they lost sizable portions of Ford and Pan Am). Outwardly, it would seem that when these companies went public, they soon became much better managed. They were forced into tighter cost-control systems and higher individual productivity, and they speedily eliminated departments and specialties that could not carry their own weight. On the negative side, however, there are these important considerations. They are less pleasant as places to work. "The bastards care only about their bottom line." They are seriously handicapped in morale in part because of perceived inequities in stock distribution when the companies originally went public. "The few people on top got the stock so they could become millionaires." "Now the company is run by the 'money boys' instead of the people with real talent." These are serious faults. For advertising is a people business that calls for close working relationships and cooperation. There is another fault often and perhaps justifiably attributed to the public ad agency. "They spend all their time with the Wall Street analysts, they are not tending the store." Jim McCaffry, president of LaRoche, McCaffry and McCall, admits this is a problem. "They are waiting for me in the reception room when I come to work. And, what the hell, I have to talk with them. We are a public company." This may be a temporary situation. Eventually, the newly public agencies will have competent financial people and specialists who will handle the necessary communications with the financial community without interrupting the day-to-day work of agency management. It has been said, however, that these are the reasons why some of these firms have lost important pieces of business, have seen the resignations of key people, and have found hiring good people harder.

The big agencies have another problem, too. Let the following conversation describe it: A major packaged-goods company that spends well over $25 million a year calls the editor of a trade publication: "This is not a news lead, we ask you not to print it. But we need help. We have a new product all ready to go. All the research is done, the test market has been picked, everything is ready to go, except for the advertising. All we need is this, two TV commercials and a newspaper ad with a coupon. That's it. But we need it soon. Can you recommend a creative team?"

The editor asks: "Why can't any one of your present ad agencies handle this?"

"Frankly, they are too big, too slow, too many people involved. We hope to see some storyboards and ads back here next week. If

284

we get it to one of our agencies, it may be weeks before they get it out of committee."

Big agencies cannot afford to let assignments like this go elsewhere. This is their future. This is a serious development. For more and more of the big corporations must work fast, must grasp elusive marketing opportunities. They can't wait for big agencies to channel work up and down through layers of committees and through hours of meetings. The companies want to work closely with a few sharp, responsive young creative men. As big agencies are now organized, this is impossible. Attempts have been made to solve it, but they don't work.

Big agencies also have another problem. The whole need for large size has diminished. No longer do the big corporations look to the big agency for a department store array of services. The companies are doing most of the marketing, research, testing, developing, and planning of strategy themselves. They are not overwhelmed, as they once were, with the elaborate and impressive appearance of a great brain factory. In fact, it is often resented. For example, a major client riding up on the elevator one day at Compton Advertising with his account executive had this comment to make. The elevator made a stop at one of the lower floors. When the door opened to let a passenger out, there was a brief view of a vast sweep of desks, each piled with papers and reports, usually manned by a studious man with horn-rimmed glasses.

"Is that Compton, too?" the client asked.

"Yep," the account man answered briskly, proudly, "Our research department."

"I hope you don't charge me for any of it."

That is the trouble; all clients are charged for many of these services, whether they use them or not. Not charged exactly, but the commissions received from all clients are dispersed for all agency overhead. Clients who do their own research, merchandising, and so forth would rather see more of the 15 percent commission allowance used only on work productive to their accounts.

Then there is this disadvantage of the big agencies. Too many today are custodian operations. The executives running them are not the founders; they are the successors, the housekeepers. They

285

follow systems; they go by the book; they play it safe. They have none of the spark, the innovative enthusiasm of the young entrepreneurs who run the new agencies. Moreover, their isolation, their almost-incestuous in-growth, has limited their experience and knowledge.

Now look at the second group of ad agencies, such as Wells, Rich, Greene; Carl Ally, Inc.; DKG, Inc.; and Lois Holland Callaway. These are for the most part younger, middle-sized, and still run by their founders. They have several unique strengths. They can still offer clients direct, person-to-person service from the top. The principals themselves often create the ads or at least are closely involved. They are faster, more responsive, and generally free of committee operations and long meetings. As entrepreneurs themselves, these young creative businessmen often have more simpatico relationships with heads of companies or with product managers. Because they are younger, with more energy, they often get into the field more. An adman waiting for a car to be repaired up in New England one night was surprised when the mechanic asked, "You in the advertising business? Ever hear of a Carl Ally?" "Sure have," replied the motorist. The mechanic, before putting his head back under the hood, said, "That Mr. Ally stops by garages like this and asks all kinds of questions. Stuff like how often do the spark plugs on Volvos have to be changed? Do you have to know things like that for advertising?"

This same group of middle-sized agencies (the new, fast-growing ones, not the old middle-sized agencies, which are pretty much stagnating) has another decided advantage. They are creative-emphasis shops. Ad making is their number-one business. Most of them, such as Lois Holland Callaway, never have had media, research, or merchandising departments. The emphasis is important to clients today because this is the one part of the advertising-marketing mix that they cannot do for themselves. It helps then that the principals of these agencies are well-known, award-winning creative men.

The group, however, does have disadvantages. They are frequently run by volatile, sometimes difficult-to-get-along-with principals. Also, in their effort to get out a great creative product, they have neglected areas of client service, client costs, and administrative efficiency. Some have found themselves in severe financial positions. They also are inclined to be prima donna operations. The partners hold and guard their prerogatives closely, which often makes it difficult to hire and hold good co-workers

A further risk with the hot young agencies is their unevenness. Nearly all the agencies in the group mentioned have had spectacular failures as well as spectacular successes. Wells, Rich, Greene; Lois Holland Callaway; Case and Krone; and other shops in the group have had some notable bombs. This is probably because in their eagerness to get off to a fast start, they took bigger gambles, tried perhaps too hard. Also, it must be noted that these new agencies have nearly all been crisis shops. That is, the accounts they got were in deep trouble. Wells, Rich, Greene has picked up one disaster account after another. Some, like Personna blades, Gleem toothpaste, and Score grooming aid, were probably beyond saving. The big agencies, usually playing it safe, have fewer such swings toward very good or very bad. They keep close to middle. By and large, however, this creative-emphasis, smaller-size ad agency stands the best chance to grow and prosper in the next decade.

The strong regional ad agencies mentioned earlier in this chapter also have a good chance to survive the coming changes. They are for the most part well-established, solidly managed operations. They are important firms in their areas, which is often the reason regional companies prefer them to outsiders. Most of them are professionally competent. They can and do hire top people from the main advertising centers. They can avail themselves of nearly any supplier services available to the big city shops. Their disadvantages are mostly those of attitude. Some of them are reluctant to move as fast or be as responsive to changes in advertising as they should be. They tend to be insular, self-satisfied. This handicap limits their growth to like-minded clients in their areas. One such agency's president was heard to say, "Our clients wouldn't buy that razzle-dazzle stuff, they like a good, solid, midwestern brand of advertising." He was wrong. He but not his client likes "good, old-fashioned, safe advertising."

A promising area is the black owned ad agency. There are now more than a dozen nationwide. Some naturally sell their black market expertise, but others like Junius Edward, Inc., serve a diversified list of accounts. Zebra, as its name implies, is composed of black and white employees. The number of blacks working in regular ad agencies is increasing. In New York City the percentage has recently reached 11%. There is also a black veterans' training program for professional positions run by the 4As and coordinated by Don Williams of Doyle Dane Bernbach.

There is a final group of ad makers who can be pegged vaguely between small creative agencies and free-lance creative people. There are about forty or so of these units, which call themselves "creative cells," "think tanks," "independent creative teams," and the like. The good ones here—Bernard Kahn, Assoc.; David Deutsch, Inc.; the Creative Roundtable; the Project Group; Dunham & Marcus; Marie Baumgartener Associates; Warren Pfaff, Inc.; Bill Casey; and Will Graham Associates—are generally hired on a per-assignment basis to carry through a new-product introduction, a brand-revival project, or any individual creative job that clients do not feel they want to give to ad agencies. Their relationships are very close, person to person. The results have often been highly satisfactory to clients. They are paid by fees or in a few cases by retainers or royalties on commercials when they begin to run. It is an area to be watched. There is tremendous flexibility and responsiveness here that clients like.

A problem facing all agencies, and one that appears to be getting worse, is the lack of professionalism and training. More than 65 percent of the cost of running ad agencies is taken up with salaries. People are the most important assets agencies have. Yet almost no major agency and none of the smaller agencies have programs to train and develop people. "We won't hire anybody except pros," says Mary Wells Lawrence, emphatically. "One of the main reasons I left PKL to start my own shop was to get away from all the amateur crap the young kids were bringing in all day long," says George Lois. "Why should we invest good money training young people just to see them go elsewhere and get a better job?" says a J. Walter Thompson personnel executive.

The result today is that big agencies, except for a few junior account executive rotational plans, have given up training programs. The small agencies have never had them. And the hot new

288

shops are dead set against it. "No time for teaching here, besides it's not fair to clients to let somebody train on their accounts." True, a few major agencies still do run some sort of educational or orientational programs. Leo Burnett has a two-year program. Campbell-Mithun in Minneapolis has what is considered a very successful routine. Benton & Bowles has several independent training programs, and J. Walter Thompson still encourages young creatives with after-hour seminars and a Compusand speech and presentation-making course. Grey Advertising shows its people a ninety-minute film, then sends them to work.

Another problem: there is a dangerous informational gap between ad agency people and clients. Agencies no longer have the informational edge they once had when they were privy to, or first to receive, marketing intelligence, copy research reports, and special audience studies. Clients get these for themselves now and often keep them to themselves. The weakest gap seems to be among senior account management types. The obsolescence here is appalling. Many of these so-called marketing experts are completely inept. A trade paper reporter has many times found that they do not even know the size of their client's market, the true position of the brand, or the specific objectives of the advertising. They are, as is often said, "glorified messenger boys" at $40,000 to $50,000 a year.

Most ad agencies are peculiarly disinterested in closing this information gap. Their own libraries and information sources are woefully inadequate and difficult to use. Almost no ad agencies will pay for courses to update their executives. The few exceptions: Foote, Cone & Belding will pay up to 75 percent of the tuition; Bates and Grey have similar deals; and N. W. Ayer has sent men to M.B.A. schools. Agencies seldom pay for subscriptions to trade publications their executives ought to be reading. They may subscribe to one or two copies, which take weeks en route to dozens of individuals. The exceptions here are BBDO, SSC and B, Warwick & Legler, Cunningham & Walsh, Grey, and a few others who pay for group subscriptions. New textbooks and trade books are seldom purchased for employees, although David Ogilvy presented a copy of his own book to all his workers.

Ad agencies also trail their clients in attendance at business seminars, conferences, and trade forums. Again, it is a false economy. Many of these events, especially those put on by the American Management Association, the American Marketing Association, and the Association of National Advertisers, and the creative seminars given twice yearly by the trade publication AD DAILY and the workshop put on by *Advertising Age* each summer are all excellent chances to update ad agency executives. Agency attendance, however, is spotty. In general, the attitude is clear: Professionalism is an individual responsibility.

The end result is that piracy is a way of life among ad agencies. Rather than train or develop people, they hire them away from rival agencies. In this they have the eager assistance of a large colony of head hunters who serve the agency business. Many of these personnel experts serve them well; some, however, serve them badly. Agencies, as a rule, place too much dependency on them. They literally turn over their entire personnel policy to these employment agents and management consultants. It is a grave risk. Especially since people are the prime asset of agencies. Many a shop has been staffed from top to bottom by unqualified or badly matched people. Often this is controlled or directed by an incompetent within the agency, who can cause untold damage. J. Walter Thompson for years had an out-to-pasture account man who hired and fired hundreds of creative people without any qualification for the job. His negative personality turned off many of the best applicants. Young & Rubicam also for long periods gave this critical post to a series of aging time servers.

A further danger (discussed earlier) is the inexplicable trend toward the de-emphasis of the creative function. This is reflected in the publicly announced plans to star the product instead of the idea, to discourage or abandon award contests that stimulate and elevate creative standards, and to underplay the role of the creative man. The gravest danger here is to the ad agencies that have built their growth on their creative reputations, notably, Doyle Dane Bernbach; Wells, Rich, Greene; Young & Rubicam; and Foote, Cone & Belding. One early result has been a desertion of some important creative people from some of these ad agencies. For example, in one week recently, Young & Rubicam lost four key men whose salaries totaled nearly a quarter of a million dollars. Doyle

Dane Bernbach has seen more people leave its creative ranks in the past year than at any time in its history. This trend may be arrested if it was caused, as some believe, by the 1970–1971 recession, during which time creativity somehow was associated with excessive costs.

The immediate destiny of the advertising business will be determined by the current leaders and those close in their footsteps. How they think, what they try to do, and what they accomplish will decide the course advertising will take. It is a scary responsibility. Here is a closer look at these, the most powerful people in advertising.

Many of the senior men discussed through this book will be retiring soon. Although they may continue to make contributions, the future will be shaped by others. Among the men expected to retire during the seventies are: Tom Dillon, BBDO; Dan Seymour, J. Walter Thompson; Al Seaman, SSC and B; Adolph Toigo, Lennen & Newell; Archie Foster, Bates; Bill Bernbach, Doyle Dane Bernbach; Clint Frank, Clinton E. Frank; Norman B. Norman, Norman, Craig & Kummel; Victor Bloede, Benton & Bowles; David Ogilvy, Ogilvy & Mather; Bob Healy, Interpublic; Bart Cummings, Compton; Paul Harper, Needham, Harper & Steers; and half a dozen other leaders. These were the men who shaped the business during the sixties.

The admen who will be shaping the business in the seventies are a slightly different breed. The upcoming leaders include more self-made, hard-driving types whose backgrounds are more likely to be a night school, retail, new ethnics, and creative. There will be a sprinkling of M.B.A. types, midwestern university grads, and some who are basically excellent salesmen. But the mix is weighted toward a less stereotyped, more independent behaving executive. For example, the new crop of leaders will include men like Ed Meyer, forty-two, president of Grey. He's from retail originally, is solid now in packaged-goods selling, and manages a big, growing agency very profitably. Then comes Joe Daly of Doyle Dane, successor to Bill Bernbach, who without the creative charisma will find it none too easy in the decade ahead to keep up the momentum this shop has had for the past ten years.

Next is Mary Wells Lawrence; although very rich already, she is still in her early forties. She'll undoubtedly continue to lead her shop in standout dramatic advertising. Others include Richard Ney, young president of Young & Rubicam, who will face a tough decade. His success will depend upon holding Y&R's once-fine image as "the most creative of the big agencies." Jim Jordan, new executive vice-president and creative director of BBDO, is expected to be its next president. If so, he will follow a long line of creative men who have headed this agency. His creative philosophy—"hard product sell, repetition of theme, and break the boredom barrier"—is sound. His main problem will be to steer clear of the spurious demos his shop has been plagued by recently.

Carl Ally and his strong men Jim Durfee and Amil Gargano are on the crest of a wave now. They could be very successful. Their brand of advertising is unique in force, directness, and candor. Shep Kurnit, Dick Gilbert, William Free, and George Lois are all young agency heads who have well-established creative reputations. If creativity stays in style, they will prosper. Another group of young key men are those who will represent the hard-sell type of ad agency. This includes Bob Jacoby and Irv Sonn, of Ted Bates; John Peace and Bob Betts, of William Esty; Walter Bregman, of Norman, Craig & Kummel; and Stu Mitchell, Paul Cooke, and Milt Gossett of Compton. These executives will find the seventies harder than the sixties because they are all still relying on creative and selling techniques that were already old in the late sixties. They will need new approaches.

Other executives who will guide advertising in the seventies include Andrew Kershaw, president of Ogilvy & Mather, a shrewd and knowledgeable adman; Paul Foley and Bob Marker of Interpublic and McCann, respectively, both hardworking, ex-creative men; Fred Sulcer and Jim Isham, of Needham, Harper & Steers, who will have some problems inheriting Paul Harper's capable administration; Victor Bloede, John Bowen, and Alvin Hampel, of Benton & Bowles, who at this point are still fighting to win more new business. It is a strong team though. Stan Tannenbaum, Leo Kelmenson, and Peter Frantz, of Kenyon & Eckhardt, are all young men at the helm of an old but still-respected agency. John O'Toole, forty-two, will have his work cut out for him at Foote, Cone & Belding. This big public agency has been plagued with bad luck. Larry Dunst, barely thirty, will guide Daniel & Charles.

Among the smaller but fast-growing young men who will certainly be heard from in the coming years are: Jerry Della Femina and his partner Ron Travisano; Ron Rosenfeld, Len Sirowitz, and their new able partner Tom Lawson; Ed McCabe and his partners Gene Case and Helmut Krone; and the three principals at Kurtz Kambanis Symon. All represent the new wave. As do Chiat/Day, on the West Coast; Mike Sloan, in Miami; and Dean Lierle of Van Brunt in Chicago.

There are others, of course. These, however, are pacesetters. Their actions and policies will be aped by a sizable percentage of all other ad agencies. As noted before, it is a scary responsibility.

Or maybe the real heroes of the seventies have yet to arrive on the scene. Since success in advertising is often mercurial, bright, colorful (possibly somewhat unorthodox) individuals are out there now waiting on tables, selling shoes, riding subways to night school, or who knows, getting fed up with commune living, and who will ride into Madison Avenue with the new message.

Index

Index

297

Index

Kellogg, H. K., Kellogg's, 91, 101, 103, 228
Kelly, Dick, 270
Kelly, Nason, 150
Kelmenson, Leo, 258, 292
Ken-L Ration, 5, 97
Kennesson, Frank, 264
Kenyon & Eckhardt (K&E), viii, 29, 61, 75, 76, 127, 189, 194, 197, 241, 267–68
Kershaw, Andrew, 263, 292
Ketchum, MacLeod & Grove, 265
Kingsley Manton & Palmer, 257
Kirkwood, Ron, & Associates, 257
Knickerbocker Club, 138–39
Knox Gelatin, 85
Kodak, 134
Koenig, Julian, 52–53
Kollewe, Charles, 161
Korda Foods, 127
Kraft Foods, 127
Kroll, Alex, 163, 254
Krone, Helmut, vii–ix, 32, 65, 70, 293
Kurnit, Shep, 47, 195, 254, 263, 264, 268, 292
Kurtz, Don, 267
Kurtz, Kambanis Symon, 59, 70, 71, 150, 265, 293

Lambert & Feasley, 190
Lanvin, 66
LaRoche McCaffry & McCall, 67, 84
LaRosa, Joe, 261
Lasker, Albert, 24, 77
Lavin, Leonard, 104
Lawrence, Harding, 67, 241
Lawrence, Mary Wells, vii, 32, 54–55, 64, 66–67, 69, 70, 73, 149, 160, 162, 185, 266, 276, 288, 291–92; and Gus Levy, 84; marriage, 67, 241; mother as receptionist, 155; and the press, 263, 264
Lawson, Tom, 66, 254, 293
Lazrus brothers, 118
Leber Katz, 61, 250
Lee, Sara, 91
Lefton, Al Paul, Jr., 75
Lemont, Fred, vii, 64, 254, 266
Lennen & Mitchell, 26
Lennen & Newell, 30, 71, 75, 85, 263
Lestoil, 103
Lever Brothers, 19, 95, 103
Levitt, Betsy, 264
Levy, Gus, 84
Levy's, 51–52
Lewis, Tom, 241
Libby foods, 3, 234
Lierle, Dean, 293
Lintas, 82, 130–31, 271–72

Lipsitt, Marty, 256
Listerine, 273
Listfax, 84
Livingson, Lida, 264
Lloyd Hall Company, 228
Lois, George, viii, 46, 53–54, 56, 69ff., 73–74, 162, 263, 264, 272, 288, 292
Lois Holland Callaway, 16, 71, 247, 286, 287. *See also* specific personnel
London Creative Circle, 81–82
London Fog, 47
Longchamps of Florida, 268
Lorillard, 139
Louis, Joe, 54
Love cosmetics, 55
Lowenstein, Larry, 264
LPE, 82
Lucky Strikes, 170
Ludgin, Earle, agency, 272

McCabe, Ed, 293
McCaffrey, Jim, 267, 284
McCaffry, Bill, 61
McCall, David, 267
McCann, H. K., 44
McCann-Erickson, 28, 41, 59ff., 75, 81, 82, 115, 129–30, 138, 150, 188–89, 204, 243. *See also* specific personnel
MacDonald, Myron, 66, 67
McGrath, Jim, 275
McGrath, Pat, 65
McGraw, Hank, 238
McKeechie, Bill, 184
McManus, Ted, 25
MacManus John & Adams, 75, 76, 85
Macy's, 49, 50
Mahoney, Helene, 244
Malt-teasers, 235
Man of La Mancha, 267
Manaloveg, Herb, 31
Manoff, Richard K., agency, 61
Mantle, Mickey, 54
Manuche, 243
Marco Polo Club, 243
Marie Cin Cin, 243
Marker, Bob, 292
Marlboro cigarettes, 4, 202
Mars candy company, 138
Marschalk, 61, 253
Marsteller, Gaynor & Ducas, 83
Masson, Paul, wines, 256
Mathes, J. M., 76
Mattimore, Mat, 275–76
Maxwell House, 127
Maxwell's Plum, 241
Mayle, Peter, 258
Maypo, 54

Index

Index

Virginia Slims, 201, 221
Vim, 95
Vitt, Sam, 31
Vivarine, 8
Volkswagen, 40, 47, 52, 53, 130, 213, 228, 250
Volvo, 53, 78, 250
Voss, Phil, Jr., 75
Vote, 101

Wald, Judy, 60, 252, 253, 258, 262
Waldorf Hotel, 242–43
Wall, Bill, 61
Warner, Bicking & Fenwick, 84
Warner-Lambert, 99, 104, 135
Warwick, John, 75
Warwick & Legler, 289
Wasey, Erwin, 82
Weilbacher, Bill, 67
Weiner, Joe, 109, 256
Weiner, Richard, Inc., 264
Weiner & Gossage, 257
Weir, Tony, 76
Weir, Walter, 267
Weir, Walter, Agency, 85
Weiss, Edward H., 263
Wells, Mary. *See also* Lawrence, Mary Wells
Wells, Rich, Greene, 16, 32, 64, 67, 73, 75, 81, 84, 149, 155, 160, 198, 286, 287, 290. *See also* specific personnel

Wenatchee Apple Growers Ass'n, 156–57
Wesson biscuits, 271–72
West Weir & Bartel, 85, 267
Western Union, 145
Wexler, Norman, 160
Whipple & Carlson, 264
White, Ab, 156, 260
Willens, Doris, 200, 264
Williams, Don, 288
Williams, J. B., 8, 99, 117
Wilvers, Bob, 247, 265
Wolfe, Janet, 233
Wolf's, Manny, 243
Wonder Bread, 2, 131
Wood, Ray, 264
Wrigley, William, Jr., 24–25

Xerox, 54

Yankelovich, Dr. Daniel, 227
Yanow, Jo, 264
Yellowfingers, 241
Young, Loretta, 241
Young & Rubicam, 26, 30, 61, 62, 71, 75, 76, 82, 84, 111, 128, 195, 235, 249, 256, 257, 290; personnel management, firings, 188, 189, 198

Zebra, 288
Zerex, 205

302